LOOTED

The Philippines after the Bases

Donald Kirk

St. Martin's Press
New York

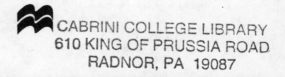

LOOTED
Copyright © Donald Kirk, 1998, 1999. All rights reserved. Printed in the United States of America. No part of this book may be used or reproduced in any manner whatsoever without written permission except in the case of brief quotations embodied in critical articles or reviews. For information, address St. Martin's Press, 175 Fifth Avenue, New York, N.Y. 10010.

ISBN 0-312-17423-3 (cloth)
ISBN 0-312-22769-8 (paper)

Library of Congress Cataloging-in-Publication Data

Kirk, Donald, 1938–
    Looted : The Philippines after the bases / Donald Kirk.
        p.   cm.
    Includes bibliographical references (p.) and index.
    ISBN 0-312-17423-3 (cloth) ISBN 0-312-22769-8 (paper)
    1. Philippines—Politics and government—1986– 2. Philippines—
Foreign relations—United States.   3. United States—Foreign
relations—Philippines.   4. Philippines—Economic conditions—1986–
I. Title.
DS686.614.K57   1998
327.599073—dc21
                                                                    97–21844
                                                                        CIP

Internal design and typesetting by Letra Libre

First edition: January, 1998
First paperback edition: December, 1999

10 9 8 7 6 5 4 3 2 1

Contents

FOR
Susanne Brooke Kirk

Preface

One of the Philippines' best-known writers, Nick Joaquin, once commented that American theater and cinema, music and literature reflect very little of the American era in the Philippines. There are all types of American musicals with Latin American and European motifs from the 1920s and 1930s, but none are set in the land of America's greatest colonial adventure—no dances, no lilting tunes, no "Manila Nights" or "Cebu Swing" embedded in the popular subconsciousness.

So far away is the Philippines from American awareness that an editor once inserted the phrase "the tiny Asian country" in a story that I had written while covering the People Power revolt of 1986. The editor, looking for a way to describe such a remote land, apparently believed that description would give readers a sense of the dimensions of the place. Fortunately, I was able to persuade another editor to delete the phrase, but I have never forgotten what it said about our national ignorance of the Philippines. Here is one of the world's larger, more complicated countries, with about 70 million people and 8,000 islands, where we once based tens of thousands of troops and fought two wars, and an editor still conjured the image of a "tiny" isle off in the South Pacific!

These observations are all by way of suggesting my varying responses and feelings during visits to the Philippines beginning in 1968. When I first got here as correspondent for the *Washington Star,* soon after having covered the disastrous Tet offensive in Vietnam, there was a sense of optimism. Ferdinand Marcos was riding high, still new in office, young, dynamic, adept at saying the right things to Americans, impressing them with plans and promises. (He told me he was about to declare a "declaration of independence" from security and economic ties with the United States. When I asked for an interview with his foreign minister, Carlos P. Romulo, "CPR" took the phone and talked to me for an hour.)

In that halcyon time, Filipinos were amazingly friendly, and the country was exciting and diverse enough to offer a welcome contrast to the miasma of Vietnam. We all were aware of simmering revolt in the boondocks (one of the few Tagalog words introduced into English). We had read of periodic "salvaging," Fil-English for assassination. For all that, we believed here was a country we could count on. Here, where American arms and men had first intruded on Asian soil in 1898, lay hope.

Each time I visited the Philippines over the next few years, the indicators showed how inaccurate were some of those first impressions. Filipinos might mimic American styles, customs, songs and movies, but Americans knew or cared little about Filipinos or the Philippines. We knew far less about the place, as Joaquin had suggested, than we did about our European allies, from which most of our ancestors had emigrated, or about Latin America or Japan, often romanticized in the first generation after World War II.

American views and concerns about the Philippines seesawed wildly as the problems generated by Marcos' corruption and cruelty escalated to unmanageable levels. From unconcern and unawareness, emotions plummeted to disgust and disillusionment. Then, suddenly, all was well as good triumphed over evil in the revolution of February 1986. It was just as easy then as in the 1960s to fall into the mood of the moment—and fall for the rhetoric. Anyone who had seen the throngs on Edsa bring down a seemingly indomitable dictator knew the heady, boundless optimism that had captivated the country.

So little are Americans really attuned to the Philippines, after nearly a century of intimate involvement, that the sense remains of a distant land doing fine after the purge of People Power—doing even better if you believe all the hype of economic reform. The country, however, is mired in problems that predated Marcos or even the advent of American colonialism. So endemic is the culture of corruption and nepotism, so diffused are groupings from one region to another, so deep are class distinctions as to counter any attempt seriously to replicate more than the forms of democracy as seen and practiced, some of the time, in some Western countries.

This book shows the failure of democracy in the Philippines not through the maneuvering of elitist political parties but in the machinations of an upper class as dramatized in the fate of the American bases at Clark and Subic. It examines the corruption and nepotism that overshadows the mystique of the Edsa revolution. It recounts the drama of the eruption of Mount Pinatubo, looming 10 miles west of Clark and 25 miles northeast of Subic, as the beginning of a period of looting and exploitation—and, in that context, analyzes and contrasts efforts at resolving guerrilla revolt. At the same time, it looks ahead to the promise—and dangers—of new frontiers to the south and west.

Halting efforts at coming to terms with Muslim and communist revolt and "reforms" that do little to redress underlying ills all reflect the looting of a system that American leaders love to cite as a model of a democracy. In traveling around the country, one also senses the dynamism of growth and new dangers, as epitomized by General Santos City in Southern Mindanao and the Spratly Islands in the South China Sea. This society may never become an icon of American pop culture, but more than ever it is a matter of concern—militarily, economically and culturally, too.

For this report on the Philippines today, I met and interviewed several hundred people from 1995 through 1997. Dr. Alex Calata, executive director of the Philippine-American Educational Foundation in Makati, not only read the manuscript but also was adviser and friend while I was in the country on a Fulbright research grant in 1995 and 1996. Leon Howell in Washington and John Sidel at the University of London's School of Oriental and African Studies made comments and corrections.

In Manila, two noted editors and columnists, Max Soliven and Amando Doronila, shared insights. Among the foreign journalists there, Thomas Diethelm and Barry Riddell helped with facts and opinions. Elmer Cato, former national editor of *Today* newspaper, and Roy Padilla of the Philippine National Council of Churches showed me around their hometowns while offering many useful observations. June Verzosa of the Malacanang media staff provided valuable research, as did Helen Ives of the American University library in Washington. Finally, I am grateful to the Protacio family of Paranaque, notably Romeo and Carmencita Herman, and to Virginia and Christian Daryl for their hospitality and kindness.

Beyond these friends, I am indebted to sources and contacts too numerous to list in entirety. All quotations and descriptions, unless otherwise cited, reflect my own first-hand conversations and observations. While absorbing a wide range of information, however, I remain solely responsible for the factual material as well as the views and conclusions expressed here.

Donald Kirk
Manila, 1997

Laoag

Vigan

Luzon

Philippine Sea

Bagulo

Tarlac

Mt. Pinatubo ▲ Angeles/Clark
Olongapo/Subic ● San Fernando
Metro Manila ● Quezon City
Makati
Cavite

PHILIPPINES

South China Sea

Mindoro

Marinduque

Legazpi

VISAYAN
ISLANDS

Samar

Panay

Leyte

Spratly Islands

Palawan

Iloilo ● Bacolod
Pontevedra

Cebu

Negros

Bohol

Puerto Princesa

Sulu

Sea

Cagayan de Oro

Mindanao

● Marawi
● Camp Abubakar
● Cotabato

N

W   E

S

Zamboanga

Isabela   *Basilan Island*

Mt. Apo ▲ ● Davao

▲ Mt. Parker

Jolo

● General Santos City
Sarangani Bay

Tawi Tawi   *SULU ARCHIPELAGO*

Map: Don Kirk

ONE

Worlds Apart

Shoppers saunter through the great department stores and malls, watching the ice-skating, playing with their kids, lining up for fine dining or snacks, hunting for bargains or spending with reckless abandon. There is something for everyone in Greenbelt or Glorietta, in Megamall and Shangri-La Plaza and Robinson's Galleria on nearby Epifanio de los Santos, Edsa, the bumper-to-bumper 12-lane boulevard where hundreds of thousands staged the "People Power" revolution that propelled Corazon Aquino to the presidency over the profligate Ferdinand Marcos in February 1986.

More than a decade later, the revolution is history, a few days of rage fast fading into an ancient past, little remembered by a new generation while an affluent elite read about liberalization of markets, rising foreign investments, growing foreign trade zones. Even older Harrison Plaza near Roxas (*née* Dewey) Boulevard, coursing by Manila Bay, is spruced up and modernized—equal if not superior in tone and range to most any mall in suburbia USA.

The great labels, the world-famous brands, the fast-food outlets, all the styles reflected in the foreign media are represented in these monuments to the good and fast life, shielded by glistening walls and shaded windows, soaring atriums and arches, as well as enough air-conditioning to create a world apart from that of drenching monsoons, suffocating heat, squalid shantytowns, fetid rivers and rickety, smoke-belching buses on the crowded avenues on the other side of the seas of parked cars.

So different are these worlds, you almost forget where you are. Here is a Third World nation mired in rising poverty, joblessness and underemployment, with near-famine in urban slums as well as in distant farms and jungle. Here crime and corruption exist on such a routine, colossal scale as even to raise eyebrows in a society in which nepotism, bribery, gift-giving and exchange of favors are the rule, not the exception. Read one day about the gross national product (GNP) rising by 7 percent after years of decline under

Marcos, and you read next how little the figures mean to nine-tenths of the nation's 70 million people.

"Child labor in the Philippines is increasing at an alarming rate and is estimated at more than three percent every year," read a story on the back page of *Today,* one of Manila's two dozen daily newspapers, during the terrible 1995 monsoon season. "This year's number of child laborers is expected to reach 5.7 million by year's end, and most of them are girls."[1] That revelation, hardly worthy of notice in the other papers, followed a week of reporting on a "rice crisis" in which the government awoke to a severe rice shortage as bureaucrats blamed each other for not importing more—and everyone held a "rice cartel" of Filipino-Chinese merchants responsible for deliberately driving up prices by hoarding stocks.

Cielito Habito, the social economic planning secretary and director-general of the National Economic and Development Authority, saw little to worry about as he triumphantly revealed that the GNP had risen by 5.2 percent in the first half of 1995—up from a 4.7 percent increase in the first half of 1994, on the way to 7 percent for 1996. "The slowdown in the agricultural sector was more than offset by the performance of the rest of the economy, particularly the industrial sector," he remarked happily.[2]

The theme of triumph reached an apotheosis of sorts with the gathering in Manila and Subic, for just two days, on November 24–25, 1996, of the Asia Pacific Economic Cooperation group, APEC, of the leaders of 18 "economies" from both sides of the Pacific Rim. The letters "APEC" appeared so often in newspaper headlines, on television, on billboards as to turn the acronym into a watchword for the renaissance of a leadership wanting desperately to show off. Did it matter if the authorities had to remove thousands of angry squatters from their flimsy shacks on some of the main avenues leading to the site of the sessions at the Philippine International Convention Center on reclaimed land by Manila Bay?

Did anyone care if thousands of soldiers and policemen had to set up barriers to blockade a caravan of anti-APEC demonstrators on the road to Subic, once the site of America's largest naval base, now a free port dominated by the buccaneering grandson of an American marine? For that matter, who noticed the hordes of young men swarming the streets of Olongapo, outside the base, brandishing sticks and baseball bats in order to "protect" the APEC dignitaries, ensconced deep within the base, from a few protesters in town?

For the Philippine president, Fidel Valdez Ramos, the American-trained soldier and engineer who had won a six-year term in 1992 and led the way in "liberalizing" and "opening" his country to foreign investment against a host of powerful protectionists, the APEC conference represented the chance he craved to showcase himself and his policies before his own people as well as the region and the world. No sooner was it all over than the papers were again full of speculation about Ramos' chances of succeeding himself in office—all ritualistically denied by Ramos—and reports of still more increases in the GNP.

Within a year, however, Philippine leaders, like those in Malaysia, Thailand and much of the rest of the region, were scaling down their rosy estimates. Whether business was hurt by a burgeoning political crisis surrounding the uncertainties of presidential politics or was catching the fever that was spreading a chill through nearby economies, Habito by the fall of 1997 was saying the Philippine's economy was in such a "state of flux" that it would grow by only 5.6 percent in 1997 rather than 7–8 percent as previously predicted. The best he could offer was that the downturn "won't be as dramatic as Thailand's," where the GNP forecast had tumbled from 6.7 percent to 1.9 percent.[3]

No one in authority in the Philippines thought to credit one source of income that supports the economy in good times and bad. The GNP depends in significant part not on investor enthusiasm but on remittances sent home by more than 5 million OFWs—Overseas Filipino Workers contracted by employment agencies or companies for a stipulated period.[4] Sadly, the vast majority of them are hired for jobs that fall among the three Ds—"dirty, difficult and dangerous"—and de-humanizing too. In Saudi Arabia and Kuwait, they are routinely beaten by their masters (and mistresses); in Hong Kong, they are beaten less often but are molested and sometimes brutalized sexually; in Japan, they serve as hostesses and striptease dancers, bargirls and masseuses, latter-day sex slaves controlled by *yakuza* gangsters who acquire them through numerous agencies recruiting "entertainers."

Ironies abound. In September 1995, a typhoon spent its force in the hills and rice paddies and villages north of Manila. The stories were the same as those published after the last typhoon. The rains, as usual, loosed the great lahar flow on the slopes of Mount Pinatubo. As usual, the lahar, a hideous gray mass of mud coughed up over miles of once-verdant hills and valleys in the eruption of Pinatubo more than four years earlier, poured into the rivers.

As usual, the porous dikes broke and thousands were left homeless. As usual, the engineers blamed the politicians and the politicians the engineers for the collapse of the dikes—thrown up, repaired and thrown up again in the path of the lahar. As usual, bureaucrats and contractors made off with a considerable percentage of the funds controlled by the Mount Pinatubo Commission, an agency formed by the administration at Malacañang, the presidential palace once occupied by Spanish and later American rulers.

The funds—10 billion pesos, $400 million—were about to run out with no viable plan for finding homes for more than 40,000 families left homeless and several hundred thousand others huddling in makeshift shelters and camps. Herminio Aquino, a congressman and uncle of the martyred Benigno "Ninoy" Aquino, hoped that the damage would "erase a growing reluctance among many quarters to provide funds for lahar-devastated areas"—but two years later said official disinterest was "even bigger" amid "anomalies and corruption."[5] Not a few wealthy Filipinos, it seemed, viewed the refugees as whiners who should learn to "help themselves." Why are people forever "complaining," asked the gracious, simple, nonostentatious Amelita "Ming" Ramos, wife of President Ramos. "They should learn to do more for themselves."[6]

Ten days after hearing these remarks, on what had begun as a sunny Sunday, I taxied to a town 30 miles northwest of Manila on the main road to Subic Bay, once the largest U.S. Navy base anywhere, abroad or in the United States, now a free port and special economic zone providing space for duty-free shopping centers alongside assembly operations set up by companies from a dozen different countries. By the time I got there, a steady drizzle was falling and lahar was washing across the road after seeping through a dike foolishly built of the same lahar by corrupt and incompetent contractors. Somewhat recklessly, at my insistence, my taxi sloshed on through.

We stopped at a restaurant on the other side, and I chatted with the manager about what was happening to all the funds for slowing the flow of lahar and guaranteeing the safety of thousands in danger of losing their homes. "You know the Philippines," he remarked. "The money, it goes somewhere else." He suggested that Ramos "give the money to those lahar people"—meaning the ones driven off the land by the onrushing flood—"so they can transfer to another place rather than give to those politicians and bureaucrats." The conversation typified the scorn heaped upon authorities, never quite specified, often unknown. "They say the dike has broken because the budget is very small," said Noel David, who owned a small business in the next town, also threatened by the lahar flow. "They cannot make it very strong."[7]

How about a massive effort to build permanent restraining walls during the dry season? "After the rainy days, they will go home," David responded. "They have no budget; they say that's why." When told the president's wife believed the people should work harder for themselves, he did not altogether disagree. "The people want help, the people wait for food and clothes. Maybe it's better to give them work." His reason for this suggestion, though, differed from that of the first lady. "The government will give for the food, but it will go first to the official," he said. "If you give them ten cans of corned beef or canned goods, maybe one or two cans will go to the people. The rest they sell to the stores."

As the storm intensified to typhoon level, I asked the taxi to drive David to his home, down streets already several inches deep in water. I met his relieved family, then left amid qualms as to whether the taxi could make it back through the lahar. By the time we had crept past a long line of waiting traffic, slithering on the shoulder or on the opposite lane, the message was clear. The road was by now entirely closed, and we were in for a night at a roadblock manned by local police. The word was that the road wouldn't open in the morning.

Come the dawn, however, and the word was worse. A walk past a police roadblock revealed a dozen bulldozers and trucks standing idle while a single truck carried rocks to pile up on the submerged roadway. Hundreds of people were slowly wading hip-deep through the lahar, still pouring across the road. There was no other way to get into San Fernando—no other route from the port of Subic to Manila but this two-lane highway, never widened and hardly improved for years. The sight of shining new Federal Express tractor-trailers caught in the long line of traffic epitomized the dilemma. For months officials had boasted of persuading Fedex to turn the air strip at Subic, once the legendary repair facility for U.S. Navy ships in the Pacific, into the Fedex regional hub.

The failure of engineers to shore up the dikes, to build up the road as promised, meant that not only Olongapo but also three of the most important provinces were cut off from Metro Manila and the country's 75 other provinces. The question was how to get around or through the lahar flow. There was one other route, upstream. The taxi drove through the fringes of the town of Porac, once a center of activity for the communists' New People's Army, a seemingly dormant force ever since the fall of Marcos and then the withdrawal of the Americans from the bases had stripped its elitist leaders of their easiest talking points. Now much of Porac, like other towns and villages, was lost to lahar.

With the rain abating, we followed the treadmarks across a moonscape of congealed mud to the edge of a ravine. Below, a steady line of people filed across a narrow steel suspension bridge—the only way to get to the main highway leading to Manila without wading into the lahar. I paid the taxi driver for two days, promised to call his boss in Manila and joined the crowd walking to the other side. There a row of jeepneys, those uniquely Filipino passenger vans originally pieced together from cast-off American jeeps, waited to pick up passengers for the bumpy ride to bustling Angeles, the city built up outside Clark, in its day the largest American air base beyond the United States.

Back in Manila that night, I expected to see banner headlines reporting on the disaster of lahar. The story merited page one but took third or fourth position behind the kind of news that appeals to the hearts of those with enough pesos to buy newspapers. Most people, to judge from the press, were more interested in the latest debates in the congress over moves by Ramos' people to rearrange the constitution to enable him to seek a second term when his current six-year term expired in 1998 and he had to retire under the post-Marcos constitution.

It was a typical debate in which factions were determined by personalities and real issues got lost. Nobody talked about the problems of poverty and corruption. Lahar for today was worth a few stories and pictures—and not a word about the economic impact on millions of peasants as well as glossy economic plans and dreams for opening the entire region north of the capital to commerce and industrialization on a grand scale.

Max Soliven, publisher and prolific columnist for the *Philippine Star,* caught the mood. "The nation has begun to suffer compassion 'fatigue' from the never-ending calls for prayers and generosity," he wrote, even though the politicians were content. "The more lahar, the more appropriations, they believe, for bigger and higher dikes and larger lahar catchment basins. Naturally, the big contractors and public works and highway engineers in league with them are not weeping crocodile tears over the annual lahar rampages. But even they must realize that the time is near when the national government and our do-gooders will exclaim 'No more! It's no use pouring money into a bottomless pit.'"[8]

The scandal of abuse of lahar funds symbolized the dilemma of a society at the threshold of a new era—but hopelessly mired in the habits of the old. For the Philippines, the new era had begun not with the fall of Marcos, who looted the treasury of at least $10 billion, most of it never recovered, but with the departure of the Americans from the bases, notably Clark in November 1991 and Subic a year later. The fall of Marcos, the one-time darling of American presidents and CIA chiefs for his uncanny ability to talk democracy while bullying and robbing his own people, was only the dramatic opening, a prelude, to the real struggle for change.

It was not until Marcos' successor, the widowed "Cory" Aquino, heir to the Ninoy legacy, sought to bring back the trappings of democracy that skeptics realized the system was still in place—the rulers of the haciendas, the old cronies, the inheritors of fortunes in banking and stocks, real estate and hotels, sugar and coconuts, beer and electric power remained as they were. One crony might undermine another, but the pattern endured—"a kind of rent capitalism," political scientist Paul Hutchcroft observed, "based, ultimately, on the plunder of the state apparatus by powerful oligarchic interests."[9] The term booty capitalism, he suggested, best described how the oligarchs were "plundering the state."

Aquino might despise cousin Eduardo "Danding" Cojuangco, one-time coconut king and one of Marcos' closest associates, but she as much as he was born of the system. A Cojuangco, she could retreat, for solace and relief, to Luisita, the hacienda in Tarlac Province, north of the lahar, that she was not about to abandon to a spurious land reform program long advocated by the anti-Marcos partisans who once so adored her.

What could not survive the Aquino era were the bases. In the face of a barrage of American propaganda, of the Americans' insistence on their value to the Philippine economy, of fears of poverty in the raunchy base towns of Subic's Olongapo and Clark's Angeles City, Philippine senators responded with even louder denunciations. What better way to vent nationalist steam, to divert attention from problems on the home front, to assert machismo and appear heroic than to speechify against the great one-time colonial power that had insisted on taking over the entire country from the Spanish after Admiral George Dewey's fleet had trounced the Spanish on Manila Bay in 1898?

The outcry among politicians at first seemed less than alarming. American negotiators were inured to periodic outbursts, often quite justified, always for some rhetorical purpose that served the interests of the politicians but not necessarily the country. The Reverend James Reuter, a Jesuit from Jersey City, New Jersey, the product of a Catholic college near Baltimore and survivor of three years and three months in Japanese internment camps during World War II, placed the schizophrenia about the United States in historical context.

In a conversation in the Jesuits' Xavier House, overlooking the polluted waters of the Pasig River, upwind from Malacañang Palace, Reuter reminded me of the words of Manuel Quezon, the oratorical dandy and clever politician who got himself elected as the first president of the Philippine Commonwealth in 1935. (The country was still an American fiefdom ruled, as far as Americans knew or cared, by General Douglas MacArthur—himself often subservient to Quezon.)[10]

"'I would rather see the Philippines run like hell by Filipinos than run like heaven by Americans,'" Reuter quoted Quezon as having said. Less ostentatiously, however, Quezon cautioned MacArthur and others against rushing headlong into independence—an eventuality that happened in 1946 amid a bout of American and Filipino speech-making on the American independence day, July 4. For the Philippines, the great day came less than a year after the atom bombing of Hiroshima and Nagasaki had forced the Japanese to surrender. Memories of the bloody struggle to rout the Japanese out of Manila—after Warsaw it was the hardest-hit urban battleground in the war—were still fresh.

Reuter, 30 at the time of independence, saw a parallel between Quezon's bombast and that of latter-day politicians. He doubted if all of the critics had really wanted the Americans to leave in such haste, even if denouncing them was the thing to do. In any case, the politicians, representing wealthy vested interests in their own milieu, were far out of touch with most of the people they claimed to represent. "The Philippine people never wanted the bases withdrawn," said Reuter. "Politicians who were screaming about the bases did not represent the people."

Reuter couldn't have been righter. Poll after poll showed that a majority wanted the bases back, wanted the Americans to return with their money, their jobs, their arms and their sense of security, both economic and military. So deep were the ties, built up despite an inauspicious beginning in what the American history books still call "the Philippine insurrection," that many Filipinos revere General MacArthur more than their own national heroes.

Cries of "Hey, Joe," invoking the era of GI Joes from the American bases, still greet foreigners in obscure towns and villages. American clichés, many of them discarded years ago by American editors, still emblazon the front pages of a largely English-language national press, which is available to all but is really the mouthpiece of an educated elite. American pop songs, including the latest rap numbers, waft through buses plying the remotest routes, and American films dominate the marquees of movie theaters—often more popular than the local hits, themselves knockoffs of Hollywood's worst.

Newcomers from abroad are amazed by the signs of Americana they see permeating the life, the culture and the language. To headline writers, local councilmen are town "dads," councilwomen are "lady dads," and members of the Congress, with an American-style "senate" and "house of representatives," are "solons." Scandals are "bared," details "aired," and cars don't flip over in accidents, they "turn turtle." Not only that, but everyone has a nickname—"Lulu" or "Hermie" or "Chito" or "Joker," "Boy" or "Girlie" or "Baby" or "Beauty"—except, of course, when aides and hangers-on refer to "the boss" (another common term) as "director" or "general" or "secretary" or "ambassador" or "senator" so-and-so, even if the great man hasn't held any such exalted post for years.

"They love the Americans here," said Roberto "Bobby" Romulo, a former foreign secretary, now chairman of one of the country's most successful enterprises, the Philippine Long Distance Telephone Company, which has prided itself for years for its listing on the New York Stock Exchange. "Twenty years from now, I can see the Americans back on the bases."[11] Romulo was speaking from a rather biased family background—as the younger son of Carlos P. Romulo, World War II propagandist for General MacArthur, postwar signer of the UN charter, president of the UN General Assembly and, for 14 years before his death in 1985, foreign minister under Marcos.

Understandably, Bobby Romulo looked with contempt on the outcome of the bitter debate that preceded the September 16, 1991, balloting on a treaty that would have provided a ten-year extension for the American bases. Needing a two-thirds majority, the Philippine Senate fell far short of approving the deal. The vote of 12 against the treaty and 11 in favor not only scuttled the American bases but also cost the Philippines hundreds of millions of dollars in loans and grants—and compelled Aquino to abandon a pro-bases policy that she had belatedly but forcefully espoused.

Among those who most reveled in the denunciations of American influence were two veteran politicians and Marcos foes, the Senate president, Jovito Salonga, who cast the twelfth and final ballot against it, and Aquino's foreign secretary, Raul Manglapus. Salonga and Manglapus had one thing in common—both had escaped martial law under Marcos by going into self-exile in America, spending much of their time abroad denouncing the Marcos regime, to the delight of their American hosts. There was, however, a crucial difference between the two: Salonga wanted to get rid of the bases entirely; Manglapus simply wanted more money for them.

Manglapus and his cohorts believed that if they bargained hard enough they could hold the United States to an agreement for $1.5 billion annually in economic and military aid—more than a billion above the $450 million level set by U.S. negotiators for both Clark and Subic. Although they were not on the side of the treaty's never-say-die foes, the Philippine team made the entire exercise almost as unpalatable to U.S. negotiators as to Filipino critics.

By the time the American ambassador, Nicholas Platt, had left, a month after Pinatubo erupted, the Americans were fed up with Manglapus. "His position moved frequently," said Platt, who departed for a posting as ambassador to Pakistan. "It was a very torturous process. They wanted the best possible deal. All their complicated feelings about Uncle Sam were clustered in the negotiations." As leader of the Philippine team, Manglapus impressed Platt as "kind of wiggly."[12]

Manglapus returned the critical sentiment, especially in his dealings with Richard Armitage, the American negotiator on what was called the "Treaty of Friendship, Cooperation and Security." He "stuck to a position which we thought was inadequate," said Manglapus, later rewarded for supporting Ramos politically with appointment to the lucrative post of president of the Philippine National Oil Company.[13] The final draft, agreed on after the United States decided that the air base at Clark was not worth the multimillions needed to repair the damage from the ashfall of Pinatubo, called for Washington to pay only $203 million a year for ten years for the privilege of using Subic and two smaller bases.

Neither side was happy. "I did not know if the treaty would survive or not," said Platt, but he was glad to get out when he did—before the signing. "I left in a great flood of relief. I knew that public opinion was in favor." He has long since recovered from the shock of rejection. "I have no antipathy or rancor in retrospect," said the ex-diplomat from his postambassadorial aerie as president of the Asia Society in New York. "I felt if their side hadn't knocked it down, ours would have. The year we concluded our deal the United States was closing 80 bases. If we'd gone to them [Congress] with a treaty costing $2 billion over ten years, I don't know if they would have approved it."[14]

Had the Philippine Senate finally authorized the arrangement, President Bush would have avoided having to persuade two thirds of the U.S. Senate also to ratify it by signing it as an executive agreement. There was solid precedent for resorting to that device. The original bases agreement of 1947 was approved on the American side just that way—by executive agreement signed by President Harry Truman. At that time, Congress was all in favor of paying for U.S. bases in the Philippines, newly retrieved from the Japanese, but 45 years later the White House would have had much more difficulty persuading Congress to authorize funding.

Philippine negotiators, insensitive to these realities, did not at all like the idea of "executive agreement." They said that the U.S. Senate should ratify it, just as they were pressing their own senate to do. Manglapus, who had resigned his senate seat to become foreign secretary, sensed the reality at home—the Philippine Senate would disapprove any deal acceptable to Armitage before it ever got to Bush. "A treaty was signed, but it was inadequate," he told me four years later, even though he had reluctantly agreed to it after "all the surveys showed overwhelming support."[15]

Following the Senate rejection, Aquino called for a nationwide referendum on the treaty but abandoned the idea for fear that the protests would fuel rebel movements. Proof of the potentially divisive impact of a popular vote on the bases was the opposition of two senators: Cory Aquino's brother-in-law, Agapito "Butz" Aquino, Ninoy's younger brother, and Juan Ponce Enrile, the wealthy former defense minister and Harvard-trained lawyer who had sided with Aquino in overthrowing Marcos and then turned against her. Both joined the majority against the treaty.

After surrendering on the treaty, "Cory was in favor of giving an extension" for the American base at Subic, Manglapus noted, but debate between U.S. and Philippine negotiators on a three-year lease on life got hopelessly bogged down. Yes, the Aquino administration was willing to give the Americans three years to make an orderly retreat, but Aquino's people wanted the Americans to present an exact timetable for pulling out all that equipment, including the world's best military ship-repair facilities.

The Americans not only balked at committing the next U.S. administration to such demands but also did not look forward to what they knew would be more anti-American posturing in the Philippine Senate, which they figured might not approve the three-year extension, either. Instead, the new American ambassador, Frank Wisner, handed over a letter signed by President Bush saying that the Americans would be out in a year. There was grumbling among Americans, notably Defense Secretary Richard Cheney, about not staying "where we're not wanted," as if they were talking about an invitation to a party, but the response clearly reflected the administration's outrage over the Philippine position—*plus* the reality that the bases, at that juncture, did not seem so important any more.[16]

The rhetoric of Salonga and his colleagues was matched only by that of American officials. They sought to portray the bases as the front line against communism long after the United States had abandoned the fight in Southeast Asia by withdrawing its last combat forces from Vietnam in 1973 and then refusing to defend its South Vietnamese ally against the climactic, victorious North Vietnamese offensive of February, March and April 1975.

During a protracted U.S.-Philippine "review" of the bases agreement begun shortly after his arrival in the Philippines in 1987, Platt had raised all the old fears. The bases, he argued, were "an essential element of the external defense of the Philippines as provided for in the Mutual Defense Treaty of 1951 and the Philippine-US Mutual Defense Board."[17] Such echoes of cold war rhetoric resonated indistinctly, however, after all the funding and support the United States had lavished on the profligate Ferdinand Marcos. The successors to Marcos could not be all that impressed by an American establishment that had poured more than a billion dollars a year into Marcos' treasury largely to buy his support of the bases—and the U.S.-Philippine alliance.

"The bases contribute to regional cooperation and stability," Platt declared. "The bases, like those in Japan, Great Britain, Spain, the Federal Republic of Germany, Korea, Greece and Turkey and other countries, deter potential threats to the host country, contribute significantly to world peace, global stability and the defense of freedom and democracy." That said, he sought to placate local sensitivities by defending the bases as "an integral part of the Philippine economic structure, adding about 28 million pesos a day [well over a million dollars] to the local economy, employing about 68,500 Filipinos, and benefiting hundreds of thousands of others."[18] (The "others," not cited by Platt, included thousands of prostitutes and pimps.)

The Americans' arguments, repeated with humdrum regularity to any and all who visited the bases, were about as sententious and self-serving as those of the Filipinos opposed to the bases. As barriers fell in Eastern Europe, the threat of a regional war was largely forgotten. Claims that the bases were needed for regional cooperation or as deterrence to potential threats appeared altogether specious after the collapse of communism in Eastern Europe and the Soviet Union in 1990 and 1991. Although China, Vietnam and, most especially, North Korea remained communist, it did not seem likely they would soon risk war far beyond their borders.

The retreat of American forces would undoubtedly cause economic hardship, but it also would impose a sense of urgency on a populace and a system left behind in the great rush to new prosperity reverberating through the rest of the region, including a surprisingly capitalist Vietnam. Already, Filipinos were considering the potential of the bases as free-trade zones in the country's economic revival.

"At this time the world's power is no longer based on a power system but on the inter-connectedness of economies," opined Jose Almonte, the retired army general who now was Ramos' national security adviser, director-general of the national security council and framer of the messianic concept of "Philippines 2000," Ramos' catchphrase for where he wanted the country to be, come the millennium. "We have all these regional organizations, structures that promote cooperation. Smaller nations like the Philippines derive their strength from these numbers."[19]

With the settlement of the bases issue, the drive to catch up economically absorbed the attention of the president and all his aides, Almonte included. "We have been confronting monopoly cartels, the feudalistic system," he told me. "We are dismantling the old system. We have opened up telecommunications, banking, insurance, the inter-island system. We have liberated the poor. We have brought down the tariffs to an average of nine percent. We hope to make it five percent. We are dismantling all laws that are restrictive of foreign investment."[20]

Not even the strongest foes of liberalization, such as tycoon Jose Concepcion, "JoeCon," who had opposed opening up the economy while serving in the Aquino cabinet, could stem the tide, in the view of businessmen and bureaucrats. "I don't think JoeCon can confront the collective will of the people," said Almonte, dubbed Ramos' Rasputin by Malacañang journalists. Almonte repeated an earthy analogy. "The old nationalist elements said we have to own the cow. I said all we have is cow dung. Now the nationalism that we have is a nationalism where we share in the milk of the cow. When we become stronger, maybe we can own not merely the cow but the ranch."[21]

Few outside the ruling structure, however, really believed "the system" had changed. There was a growing fear that Ramos, for all his seeming fortitude and forthrightness, might follow the example of Marcos and become a dictator, if not somehow perpetuating his own presidency, then working to install a successor amenable to his will. Nobody forgot that Ramos, as the general in command of the Philippine Constabulary, had been a key player in enforcing the martial law decree declared by Marcos on September 21,

1972, after he ordered Ninoy Aquino's arrest. Nor did anyone forget the fidelity with which Ramos had lived up to his first name, serving his boss while doing and saying nothing about the assassination of Aquino as he stepped from the plane returning him to Manila from exile in America, via Taipei, on August 21, 1983.

Hiding behind his military rank, Ramos did not appear involved in the campaigning preceding the snap election called by Marcos for February 7, 1986, in a test of power against the widowed Cory, the overwhelming people's choice. Not until several hundred thousand demonstrators had engulfed Edsa on February 22, 1986, as Cory campaigned to overturn the fabricated election results, did Ramos emerge on center stage with Enrile, Marcos' old-time ally and defense chief, both suddenly national heroes willing to do or die for Cory.

Ten years after those great events, the twin evils of poverty and corruption were as terrible as ever. Ramos longed for respectability for himself and his country, as reflected in the fuss he made of APEC—by coincidence convened on the fourth anniversary of the turnover of Subic to Philippine authority. From that lofty perch of international publicity, however, the benefits hardly trickled down. Almost half the people lived on or below a poverty line demarcated by an income of about six dollars a day for a family of six, whereas bureaucrats routinely earned 10 percent kickbacks on contracts—and sometimes much more.

Public works remained the worst offender, but such entities as immigration and customs were also so rife with bribes and thievery that Filipinos laughed at the stories. The problems with customs reached one comic high, for all but the victim, when a passenger discovered $4,000 in cash missing from his briefcase in the time it took to go through the x-ray machine at the international airport, named for the martyred Ninoy. Almost any businessman had stories to tell about the bribes paid to expedite cargo, both imports and exports, that might otherwise have been delayed for weeks or months—if they got through at all.

The Philippine National Police (PNP), incorporating the old Philippine Constabulary as well as all the country's police forces, was the stepping-stone from which Ramos had leaped to national power. As much as any other government entity, however, it too was powerless to do much about anything. PNP chieftains were linked to *jueteng,* a numbers game from which not only they but a network of officials earned fortunes for themselves and the mobsters behind them. The more questions one asked about *jueteng,* the deeper one learned were its roots on all levels, from a ruling structure that profited from it to impoverished workers and out-of-work street people who dreamed of getting rich quick on their lucky day.

Although *jueteng* sometimes dominated headlines, killings and assassinations were front-page staples. On one dark day in December 1995, a communist death squad gunned down an 82-year-old Filipino-Chinese industrialist and the 5-year-old son of a Singapore businessman. The killers threatened more as long as the rich exploited the poor.

In pursuit of thieves and criminals in high places, reporters, researchers and others with probing questions are often greeted by the challenge, "Can you prove it?" Seldom was proof available, even in cases in which thousands of dollars changed hands to spring an accused criminal from jail or do away with a political enemy, but the perception persists that corruption is intrinsically related to what many outside the topmost ranks of government see as a national crisis. The crisis has nothing to do with a foreign enemy, the kind the Americans staunchly maintained they were guarding against by clinging to the bases. The enemy is here, there, everywhere—not only the New People's Army or the Moro rebels in Mindanao. The worst enemies are the pillars of the establishment.

Ben Serrano, a columnist for *Gold*Star Daily,* published in northern Mindanao, also delineated the foe even though he offered no proof. "I'm really amused on the people's complaint about the recent crisis we are facing today," he wrote in Fil-English. "After plans to petition of some equally greedy oil companies, to foot and mouth disease, to formalin-using of some vegetable and fish traders to extract more and more profits, to sugar price increased [*sic*] that soars high like a flying Philippine Eagle, basic commodities price screwed-up, and the most devastating event that really hit us, especially poor people like me, the unabated high price of rice that cause an uproar of our citizenry, all of these have one common denominator, and all bogs down to local officials and government agencies' inutile, efficient and ineffective governance."[22]

Serrano sardonically refused to hold the man at the top responsible: "Who's to blame? President Ramos, I don't think so! And I firmly believe it is US, the people." The columnist pointed at those widely viewed as the real culprits—the people around Ramos, "feeding the President wrong information" and "wrong direction by issuing policies that are for their own benefit and not for the people."[23]

One immediate crisis sprang from the shortfall of rice. The country was supposed to be a rice bowl, with three-quarters of its people working on farms, but by late 1995 the populace found itself short of the staple of life. The price of rice rapidly rose, from ten pesos (about forty cents a kilo) to more than twice that amount—no problem for those who dictate policy but enough to compel millions less fortunate to go hungry.

As usual, payoffs were presumed responsible. Officials at the notorious National Food Authority were oddly reluctant to buy American rice at a tremendous U.S.-subsidized discount. They preferred to forage elsewhere, perhaps for rice from Thailand of inferior quality after having been stored too long, for one reason: the Thai would gladly remit the usual 10 percent kickback to Philippine importers and those behind them. Then there was that other fear—that Chinese middlemen in collusion with bureaucrats were hoarding rice to drive up prices. True, these "middlemen" were Filipino citizens, but in the popular view they were the enemy gnawing away at the fabric of society.

The fear goes much deeper. All the Philippines' wealthiest families are ethnically Chinese or partly Chinese, with the notable exception of several extremely rich families of Spanish heritage. The list of the ten wealthiest Filipinos comprises ethnic Chinese in control of department stores, hotels, real estate, banks and insurance companies, vast agricultural estates and factories, plus the old Spanish names—Soriano, the San Miguel brewing family, and Zobel de Ayala, in banking and real estate, among other things.

Cory Aquino has a Chinese great-grandfather and is ethnically probably half-Chinese. Her cousins, "Danding" Cojuangco, her sworn enemy, and the late Jose Ramon Cojuangco, owner of the Philippine Long Distance Telephone Company, bear a Chinese family name—the "co" suffix is a giveaway for a Chinese *mestizo* of means in the Philippines. Marcos and Ramos, born and raised in northern Luzon, are also partly Chinese if a few generations removed. (They are blood relatives, second cousins, even though Ramos, after so faithfully serving Marcos, helped overthrow him.)

Thus the rice crisis symbolized an entire relationship between the most unscrupulous exploiters, growing in strength and national visibility once the Americans were gone from the bases, and the government with which they were in collusion. It symbolized the wealthy landowners, refusing or reluctant to give up their land under a pathetically ineffective land reform program, eager to take it back when poor farmers proved unable to pay the authorities, who sold it to them at reduced prices. It also symbolized the store owners selling overpriced goods, charging interest that most people could not afford. And it symbolized the banks, growing in size and prominence, the bailiwick of a moneyed class with far more pesos to spare than 95 percent of the people—an underclass too poor for banks, relegated to city shantylands or rural slums.

Through it all, American officials were relieved that the American bases did not become scapegoats. No longer could politicians like Salonga sell themselves on TV and in headlines by denouncing the bully America. The bases issue was over. A measure of the public view of Salonga's rhetoric was that he ran far behind the front-runners in the 1992 presidential election in which Ramos led the field with a mere 23.6 percent of the votes—not exactly a ringing endorsement.

Yet the government managed to invoke fear of foreigners in different ways. One was to attack the bars in Ermita, an old-time entertainment and red-light district in which foreigners once predominated as customers and owners. The mayor of Manila, Alfredo Lim, former senior official of a thoroughly bribe-ridden Manila police force, made a great show of closing down these dens of iniquity, where girls danced nearly naked and were available for the cost of the "bar fine," Fil-English for the fee the customer pays the bar for the privilege of checking one of them out for the night. Once the bars shut down in Ermita, the spotlight shifted to foreign bar districts outside the main gate of Clark and in one barrio of Olongapo, the world's freest port of call for American sailors on the town when Subic was under American control.

Ramos himself in 1995 and 1996 ordered crackdowns on "prostitution," which sounded all very well, except that girls are still available in massage parlors, bars, brothels, parks and streets in every city and town, and there is no prospect of the evil going away amid highly publicized raids. The hypocrisy is all the more evident in the plans of authorities, in league with businessmen, for the areas they supposedly cleaned up.

For Americans, the good news about the crackdown was that most of the culprits appeared to be another breed of arrogant foreigner, not American but Australian, who flocked to Manila, Angeles and Olongapo on tours whose sole purpose was cheap sex—cheap to them but big money for the bars and the girls who worked there. With the pressure off the United States, American officials and businesspeople believed that they would have far less difficulty than before in trade and investment. They were proud of an aid program that cost a fraction of the $900 million in "rent" the Philippines once demanded in aid as the price for renewal of the bases treaty.

American aid in the '90s was still going strong on the country's newest frontier, the giant southern island of Mindanao, opening up a brand-new port in General Santos City, named for the military figure who led a wave of settlers there in the 1930s. U.S. companies, with Agency for International Development contracts, constructed a 10,000-foot airstrip and seaport facility that might some day turn the once-distant outpost into a world-class center at the heart of Southeast Asia, bound economically by an increasingly active ASEAN (Association of Southeast Asian Nations). American aid appeared more carefully directed, easier to identify, more certain of results than before despite such vague programs as GEM (Growth with Equity in Mindanao) and GOLD (Governance of Local Development)—cesspools for perpetuation of a system the programs, on paper, were designed to change.

The United States, however, encountered suspicions and resentments that might worsen under stress or criticism. A sorry debate over facilities at Ninoy Aquino International Airport showed how the Americans were still convenient whipping boys regardless of political shifts. After a team from the Federal Aeronautical Administration denounced the airport as a security risk, Filipino officials, led by the transportation secretary, charged that the FAA investigation was a cover to force the government to acquiesce to an open skies deal under which U.S. planes could travel more or less as they wished to the Philippines and beyond.

To Max Soliven, educated at Fordham and often full of praise for the United States, these Americans were easy targets. "Now, those interfering Yankee bozos had better have a care," he inveighed. "We're not a colony of the US any longer. . . . We won't countenance being pushed around by the Great White Shark in our corner of the Pacific Ocean and the South China Sea."[24]

On a larger scale, the government focused on politics as usual in a style with dire implications for the future after Ramos. The question, "after Ramos, who?" was all-consuming. The purpose of the single-term provision, for which Aquino would fight as she never had for land reform, was to keep anyone from remaining in power for too long, possibly for life. It was a re-action to Marcos, who had every intention of remaining where he was from the time he won his first tainted presidential election in 1965 and on through martial law, which he lifted in January 1981 but tried to keep in place until his final defeat and overthrow. The trouble with the term limit, as critics noted, was that six years was too long for a bad president—and not enough for a good one.

Once she restored a semblance of democracy, Aquino was widely seen as falling into the category of a bad president. "She had every opportunity, but she did nothing," observed Bobby Romulo. She was, clearly, a victim of her narrow upbringing as the darling of a wealthy Catholic family, educated in Catholic schools and a confined Catholic college in New York and by the environment and circles in which she moved at home.

Cory's principal advisers were brothers Pedro "Pete" Cojuangco, a banker, and Jose "Peping" Cojuangco, a politician. Both of them were stubborn foes of serious change, notably land reform, to which they all paid lip service. Land reform, they feared, would tear apart the estate in Tarlac and numerous other holdings, the inheritances of not only the Aquinos and Cojuangcos but of all the ruling clans, friends and enemies alike, banded together by history, habit—and greed.

Ramos, by comparison, was a doer. A West Point graduate, with a master's degree in engineering from the University of Illinois, he had a practical mind that perceived the need for change. But how much change could he bring about—and how quickly? Ramos's oft-stated denials of any scheme for extending his term were less than convincing. In any case, legislators appeared to have far more fun talking over the topic, amid party "revolts" and "defections," than digging into issues. They were not about to vote for real changes that might undermine their roles as both members and representatives of a moneyed class. Their otherwise low-paying positions were, after all, extremely profitable—worth buying off, certainly, in any campaign.

Into the legislative maelstrom, toward the end of 1995, stepped a figure from the near-forgotten past—the widow Imelda Marcos, permitted by Cory to return from exile in Hawaii after the death of her husband in 1991 to bury him in his beloved homeland of Ilocos Norte. Easily the winner in the May 1995 race for the lower house seat as representative of her native island province of Leyte, she was prevented from taking her seat by the Commission on Elections (Comelec), whose members noted she had hardly resided in Leyte since childhood. Four months later, the Supreme Court ruled eight to five in Imelda's favor—and ordered Comelec to proclaim her the winner.

There were the inevitable rumors of payoffs, especially since the court postponed rulings that would decide whether she was to go to jail for a number of years for stealing billions from the national treasury as the First Lady of Malacañang. Nor was there much doubt her money would count once she assumed her seat in the lower house and bid for power among her peers. "It's so good to be back," she remarked charmingly, appearing for the press in her condominium, above that of the American embassy's public affairs officer, in Metro Manila's high-rise business and residential city of Makati.[25]

It was as though all was forgotten as Imelda, once the governor of Metro Manila while Ferdinand ruled the country from Malacañang, again posed a real threat in the money politics that prevailed as much now as in the old days. Although many refused to take her seriously, many more viewed her as a mythic figure from the past, forgetting her enormous crimes, forgetting even the assassination of Ninoy, which she undoubtedly had had a hand in engineering. The dream of a new Philippines, "Philippines 2000," as Ramos, thumbs-up, loved to repeat before audiences at home and abroad, faded in the nightmare of the Marcos era.

The wonder was that the Philippines still clung to the specter of American military power like a security blanket—frayed and thin but still there to pull out of the closet in case of serious threat. Astonishingly, American and Philippine forces, five years after the Americans had to withdraw from the bases, conducted joint exercises. A report that U.S. Navy Seals, experts in deep-sea diving, were training Filipinos in war games in the South China Sea was embarrassing. Could it be coincidence that such training went on while China claimed the Spratly Islands as Chinese—and in late 1994 built some ominously shaped octagonal structures on what a British navigator had dubbed "Mischief Reef"?[26]

Philippine and American officials cited the existence of the 1951 Mutual Defense Treaty as a guarantee of the Americans' pledge to come back if the country were seriously threatened. The words of General MacArthur,

"I shall return," when forced to flee the rocky island redoubt of Corregidor, at the mouth of Manila Bay, after the Japanese invasion of December 1941, still resonated. For several years after the closure of the American bases, a few thousand Philippine and American troops reconfirmed the tie in annual exercises called Balikatan ("Shoulder-to-Shoulder"), even as Washington ended a yearly outlay of $200 million in military assistance. Overall, U.S. aid plummeted from $500 million a year before the departure of U.S. forces to $157 million in 1993, en route to one-third that amount by the mid-90s.[27]

While Imelda ("Imeldific," to the Manila media) was staging her comeback, West Pointer Ramos dramatized the yearning for old ties in a new era. Like a voice from the cold war, Ramos, in Honolulu in October 1995, begged the United States to flex its muscles against China's new military, economic and political power. "Only with U.S. help, only with America's leadership, are we to have lasting regional stability," he said. "Over the next quarter century, China will unavoidably press—politically and military—on East Asia."[28] The message, anachronistic in a context of a superficially rising GNP, political violence and rampaging corruption, resonated among an elite not quite weaned from all the aid they had once lapped up so hungrily from Uncle Sam.

In the impasse between a Republican-led Congress and a Democratic White House, however, longstanding U.S. programs had joined the ranks of endangered species. American power—and interest—in Southeast Asia had never been at a lower ebb since the Spanish-American War nearly a century before. The United States, after withdrawing its last forces from South Vietnam, had been retreating steadily ever since—even as the economies of Southeast Asia and East Asia were in dizzy ascent. Further erosion of American military strength might lead to unforeseen displays of Chinese, even Japanese, strength. What if the Americans had to close their bases in Okinawa, wrested from Japan in the terrible battle of June 1945, then "reverted" to the Japanese in 1972?

The drama of Northeast Asia appears far removed from the Philippines—a cloud on the horizon. A look at a map, however, shows the close links between two regions. Taiwan is the nearest neighbor to the north. The memory of World War II may have dimmed, but Japan also views the Philippines as key to its regional security—not so important as Korea, to be sure, but no place to ignore in a showdown of strength or a power vacuum created by the Americans' absence.

The bases are gone, but the factors that had given them such importance are as relevant as ever. The Philippines, overrun by Spaniards, British, Spanish again, Americans, Japanese, Americans again, as well as waves of Chinese entrepreneurs, cannot endure in isolation. "What worries me are developments we have no control over," Defense Secretary Renato de Villa told me in an interview at Camp Aguinaldo, named for the national hero, General Emilio Aguinaldo, captured by the Americans in 1901. When asked for specifics, he replied, "Such as the United States and any other country around here. That's what we have to worry about."[29]

The Philippines, however, has much more to worry about at home. In the post-bases era, the country's worst enemies remain as they were before—the leaders of a thoroughly corrupt ruling class far more concerned about their intertwining networks of family and friends rather than the needs of a people in distress. At the apex of society, and of commerce and finance and, by gift and bribe, of politics and governance, are 40 families—or 50 or 500, depending on who's counting whom. The names of the "first families" may change as great fortunes wax and wane, as power shifts, but intermarriage and favor-giving ensure the continuity of a society that may compromise and bend but never really change.

The Filipinos' foreign conquerors perpetuated the society they dominated. The Spanish created a ruling class of *ilustrados,* an educated elite of the "enlightened," conniving for commercial gain with the steadily encroaching Chinese—ambitious but desperately poor young men from the Chinese southeast, cast into a Southeast Asian diaspora by wars and prejudices and domination by an entrenched ruling class in their own homeland. The Americans allied with the *ilustrados* to put down the rebels, who were themselves from the same ruling class. The Japanese, in their three-year rule, did nothing to question the arrangement, importuning members of the same elite to work with them for mutual gain.

The difference now, however, is that the Philippines, ruling class and everyone else, is on its own. The Americans are dubious allies. There is no longer a great foreign ruler, leader, protector or even benefactor. The new leaders, Ramos and his allies as well as their foes, seek economic and mercantile progress within the framework of a decayed system set up and controlled for centuries by foreigners. They have no notion of real change—and radical revision may be needed to overhaul a society sickened by social diseases that may otherwise be incurable.

TWO

Rivers of Mud

The pictures lied. The photographs of the vast mudflows on the flanks of Mount Pinatubo, 8.6 miles to the west of Clark Field, were deceptive. They showed mounds and inundations, but like photographic images of an athletic event, did not quite portray the reality. One had to fly over the mudflows below the 5,746-foot peak, at the center of the Zambales Mountains that divide the inland plain from Olongapo and Subic Bay, 25 miles down the westward slopes, to appreciate the awesome power of the 42 eruptions from June 12 to June 15, 1991.

Seated behind Richard Gordon, chairman of the Subic Bay Metropolitan Authority, in a helicopter flying about 1,000 feet above the mud, I had a sense of isolation and vulnerability. A sudden downdraft could plunge the chopper into the mud, perhaps into a quicksand from which recovery was impossible. At any moment, the mudflow could erupt into small explosions precipitated by the impact of cold rain- and floodwaters on the hot materials still simmering below the surface. The green forests of the surrounding crags and peaks seemed distant, another world away from this moonscape of uninhabitable, untracked, gray and beige lava and earth—the outpouring of a volcano that had lain dormant for six centuries before it exploded at the height of political and diplomatic turmoil over the future of the bases.

At the center of it all were the slopes of the crater, dug out of the peak's western shoulder. Our helicopter veered crazily over the fringes, then soared high above the shimmering blue waters of the 2-mile-wide lake, on the surface looking for all the world like an ideal resort area. This potential resort, however, would have to wait a few decades, perhaps a century or so, before it was safe for exploitation. According to reports from those few who had dared approach the edge, the water was still warm, perhaps near boiling a few feet below the surface.

The water, moreover, was high in sulfuric content, so much so that nothing swam or grew there. Above the lake, the earth rose in brown, bare folds, no place for man, beast or tree. So forbidding was the crater that no one, six years after the eruption, had blazed a reliable trail to the water's edge. Travel agents, advertising "Pinatubo tours," would escort the curious on a six-hour hike up barren slopes to the crater's rim during the dry season but had to stop the tours after the first rains. An American scuba diver risked a plunge in the waters, reporting them warm. A French team descended the crater to test water samples, then got lost on the way back and had to radio for help, which arrived by helicopter, not land. Ordinary adventurers were advised not to risk the trek to water's edge, by land or air.

One who braved the trip, both before and after the eruptions, was Pete Soledad, a Philippine Air Force officer. He was with a party of seismologists, Filipino and American, that flew to the slopes of Pinatubo on April 4, 1991, the day after Aeta tribesmen, who had lived there for centuries and viewed the mountain as sacred, reported steam rising from five vents near the summit just two months and eight days before the first eruption.

"One square kilometer of jungle was already dead," said Soledad. "Nothing was living there. No animals, no insects. They knew something was going on below the surface"—vengeance, said the Aeta, for drilling in the area by the Philippine National Oil Company.[1] Experts from the Philippine Institute of Volcanology and Seismology (PHILVOLCS) said that what was happening was "not an eruption but a hydrothermal explosion caused by hot underground rocks." Not until April 10, six days later, after one person was killed and several others injured by sulfurous fumes, did PHILVOLCS recognize the seriousness of the threat.[2]

From then on, seismologists from the U.S. Geological Survey and PHILVOLCS risked the trip again and again. They recalled the drama in an hour-long program produced by WGBH-TV in Boston and aired by cable in the Philippines. On June 2, checking numerous tremors around the summit and slopes, the Americans worried about an eruption with no warning. The next day, their instruments showed, "a big event comes in, probably an explosion." Rick Hoblitt of the U.S. team speculated, "I think maybe we're witnessing the—the—the precursor to a—to a historic eruption." Colleague Dave Harlow replied, "Don't talk like that! I don't want to hear that!" The same day, they posted "Alert Level 2," meaning "activity more intense, eruption probable."[3]

The buildup to one of history's greatest blasts intensified by the hour. While Filipinos were beginning to evacuate towns and villages, Major General William Studer, commander of the U.S. 13th Air Force, the crucial American unit that covered much of Asia and ranged into the Middle East from Clark, had to decide whether or when to evacuate the thousands of people under his command, and all their dependents, plus all his aircraft—a move that would look ridiculous if Pinatubo failed to explode. Like a commander at war, contemplating where, when and how to retreat in order to save men and materiél, Studer knew that he would look more than ridiculous if he hesitated too long. He would be disgraced, possibly court-martialed, held derelict in his responsibility for the lives of thousands.

As the general weighed the odds, he wrestled with the logistics of mass evacuation: "We had millions of dollars worth of airplanes, helicopters, millions and millions of dollars of supplies. We had about 14,500 or so people to move in short order. All of their belongings are very important to them. Their pets are very important to them. We had a 200-bed hospital, a lot of babies. I have to tell you that if you took all of that and tried to do it in one big bite, it becomes very mind-boggling and obviously just scares the hell out of you."[4]

To the staff of the U.S. Geological Survey, the messengers of bad news, the sense of responsibility was overwhelming. "People don't want probabilities, they want black and white," team member John Ewert discovered. "'Yes,' 'No,' 'It's going to erupt,' 'It's not,' 'It's going to be big,' 'It's not,' 'We should move,' 'We shouldn't.' It's—that was, for me, the worst part, and I didn't even have . . . that sort of awesome responsibility."[5]

Hoblitt captured the dilemma in the WGBH documentary: "Our stress load was intense. There was an awful lot riding on our interpretations, and if we—if we dropped the ball, it would be very unpleasant." If the experts said that everything was okay, then thousands of people might die needlessly, as had happened on November 13, 1985, when a boiling sea of mud triggered by Nevado del Ruiz in Colombia killed 22,000 people after experts had predicted, no explosion. Conversely, if the experts said to get out and nothing happened, they would risk the rage of Filipinos and Americans alike for triggering a false alarm. No one forgot that U.S. Geological Survey team members had received death threats after predictions of an eruption near the resort of Mammoth Lakes, California, in 1982 turned out to have been wrong—and thousands had fled.[6]

By June 7, the experts were sure things would get worse—much worse—before they got better. On that day the instruments picked up "continuous or nearly continuous earthquakes" and one non-stop shaking of the earth. Seismologist Dave Harlow of the survey team decided to "call a four," meaning Alert Level 4, the highest level, with "eruption possible within 24 hours." There was no mistaking what that meant. "You know, once you declare a four, the end of the world happens," said an American colonel. Everyone within 12 miles of the crater had to leave. By then, 120,000 Filipinos were either packing, on the road or in evacuation centers. General Studer, however, was less than completely convinced. He was not going to move those planes and people without more assurance that it wouldn't all be a terrible waste of time, effort and funds.[7]

Colonel Ron Rand, 13th Air Force public affairs officer, who was on the scene before, during and afterward, said later that Studer "called the shots by gut instinct," but the general was in a quandary. He had little time to decide whether to shut the airport and evacuate the mass of Americans. The geologists, however, offered no absolute guarantees of anything. "We could never pin them down," said Rand.[8]

Studer, unsure how to assess the judgement of the civilians sent from Washington, respected the ones who did not seem to show what he disparaged as the "chicken little tendencies" of some of the others. "I had been . . . looking at the situation with one of the individuals," said Studer, singling out Hoblitt for respect. "He was describing many times to me things he had seen in other places. We went up several times several thousand feet up."[9]

On June 8, a helicopter flight over the steaming top of the mountain offered further confirmation of all the experts had been saying. "We observe a dome," said Dave Harlow. "That's indicative of the kind of magma that's very explosive. So then suddenly the equation changed dramatically." Nobody "cared to walk up and whack off a sample of this stuff," he remarked in the WGBH program, but it was "the same stuff" that "had been erupted previously in these huge pyroclastic flow sheets" four or five times in 2,000 years.[10]

For Studer, the view from a helicopter while flying over the dome was more convincing than technical analyses. The general recalled "that thump-thump [of the helicopter blades] that all of us remember from Southeast Asia," where he had done two tours during the Vietnam War, flying C-123 cargo planes out of Danang, then F-4 Phantoms from Korat, Thailand, on bombing missions over North and South Vietnam. "The doors are open, you know, you hear the wind, and you see how big it is, and you're so close to it you feel like you could reach out and touch it, but you're afraid that if you did it'd burn your hand."[11]

At 5 A.M., June 10, Studer ordered the last planes, a few huge C-5 and C-141 transports, off the base while everyone else, men, women, families and pets, scrambled into cars, vans and trucks for the drive through the Zambales Mountains to Subic.[12] There was great historical irony here—though no one noticed it. Nearly half a century earlier, on December 8, 1941, General MacArthur, closeted in his headquarters at the Manila Hotel, had failed to order the planes off Clark Field after getting word of the Japanese attack on Pearl Harbor hours before. Japanese fighters and bombers, attacking in waves that same day, destroyed almost every plane on the ground, mostly P-40 fighters and B-17 bombers.

Facing a potentially more lethal foe in the form of Pinatubo, the U.S. commander had to make a similar but distinctly simpler decision. Two squadrons of F-4s, the workhorse fighter-bomber of the Vietnam War, had already flown out of Clark for reasons that had nothing to do with Pinatubo, and there was no plan to replace them. Had the Americans stayed on, Clark would have still served a major role as a supply hub and training center for regular live-fire exercises, called "Cope Thunder," but its days as a fighter base were over.

Thus Studer downplays any suggestion of great instincts in his decision to shut down Clark in the nick of time: "I would like to take credit for some big brainstorm, but it just wasn't there. There was a time when we said, 'No one can use our base any more, no one can bring an airplane in.' We reached a point where because of the ongoing activity we did not want to risk an airplane coming in and not being able to take off." He believes the call was obvious—"there was not a lot of technology involved"—and shrugs off some of the complex technical analyses by the civilian experts: "It was more common sense."[13]

At the same time, the general was sensitive about photographs purporting to show that the Americans had left a few planes behind: "There were what we call trainers for people to practice blowing holes in and patching. Those are the infamous planes that people say, 'Oh, they didn't get all the planes out,' because they have pictures of airplanes covered with ash. One was a 105 [F-105, another Vietnam War mainstay]. They were derelict airplanes. They were used in maintenance training."[14]

Although Studer's instinct was sharp enough to prevent a loss of aircraft, he still waited longer than some second-guessers believed he should have to order evacuation of the base. The trip to Subic ordinarily takes two hours but stretched to ten in the chaos of everyone leaving at once on June 10 rather than earlier, in stages. Studer denies, however, that there was more than normal confusion—and disputes the impression that the ordeal was an all-day affair. "We got about 14,500 people out in about six hours. It was taken care of very well. It was done very professionally. Everybody did what they were supposed to do. It was a good operation."[15]

Steven Campbell, a former air force sergeant who now runs a restaurant in Angeles City, saw the scene differently. "The evacuation from Clark was a joke," he recalled. "They should have let on to the people what was happening—that they knew more than what they told us."[16]

The day-long traffic jam was only one of the more obvious problems. Campbell blames Colonel Rand for having failed to release information and then for minimizing the implications: "Ron Rand was on TV saying, 'Take three days of supplies of clothing, don't worry about your valuables, everything will be protected, we'll let you know when it's time to evacuate.' Then hours later it was time to go. People had no money. The banks were closed. Gas was rationed. We had to wait four hours in line to get five gallons."[17]

Caught between the need to avoid spreading panic and the desire for a speedy evacuation, Rand offers no apologies: "We evacuated the base so quickly, people didn't take a lot of stuff with them."[18]

By the time that Campbell, a specialist in maintaining the weapons systems on MH-53 helicopters, got to Subic with his wife and year-old baby, he found a scene of near-mayhem: "They were not prepared for thousands of people. Processing was horrible. They should have never sent everyone down at one time. We stood in the processing line. It was hotter than hell down there. There was me, my wife and daughter in line for 17 hours. We would have been better off if we hadn't moved down. There was no water-rationing for that amount of people. There was no food service."[19]

The *Philippine Flyer,* unofficial paper for the American community on Clark, gave perhaps the most objective view. "By 6 A.M., the first vehicles were rolling out the gate and a little more than six hours later, about 14,000 folks were on the road," the paper reported. The roads were jammed as tens of thousands of Filipinos joined the rush to get out of harm's way. It was not until nightfall that everyone was finally "safe at Subic."[20]

While thousands were fleeing, the American experts, huddling over their instruments, were depressed. It was not the hardship and suffering about to engulf the populace or fears for their own safety that most disturbed them. For them, their careers and their professional reputations were at stake. What if their forecasts were wrong? What if they were causing all this trouble for nothing? "That was a period of falling off in our spirits," said Harlow. "We were then beginning to really second-guess ourselves. We were fundamentally sure something was going to happen, but then we started asking the what-if—what if this waits a long time? What if it doesn't go? What if we, you know, made a huge mistake?"[21]

By early morning of June 12, there was no doubt what was happening. As ashen clouds billowed up from Pinatubo, everyone left at Clark began running to the east side of the base for fear the lava would shower down on them from the west. "I see that thing started going and I was gone," said one airman. "I think my underwear is about two and a half miles that way," said another. "It came straight up, yeah, about this fast, and that was it."[22]

Among the experts, the response was delight. "It was more of an emotional release," Harlow recalled for the benefit of WGBH. "One, it was a spectacular blast, and second . . . what we had been saying was right on about the volcano, that we had really nailed it, and then there was a lot of excitement about that." The worst, however, was yet to come. "We knew that June 12th wasn't the big guy," said Ewert. "That was just the volcano saying, 'Okay, I'm going to do it,' I'm ready, and . . . these are appetizers"—although a shower of ash and sand spreading as far as 50 miles from the volcano gave many the impression they had seen it all, and what else could possibly happen?[23]

Besides the big one, a typhoon was also on the way—due to hit "within the next 36 hours," just about the time Pinatubo was likely to erupt in earnest. Sure enough, on the morning of Saturday, June 15, "Pinatubo serves up the main course. From 2 A.M. on there's a continuous eruption, punctuated by massive explosions that send ash 100,000 feet into the air. At daybreak, when the eruption becomes visible, it appears to be over 10 miles wide. Pyroclastic flows roar down from the summit in all directions, and even from 15 miles away these flows overwhelm the horizon."[24]

Geologist Kelvin Rodolfo, arriving two days earlier from his lab at the University of Illinois at Chicago, realized Pinatubo had blown in earnest as the tephra or rock fragments began "pattering on the trees," with "walnut-sized pieces" falling amid the ash. By then, "reddish, horizontal lightning and loud thunder was unceasing, for airborne ash is laden with static electricity, which jumps from one portion of the eruption cloud to another," he said. "The lightning bolts overhead were so close that they were accompanied without lag by enormous thunderclaps. My last nap between samples was ended by an especially loud crash that brought me leaping to my feet, yelling 'Heto na!'—'Here it is!'—for the eruption was permeating my dreams." The time: "Five-thirty Saturday morning, even though it was pitch-black in the moments between lightning strokes."[25]

Then, at 6:30 A.M., Typhoon Yunya joined the tumult, metamorphosing ash and lava into gray and white mud, turning day into pitch-dark night and vastly complicating the escape from the area. The *Philippine Flyer* described the near-panic: "Instead of plumes of gray ash steadily climbing even higher, the darker than usual cloud immediately began spreading laterally. Wide-eyed ash warriors looking at the volcano that morning saw a wall of ash about five miles across rising into the leading edges of Typhoon Yunya, which just happened to be closing in on Clark with swirling winds and nearly 7 inches of rain."[26] Word spread that "pyroclastic flows—rivers of gas and pumice heated to 900 degrees celsius and moving 60 to 100 mph—might reach the base . . . day turned into night as falling ash and pumice stones blocked out the sun."[27]

It was up to a 1,500-person security force to guard Clark against a scourge the extent of which no one fully predicted—wave on wave of looters. General Studer ordered most of the security troops to the safety of the Pampanga Agricultural College to the north while he, his staff, and the civilian experts hung on, monitoring their instruments, leaving briefly, then returning after staring at the eruptions through ash-and-storm-darkened skies.

Attempts at figuring out the strength of volcanic activity stopped around 2 P.M. when the pyroclastic flow inundated the sensors out on the slopes.

Now the question was whether the experts could get out at all. "We had . . . four cinderblock walls between us and the mountain," said Ewert. "It's this great hurricane-force winds and rocks and just an awful mess, and you know, you figure if you hunker down behind a wall, maybe you'll . . . come through it. And you know, the roof will come off and a lot of debris'll fly around, but maybe you'll be okay."[28]

Nor was flight from the base necessarily a sure passport to safety. Off-base, people were also at risk—and just as frightened. "The images of Black Saturday are etched forever in our memories," wrote the *Philippine Flyer.* "The eerie midday darkness, ash falling like snow; mud and rocks raining like cats and dogs; the raging volcano clashing with a thundering typhoon; families and friends huddled together in the glow of candles and flashlights, because there was no power; everybody jumping with fear each time the earth quaked, and all of us wondering just when it would all end and things get back to normal."[29]

General Studer held back a team of 32 "after we had sent everybody else up to the college" to spend the night. "The pumice that fell on us was soft and flaky and large while the mountain was coming apart, but the biggest thing was you could not see, you could not hear, and what you could see was scaring the hell out of you." Studer would not be convinced that he and the rest of the team had to go, however, until "the frequency got to what I thought was appropriate, thousands of earthquakes."[30]

Shortly after 4 P.M., as the eruptions escalated in violence and the lava broke entirely out of the volcano's dome, Studer made the final decision to clear out the last 32 Americans, himself included. "What made me leave was a guy by the name of Andy who ran past me saying, 'General, you better put jam in your pockets, we're all about to get toasted.' When that guy . . . ran past me going the other way, I said, 'I think I'm going to follow him.'" Colonel Rand, who was driving alone, literally the last man off the base, re-called the mad dash: "It was showering like you wouldn't believe. It was pelting us. Typhoon Yunya dropped nine more inches of rain while the ash was coming down."[31]

Rick Hoblitt, getting to his van, found "a driver in there crossing him-self." No one doubted it was time to go. "We were very confident we were doing the right thing," said Harlow. "There was no question about any-body's courage left any more." Ewert did not "regret leaving at all." He looks back with a laugh, "I think if I was put in that situation again, I'd—I might have left sooner"—"just psychologically I was happy to get away, to go any-where else, as long as it was away from where that eruption was happening." Otherwise, "I might have come unglued. . . . It was a week of almost no sleep and incredible stress, and then to have this sort of constant earthquake activity was unnerving."[32]

That night, the ash was falling as far away as Manila, 50 miles to the south, closing Ninoy Aquino Airport, disrupting traffic, sending millions into the streets to watch in wonder—and millions more into their homes in search of shelter. Katherine Bruce, then a student at the International School, remembers driving through the storm: "They were playing 'White Christmas' on the radio. We were all singing it."[33]

Come the dawn, the worst was over, and a small group of Americans returned from Pampanga Agricultural College to the north where they had sheltered overnight. "But as we cautiously emerged from our shelters Sunday morning and looked in awe on the gray devastation all around us, we knew things were never going to get back to normal," said the *Philippine Flyer.* "Buried in ash several inches deep, with hundreds of buildings collapsed, Clark, Subic, San Miguel and Cubi Point were no longer able to support us. Roads were blocked by mud, tree limbs and abandoned vehicles; the power was still out; and there wasn't much food and water."[34]

To Rudolph "Tiny" Littleton, in Angeles with his wife and five children, the day after was a phantasmagorical hangover. "I was right here on this house on the Sunday the day after the volcano blew," said Tiny, an enormous man who retired from the navy as a chief petty officer, then toiled for a contractor in Saudi Arabia and ended up working for the Americans on the base. "After the volcano blew, there was no electricity, no water. We had earthquakes every three minutes." The typhoon added to a scene out of hell. "The eye passed through this area. There was a fire at the Shanghai Restaurant on MacArthur Highway. It started in the kitchen, probably a broken gas line. The staff had all run away. The fire trucks couldn't pass because the Abacan Bridge collapsed. It was like Dante's Inferno."[35]

Tiny looked for another analogy to describe the ordeal. "Imagine what the end of the world will be like. I have seen a lot of things, but I don't want to see anything like that again." Nor did the cessation of eruptions and the end of the typhoon bring instant relief. "Food was starting to go bad. My kids were getting scared for the first three or four days. We have close friends in Malolos (on the highway to Manila). We stayed with them for eight or nine days, and two housemaids stayed here to keep people from ripping things off. When I came back, I had a foot of sand and ash on the roof."

A U.S. Air Force pilot, Lieutenant Colonel Jules Ferreira, contrasted the sight from the air, before and afterward. "Before Pinatubo erupted, there was moon crater valley. They had a bunch of little craters from the last eruptions 600 years ago. Now it's lahar valley, lahar and ash. What blew was the 3,000-foot side, on the west side of Pinatubo, north northwest. It blew down to 1,500 feet. A lot of people thought it was the top of Pinatubo. The peak is still there."[36]

For all the advance notice, the death toll still climbed to about 1,000, many of them Aeta tribal people. The Aeta, for centuries the victims of discrimination by a lowland majority, were unwilling to leave their jungle homes for an uncertain existence in more populated areas. Their reluctance "would persist until the morning of the great paroxysm," Rodolfo observed, "for all the worldly goods of poor mountain people is [sic] in their homes and their small plots of land."[37]

The volcano had no mercy for those who stayed behind. One newspaper reported that 52 Aeta hiding in a cave were suffocated and may have burned to death. Other laggards may have suffered a similar fate.[38] Had it not been for the warnings, however, thousands more would have died. Left behind or left outdoors with nowhere to go for shelter, half the animals within 50 miles of the volcano were killed. Now the emphasis was on the aftermath.

The first reports dwelled on the long-range environmental impact of Pinatubo. The eruption—one of the worst in recorded history, the world's worst in 80 years, ten times the ferocity of Mount St. Helens in Washington State in 1980—sent enough ash and dust into the atmosphere to lower global temperatures by nearly 1° C for a year. Then there was the obvious spectacle of physical damage. Foot-deep ash was so heavy that bridges and roofs collapsed, roads were blocked and runways shut down. Homes were isolated as if in a blizzard. The volcano would go on popping intermittently, but it's predicted to wait a few hundred more years before erupting again in full fury.

The saga of Pinatubo was far from finished, however, after the volcano had ceased belching fire and steam and smoke, the skies had cleared and people had cleaned off the worst of the rubble and begun rebuilding homes, apartment and office blocks, nipa huts and shacks, all of which had been pounded, cracked and caved in by the showering ash and pumice. Pete Soledad, one of the first to reach the smoldering volcano before the eruption, also got a firsthand posteruption view. Flying into the crater by helicopter three months after the blast, he jumped from the craft long enough to dip a finger in the waters while a scientist scooped up a sample. "We were there for a few seconds. The water was still hot."[39]

Millions in the path of the rivers and streams pouring down the Pinatubo watershed now face an annual cycle of flooding and burial beneath the dreaded lahar. The word itself is from bahasa Indonesia, the Indonesian Malay language related to Tagalog and numerous other languages of the Philippines. A British geologist picked up the word from local Javanese after viewing the aftereffects of the eruption of another volcano, Mount Kelut on Java in 1919, and introduced it in a scientific journal a decade later.[40]

The problem of lahar caught the country by surprise. At first, it was hard to believe that lahar would do more than a season or two of damage. As monsoon rains pummeled the land in the summer and fall of 1991 and the mud widened the rivers, creating new streambeds and tearing down villages and towns, the sense was that this season of hell would be the last—the next would surely be easier; in a year or two, the problem would evaporate as the moonscape on Pinatubo congealed and life sprouted anew on what had been jungle before and would become jungle again.

The figures, though, argue differently. No one knows exactly how much lava and mud the eruptions flung up and over the countryside, but experts estimated the pyroclastic flow at anywhere between four and seven cubic *kilometers,* enough to fill four to seven boxes, each measuring one kilometer across and one kilometer deep. Or as Rodolfo graphically put it: "Pinatubo released hundreds of times more energy than the largest thermonuclear weapon ever tested, which was equivalent to the energy of 58 megatons— million tons—of TNT, over a million times more energy than the atomic bomb that leveled Hiroshima."[41] The flow in one place west of the crater was 200 meters thick, deep enough to form an entire new ridge.

Typically, the field of lahar cast over the slopes is 50 meters thick, an-chored by no vegetation and still hot beneath the surface, with a density equivalent to concrete—becoming wet, sucking ooze in the monsoon season and deceptively dry and hard in the dry season, spreading a dozen miles across, with a depth of 1–4 meters thick as far as 10–15 miles from the crater. A year later, destruction in jobs lost was 650,000, and 50,000 lost their homes—40,000 were lowlanders, the rest Aetas, many of them help-less to compete and left to beg on the streets of Manila.[42]

U.S. Air Force Colonel Arthur J. Corwin, in charge of U.S. security at Clark, summarized the destruction on base: "Clark AB was severely dam-aged with over 200 buildings partially collapsed or destroyed. Hundreds of others were on the brink of collapse under tons of ash. Utilities were out, water and sewer systems were inoperative, and rations were limited to meals ready to eat (MRE). It took months to stabilize this situation and critical problems were experienced until the base closed."[43]

Corwin painted a stark picture: "The climate/environment during the post-Pinatubo period (Jun-Nov 91) was so harsh at Clark AB (near-continuous ashfall, daily rainy season storms, mudflows, lahars, extreme heat) that continuous cleaning/maintenance of vehicles, equipment, build-ings and grounds was required." As if all that were not enough, "All facilities had to remain in near inspection order for the never ending parade of VIP's . . . coming to see the destruction."[44]

The ferocity of the blast relieved the Americans of one difficult deci-sion. Amid all the pressure from Filipino politicians to abandon the bases, Washington had no trouble deciding simply not to rebuild Clark. On July 17, Richard Armitage and Raul Manglapus jointly announced the new agreement under which the United States would withdraw from Clark and two smaller bases—but would stay in Subic for another ten years while paying $203 million a year.

The planes flown out of Clark in the weeks before Pinatubo erupted were never to return, though the landing strips, including one completed just a few months earlier, were cleared. The families shipped out of Clark on June 10 never came back, either. A U.S. security force would remain until November, but the base, post-Pinatubo, no longer had a military purpose.

The greatest reason for Americans to regret the loss of Clark may have been its rising value as a regional training center for the Cope Thunder war games, in which planes bombed and strafed the Crow Valley range to the west in remarkably realistic exercises. Although no more fighter planes would base at Clark, the idea, pre-Pinatubo, was that they would continue to fly in from throughout the Pacific region for training. "The planes for Clark were to be the primary base for Cope Thunder, which would have made it the number one training base for the Pacific," said Studer.[45]

Military strategists had big dreams for Clark. They wanted "to give it an increased and expanding role with regard to our allies, the Australians, the Thais," Studer explained. "There were plans for other countries to participate in Cope Thunder."

The Pentagon clearly had little comprehension, in the years before the loss of Clark, of the depth of the danger—not from Pinatubo but from Philippine politics. The generals were counting on staging Cope Thunder games every six weeks or so. The second 10,000-foot runway, opened less than a year pre-Pinatubo, made it possible for 120 to 125 planes to fly in and out constantly. "The two runways allows you to make simultaneous takeoffs," said Studer. "It allows you to make simultaneous recoveries [landings]. If you have a lot of airplanes taking off within seconds, if you had an emergency, it would allow landing at the same time."[46]

Nor was the second runway the only newly added attraction at Clark. "There had been a multi-million-dollar facility built specifically for Cope Thunder—an auditorium for mass debriefings, the ramp upgraded so you could get the majority of the planes parked in the same area," said Studer. "It was big business and superior training." So vital was Clark for training that the air force had to find another facility for conducting similar exercises. (It now stages Cope Thunder in Alaska, at Eielson Air Force Base near Fairbanks.)

Studer cited the cost of repairing Clark post-Pinatubo as prohibitively high in an era of peace, especially after the Soviet Union's collapse. "My estimates that I had gotten from competent authority was in the neighborhood of $600–$800 million, and we would continue to have fallout from the volcano at various times probably for the next ten years."[47] There was no way the U.S. Congress would authorize that kind of money to reopen Clark—even if the Philippine Senate were to vote, as some diplomats and pro-bases politicians still unrealistically expected, to renew the treaty.

Olongapo was another story. "Tephra shoveled or sloughed off the roofs had piled up to depths of two feet in the streets, which were cluttered with downed electric poles and wires," Rodolfo noted, but the Zambales Mountains safeguarded the Subic Bay navy base from either pyroclastic flow or lahar.[48] Washington resolved to repair Subic—though "warehouses and other steel buildings, some sheltering helicopters or jet aircraft, looked like so many stepped-on shoe boxes."[49] The resurrection of Subic was well under way when the vote in the Senate told the Americans they were not wanted there or elsewhere, any more than at Clark.

What no one fully recognized at the time was that the worst, for much of the countryside, was yet to come. The lahar, far from diminishing year by year, actually poured down the slopes and waterways from Pinatubo in ever-greater quantities.

The pattern was deceptive. The dry season between typhoons and monsoons had a lulling effect. When the rains ceased to fall, the lahar hardened quickly, in a day or two in places, a week at most, and trucks and buses could rumble across as easily as on a paved road. For the first few years, engineers believed it was the right stuff for the flimsy dikes they were throwing up in a perfunctory gesture at saving the country from next season's deluge. Lahar was even used for rebuilding roadways—with disastrous results when the rains came, as inexorably they would, and the lahar flowed again, just as inexorably.

The lahar flow was nearly at its worst when I was caught on the other side of a flood of the sticky gray stuff in September 1995, while on the road between San Fernando and Bacolor, an historic town already largely under mud and water. Officials were awakening to the reality that most of the 10-billion-peso special budget bequeathed to the Mount Pinatubo Commission two years before had been squandered. With another 136,971 families reported homeless by September 1, word was fast spreading that dikes were crumbling all along the Pasig-Potrero River, the main waterway southward from the eastern slopes of Pinatubo. No one knew what to do to stop what many resignedly dismissed as "nature's way."

Engineers at the commission talked about building "the mother of all dikes." Manuel "Lito" Lapid, the "top action star" governor of Pampanga Province, hardest hit by lahar, feared that a proposed tertiary dike would wipe out more populated areas.[50] Instead, Lapid, who spent most of his time working in films that got his picture on billboards throughout the country, called for deepening existing channels, the ones overflowing with lahar.

The popular Senator Gloria Macapagal-Arroyo, four months earlier the biggest vote-getter in the national senatorial election, daughter of Diosdado Macapagal, the corrupt ex-president notorious for his government's involvement in smuggling, whom Marcos had defeated at the polls 30 years before, called for disbanding the Mount Pinatubo Commission altogether. Better to entrust rescue and relief and recovery to existing agencies, said Macapagal-Arroyo, who liked to cite her family's roots in the lahar region, than pour more funds down a damnable, undammable drain.

At Pampanga Provincial Hospital, awash in water up to its doorsteps but still functioning, the regional director, Dr. Ignacio Valencia, noted that engineers had raised the nearby main road by three meters during the last dry season, only to see the lahar crest above it the day I got there. "The problem with this ten billion pesos is they started putting up dams and bags which are ineffective," he said. "They put some mesh wire and dikes, but they are being washed out." Like everyone else, he blamed "the contractors, probably the politicians and bureaucrats." None of them shared the terror of the bereaved and displaced, herded into resettlement areas where, the doctor observed, "people have no livelihood, no will to survive, are just waiting for alms."[51]

Valencia dared, at this juncture, to venture a view shared by many but not expressed much in public since the end of the great debate over keeping the bases. "Personally, I believed the two bases must stay," he said, referring to both Subic and Clark. For one thing, he noted, had American forces still been there, U.S. Army engineers and Navy Seabees, backed up by helicopters, fixed-wing aircraft and mobile hospital teams, would have been visible all over the region, rebuilding the roads and ministering to the victims, carrying out a massive relief operation that was clearly beyond the immediate capability of Philippine forces.[52]

Now, no one talked about American aid. It was up to the Filipinos to prove that they could handle the crisis themselves.

Again, the pictures lied. Although news photographs showed restaurants covered up to the signs on their roofs, church steeples rising from the mud, homes that appeared to have sunk of their own weight in the muck, they hardly captured all the devastation. Worst hit by early September 1995 was Bacolor. The trading community's origins preceded the arrival of the Spanish in the sixteenth century. Chinese immigrants had settled there, building it into an important center before the Spanish made it the capital of Pampanga. Briefly, in 1762, when the British took over Manila for two years, it became a Spanish colonial capital in exile.

The arrival of the railroad had given the edge to San Fernando, a relatively new community built by the Spanish in the eighteenth century; in

1904 the Philippine Commission, under the American governor-general, approved San Fernando as the new provincial capital. Still, Bacolor, a cultural center of graceful Spanish-style homes, had a cachet and heritage that time had not erased. "What Boston is to the United States, Bacolor is to Pampanga," wrote one of the townspeople at the time. "When San Fernando became the capital, thus robbing Bacolor of her right to that name, she could not fill the offices without going to Bacolor."[53]

For all its past glory, the rush of lahar in September 1995 relegated the town, past and present, to memory. One by one, Bacolor's 21 *barangay*, the Tagalog word that Marcos had ordered to replace the Spanish *barrio*, disappeared under the mud. Finally, only one was left—though hardly habitable. Townspeople did not flee until absolutely necessary. Many, fearful of losing treasured possessions to looters if not to lahar, clung to the rooftops until they were able to get out by rafts or by Philippine Air Force helicopters. In vain, the mayor, Ananias Canlas Jr., argued for reconstruction, for stopgap diking—anything to save his town. Bacolor was hallowed history, another Pinatubo casualty.

The same fate awaited portions of some if not all of a score of other towns. Guagua, an important center bordering Bacolor, was already partly under water, as was half of San Fernando to the northeast. Shops were open, but townspeople had to splash through one or two feet of water on downtown streets, sometimes paddling rafts and rowboats instead. The flooding here would not be fatal—unless the water rose significantly. Lahar was the real menace; it was capable of burying neighborhoods so deep that a passerby might not know anyone had ever lived there.

By the time the 1995 monsoon and typhoon season were over, San Fernando, center of the relief operation and the junction point for buses and trucks roaring to and from Metro Manila, through the Zambales Mountains to Olongapo and northwest to Angeles City, Tarlac and Baguio and points beyond, also ranked on the endangered list, for it was in the path of an onslaught that experts feared might worsen year by year for another decade.

While mud and flood ravaged the land, the experts, bureaucrats, politicians and contractors dominated the headlines with their quarrels over what to do about it all. One of the most outspoken was Kelvin Rodolfo, son of an Ilocano father and a German-Russian mother, who was raised in the town of San Antonio southwest of Pinatubo and educated in both the Philippines and the States. He antagonized the contractors, the director of PHILVOLCS and not a few of the politicians and bureaucrats salivating over kickbacks by arguing against doing much of anything beyond clearing the path of those in the way of the mud.

"We can ignore fancier physics," Rodolfo told one audience. "This is the earthly and laharic reality." From that verity he jumped to what he saw as an unavoidable conclusion: "We cannot make the debris destined to descend as lahars shrink or go away. We cannot make it go away by blowing it away wholesale with explosives. Even if we commanded the brute force to do so— which we by far do not—we would simply be redistributing it as a wide-spread, disastrous ashfall." That said, he asked, rhetorically, "But can we bulldoze and truck it away?"

To Rodolfo, the logic was irrefutable. Removing the lahar by heavy equipment could "be resorted to *only as a very short-term, desperation mea-sure,*" whereas dikes "serve as failed experiments that teach us what we should *not* do." In fact, he said, in a presentation backed by all manner of facts and figures, *"an inadequate hazard-containment structure is itself a haz-ard—a man-made hazard."*[54]

Rodolfo was emphatic about the most controversial proposal—the one calling for a 21-kilometer-long dike that would help to form a catchment basin in which all the lahar would collect, it was dearly hoped, until the mys-tical day when Pinatubo was stripped bare of the horrible stuff or vegetation had begun to hold it to the slopes. To the disapprobation of many bureau-crats, Rodolfo evinced an understanding that argued against any kind of dike on the basis of political and social realities, let alone finer technical points: *"A good 20-kilometer dike meant to contain* floodwater *(not lahars, which are much stronger) takes at least two years to build properly."* Already, the part of the dike "that was completed in the first year is gone, a total waste."[55]

In his role as science consultant to Richard Gordon's Subic Bay Metro-politan Authority, Rodolfo was only slightly more sanguine about building up the 2-kilometer stretch of road running southwest from San Fernando through Bacolor, by now totally impassable without engineering. To many, the proposal was absurd—as if raising the height another three meters would guarantee the flow of traffic through the next typhoon season and the next, when the last 3-meter buildup had failed so miserably.

Since the road was a lifeline for Olongapo and Subic, however, Rodolfo adopted a more tolerant view. "Whether intended or not," he advised Gor-don, "the raised stretch of road would serve as a debris dam that would pro-tect the Bacolor poblacion at the cost of further burial of the barangays [*sic*] north of the road." Rather than condemn road reconstruction as futile, he allowed as how "I do not think that this is necessarily a bad idea"—but warned "it also means deflection of dilute lahars" over the road along with "disruption in traffic" and "continued incursion of lahars into Guagua," the first town southwest of Bacolor. Then there was yet another big "if"—"if the fundamental lahar path does not switch in the upstream area . . . to flow to-ward western San Fernando."[56]

Outside expertise might be welcome on narrowly technical matters but had no effect on the politicking, name-calling and accusations among politicians and bureaucrats. "Misuse of public funds in the billions of pesos is perhaps the greater cause of the people's suffering in the area," editorialized the *Manila Standard,* echoing the popular view. "Haphazard construction of expensive dikes to control the lahar flow without success has been given priority over evacuation, relief and rehabilitation of the victims. There is money to be made by government officials and contractors in the first, none in the second. This attested to by new mansions and ostentatious lifestyles of certain persons."[57]

At the Mount Pinatubo Commission, the target of much of the criticism, Executive Director Antonio Fernando, a retired army colonel, smoothly parried all the shots fired at him. "Most of the dikes were lahar-mitigating projects," he told me in his office in a row of white frame houses, once the homes of senior American officers, facing Clark's historic parade ground. "They were made of lahar. We had only time to build the raw dike"—a handy rationale for why all of them had caved in so easily. A one-time Philippine Military Academy classmate of National Security Adviser Almonte, Fernando was puzzled by accusations of bribery in the awarding of contracts. "They were awarded through public bidding, we have a commission on audit."[58]

Still, Fernando had to admit "there was a time after Mount Pinatubo erupted when they were taking on projects without documentation"—and "there was this thing called *laharscam,*" a word coined by the media for the kickbacks held responsible by many for diversion of all those lahar funds. Noting that his commission was formed in 1992 in answer to "laharscam," Fernando was aggrieved by one columnist's description of his commission as "a band of thieves." Had not the Senate committee chaired by the gadfly Gloria Macapagal-Arroyo gone over the records and found "there are no laharscams"? Now, he pleaded, he had to coordinate the disaster effort with funds running out and bureaucrats demanding "an all-weather road" running southwest from San Fernando.

Partly on the basis of Rodolfo's advice, engineers hastily raised the elevation of the road yet again and, for a brief interim between typhoons, had it open to traffic. Rodolfo, it turned out, might have applied his advice on dike-building to road-raising. Undoubtedly, he would have been considerably less positive had he written Gordon several weeks later, after Typhoon Mameng on October 1, 1995, belted the region with enough force to bury the rest of Bacolor and endanger San Fernando. The mayor of San Fernando, fighting for the life of his city in the name of his Save San Fernando Movement, acutely mindful of the fate of Bacolor, inveighed passionately against suggestions for more road-raising, which was blamed for having already diverted the flow into half of San Fernando's *barangay.* Enough was enough.

For the bureaucrats and politicians, however, enough was never enough. As more towns were evacuated from the path of the rising lahar, President Ramos on October 12 ventured from Malacañang for his first visit of the season to the nation's most critical trouble spot. An inveterate junketeer who often flew about the country and aroused bitter criticism for his many trips overseas, Ramos had somehow not previously found time to travel 40 miles north of Manila to inspect the damage and witness the suffering. When he finally did so, he turned the expedition into a publicity stunt in which he made a show of consulting with local leaders in the company, among others, of Defense Secretary Renato de Villa, a long-time army friend who was also chairman of the national disaster coordinating council, as well as the Public Works Secretary, Gregorio Vigilar, and Senator Macapagal-Arroyo.

A retinue of Malacañang reporters ensured full coverage for the jeans-clad president, who chewed on an unlit cigar as he listened to briefings first in a resettlement camp, then at the San Fernando disaster center. The outing betrayed the flare for showmanship of a president who, outwardly, seemed rather unassuming and businesslike. Hundreds of children lined up to meet Ramos and his entourage as they arrived aboard several helicopters at the camp, in the Pampangan town of Mexico. The camp was a model of humanitarian largesse—clean cement buildings, a school, medical facilities and a central hall where Ramos, chomping away on his cigar, asked a few questions and won headlines by announcing the release of about $10 million in funds for resettling another 30,000 families.

If the president had any interest in meeting refugees or inspecting anything, however, he failed to show it. Already behind schedule, the group rushed off to San Fernando, where a trim brigadier general recited facts on the dead and missing—more than 100—and those evacuated after the latest typhoon. Ostentatiously, Pampanga Governor Lapid, ever the actor, snubbed the event, refusing to be a "mere prop." His complaint was not against Ramos' play-acting so much as the government's refusal to release funds to his own administration while channeling them through the Mount Pinatubo Commission. Which route was riskier? What would Lapid do with the money? Few of the victims dared—or cared—to guess at the lesser of the evils.

For Ramos, ostensibly unconcerned about the snub, there was no time to turn southwest a mile or two from San Fernando for a glance at the road where it plunged into water and mud, for a glimpse of the empty wasteland of lahar, for gawking at the roofs of homes and roadside stands nearly covered by mud; no time to see the lines of people slogging through lahar up to their knees, sinking into quicksand, laughing and grimacing as other wayfarers pulled them out, then moving on, antlike, toward towns and villages on the other side; no time for a pro forma look at an unfolding tragedy.

Ramos' failure to dirty himself in the muck, symbolically much less in fact, epitomized the underlying attitude of a government embroiled in petty political concerns. It was all well and good for him to declare, "The government will never abandon you," as he arrived at the resettlement center in Mexico, but to a large degree he was doing just that. His presence in the region for anything other than speech-making and political showmanship was inexplicably overdue. He had previously shown little interest in the missing funds and was only now confronting the long-term impact of a disaster that he hoped would somehow go away without diverting the public and the world from his efforts at projecting the country's budding image as an economically viable ASEAN member.[59]

Right away, Ramos had to face the question of whether to build what Vigilar had described as "the mother of all dikes." Clearly less than enthralled by Rodolfo's judgement, Vigilar confounded the naysayers by claiming a 24-kilometer wall would stave off 200 million cubic meters of lahar for the next three years if the Congress would only authorize $100 million needed to do the job. Without a backward glance at Rodolfo's controversial study, Vigilar called for a 10-meter-high concrete dike that he said would form a 100-square-kilometer basin capable of protecting an area ranging from Angeles City in the north all the way to Bacolor.[60]

His plea was intimidating. Without the dike, according to the argument, another five towns, including San Fernando and Guagua, would join Bacolor as material for future archeological excavation. Reminded that portions of these communities were already under lahar, Vigilar countered, "Those drowning now would be drowned all the more" while "areas still intact would be completely buried." He added that the plan also called for elevating roads and building bridges over special lahar spillways—all with funds to be funneled through the Mount Pinatubo Commission.

The plan was viewed with skepticism for several reasons. For starters, most senators did not want to allocate more funds. Many shared the view of the senate majority leader, Alberto Romulo, that it would be unfair for other regions to deprive them by diverting funds to a region that had already gotten more than its share. Then, too, it was uncertain if the Philippines had the engineering know-how. A German firm, Krupp, sent experts selling a plan for excavating a lahar channel 24 kilometers long, 200 meters wide and 20 meters deep with German aid funds. Foreign aid, welcomed as "scam-free," would be needed, though getting it entailed a lengthy campaign among such perennial donors as the World Bank, the Japanese-dominated Asian Development Bank and foreign governments.

One had only to watch the feeble efforts of local engineers at raising the road from San Fernando to Bacolor to realize the difficulties of carrying out such a grandiose plan. Most bulldozers were idle while one or two trundled on, laboriously smoothing out a roadway sure to wash away with the next rain. Emergency operations that should have taken a few days never seemed to end.

As the sun beat down between storms, one was amazed—not by a flurry of roadwork and dike-building but by the absence of a sense of urgency. Nor was anyone sure how many refugees really had new homes. The total of those displaced by Pinatubo and its aftermath was probably well over 500,000. The Mount Pinatubo Commission claimed that 136,000 of them were resettled in the first four years and another 80,000 were still waiting— that is, until the next typhoon, and the next and the next.

The next typhoon after Ramos' excursion to Pampanga was Rosing, the worst in more than ten years. Before, during and after Rosing, the president put on a show of appearing to be on the case while blaming others. On the night before Rosing hit Luzon on November 3, 1995, with winds of more than 150 miles an hour, Ramos was on television declaring a state of emergency. Afterward, he played the blame game, charging cabinet members with deserting their posts at the height of the storm while holding local officials responsible for a disaster in which more than 800 died, more than 70,000 houses were destroyed and 300,000 people were left homeless. Asking Defense Secretary de Villa to go after those "with non-existent, weak" or "unresponsive disaster plans," Ramos had to fight off charges from senators accusing him of drawing from fast-dwindling "calamity funds" for his numerous trips abroad.[61]

Over the entire scene hovered the living image of Pinatubo, a heaving monster not expected to re-erupt until about the twenty-fifth or twenty-sixth century but still spewing forth reminders of its wrath with alarming frequency. The volcano intermittently inspired terror with mini-eruptions when cold rainwater poured onto the hot lahar fields or into cracks and crevices still steaming beneath the surface. Sometimes the explosions billowed two to three miles high, shocking the citizenry into believing a repeat of mid-June 1991 was imminent. The drama of the volcano was a sideshow, though, compared to the destruction in Pampanga and, to a much lesser degree, Zambales, the province encompassing Olongapo—largely spared by a watershed system that drains jungle regions.

The PHILVOLCS resorted to declarations that might have seemed like scare tactics were they not also true. "Geomorphic and topographic changes," said one pronouncement, "have altered the lahar situation in the Pasig-Potrero River." Lahar might "escape" and "encroach further east" toward other towns but would also create "heightened and prolonged flooding problems in the coming years as a result of the situation of existing waterways."[62] In other words, no one knew where the lahar was going, how much would pour down—or when it would stop.

Where official efforts failed, however, improvisation was the order of the day. The mayor of Porac, between Bacolor and Angeles City, got quarry operators to scour a long, dusty road over the lahar field to a newly formed canyon through which flowed the lahar-swollen river. First, he set up a footbridge that was hoisted and held in position by a winch on a truck. Then, several weeks later, from Subic came a vestige of the reviled American presence—a Bailey Bridge, a movable steel structure named for British engineer Donald Bailey, this model left behind by U.S. Navy Seabees.

Once the bridge was hoisted into place in the Porac lahar field, traffic again moved between Manila and Olongapo, via an awkward route, one lane at a time, but better than nothing. The span held only ten tons, but when the water was low enough heavy buses and trucks forded the river, struggling up and down banks carved open by bulldozers. Within weeks, the span was washed out in heavy rains. Briefly, U.S. largesse, more than four years after the Philippine Senate said no to the bases, provided a stopgap link where engineers, contractors, bureaucrats and politicians had failed.

That was a message that no one acknowledged or dared mention amid all the recriminations, accusations, self-promotion and breast-beating as the Philippines faced its greatest challenge since the fall of Marcos. Indeed, none of the statement-makers evinced any knowledge of the existence of the span. Probably, they were not aware of it since none of them stood to profit from it or had even seen it—and no one would be so politically incorrect as to resurrect the image of a power they loved to revile for whatever the bases had done to or for the region and the country.

The real question was who was going to run off with the most money from the dike construction. The papers were full of charges and counter-charges as bureaucrats, contractors and everyone else with a stake, or a desire for a stake, accused each other of paying off, or accepting payoffs, for a slice of the pie in the days of sunshine before the onset of the 1996 monsoon season. Just about any way to buy or sell a contract was legitimate, as long as it worked. The chances were that all the charges had more than a shred of truth. "We have to expose the corrupt contractors," said an idealistic local journalist. "To silence a reporter, a contractor will give money. Or if I'm a reporter, and you're an official, the reporter gets the contract—and sells it to the contractor."[63]

Most of the contractors who won the initial bids were already blacklisted for having been involved in corrupt dealings earlier on. Long before the work began, there were reports and claims of lack of funds. "They are supposed to put concrete in the megadike," said the journalist. "You never know how they will build it. They say there is not enough money." As the 1996 monsoon season approached, construction companies were divvying up a windfall of $100 million worth of contracts after having procrastinated for precious dry-season weeks. Ramos, accompanied by a retinue that included Vigilar, drove through what was left of Bacolor, issuing "orders" for the construction companies to get the job done before the rains came—a gesture that no one believed would stop the bickering over the spoils.[64]

This time Governor Lapid, in a black jumpsuit, was there too, playing his role. Vigilar assured them both that the 54-kilometer-long dike complex—a transverse dike intended to form a sort of dam at the bottom of the catchment basin and a tail dike below that—would be finished by the end of May. "The dike will be 90–95 percent complete," the Pinatubo Commission's executive director, Antonio Fernando, told me as helicopters bearing Ramos and his cabinet touched down at the base of a dike, its top glistening with cement poured several hours earlier. Fernando also warned, however, of "flooding if we don't do it properly"—especially if contractors did not live up to all their plans for a project likely to cost $100 million.

In any case, neither Fernando nor the engineers for both the government and the private contractors believed that lahar could breach the dike's walls, which were ten meters high and eight meters across at the top—wide enough for a roadway—and spread 60 meters across at the bottom. Megadike still consisted largely of lahar, but the sides for the first time were made of concrete reinforced with steel bars—something not attempted on the previous, porous lahar dikes piled up on either side of the river. "If we erred in terms of the capacity of the catchment basin, we are in trouble," said Fernando, "but this won't break."

Ramos did not walk up and down the dike to see what it looked like or what was happening. He listened as Vigilar, in front of a map, told him, "We feel confident that the necessary protection will be in place" and pronounced himself "delighted."

Considering the record of the last few years, though, it was difficult to convince the skeptics. "Megadike, Mega-doubts," headlined the report at the top of the evening news one night on ABS-CBN, the country's leading television network. The report said that another 20,000 people would be leaving their homes as the season's first typhoon loomed large off the eastern coast in mid-May. Vigilar admitted it was conceivable the combination of the lahar already in the field and the millions more tons visible as a gray gash on the slopes of Pinatubo might lap over the top, endangering San Fernando and other towns. As to what would happen, he said, "Only God can guarantee."

Engineers and contractors cited endless problems. It was difficult to recruit workers to labor under the hot sun for hours on end. Some contractors had to quit after failing to acquire proper equipment. Hundreds of people refused to abandon their land to make way for the dike, claiming that the government did not offer enough and might avoid compensating them at all. The director of PHILVOLCS, Raymundo Punongbayan, warned that all San Fernando would be "at immediate risk" if the megadike were not completed. San Fernando Mayor Reynaldo Aquino called on 200 families upstream in Porac, across the lahar field, to show "sobriety, compassion and heroism"—an appeal not likely to do much unless supported by cash.[65]

The Mount Pinatubo Commission, with authority over the Mount Pinatubo Rehabilitation Project Office, was probably the worst offender. "That's where most of the corruption takes place," said my journalistic informant. "Most of the government engineers have new cars. Some have big four-wheel drives"—the real status symbols these days. He did not expect to see any exposés. "Even before the project takes off, if I'm an official, and I smell you're going to write a story, I'll pay you off as soon as possible."[66]

Next time I was passing through, toward the end of 1996, the road was clear and traffic was moving, at least on one lane. Some of the worst fears, however, had come to pass. Cascading waters had breached a transverse dike linking the east and west dikes, creating a yawning chasm 65 meters wide. "The transverse dike was not made correctly," said Executive Director Fernando. "It was made of compacted lahar with concrete armor [as indeed were the east and west dikes]. This project is not yet under control."

For the great megadike—spared another monsoon as rough as that of 1995—the worst lay ahead. "We do not yet have the supertest for megadike," said Fernando. "If we got a typhoon like last year, the whole thing would have gone."

Kelvin Rodolfo, now a visiting professor at the National Institute of Geological Sciences, derided the claims of government experts—and criticized them for raising hopes. "Official assurances that [the megadike] is strong are only making matters worse by encouraging a false sense of security in the threatened communities," he concluded in late 1997. The erosion "had gotten worse" with gaps in four key towns in the path of the flow, he said, estimating that 60 percent of the dike was porous lahar, unprotected by concrete and "most vulnerable" to washout.[67]

As long as the government was so lax in emergency planning, Rodolfo advised those in endangered areas to prepare for any contingency on their own. Before the dikes broke, he said, "send very old, young, ill or pregnant family members to visit with relatives in safe places until the rainy season was over."[68] No one knew for sure when the next killer typhoon would hit, but one thing was certain: the contractors looked forward to years of easy profits and payoffs as the waters rose and fell, dikes collapsed and were rebuilt—and the people in between waited only for Pinatubo finally to dispose of all its lahar in the valleys below.

THREE

Scandal of Angeles

The humiliation at Clark Air Base was a disgrace for both the United States and the Philippines. The evidence of the disgrace was there for any visitor to see. A drive around the base, converted after the pullout of the last Americans in November 1991 into the Clark Special Economic Zone, revealed gaping holes in place of large windows in barrack walls. Doors, hinges, locks were gone. A walk inside exposed bathrooms without toilets, basins or showers, ceilings gouged out for copper wiring, floors stripped of tiles. The looting of Clark had begun as the ashes were still falling from the eruption of Mount Pinatubo in June. So meticulous, thoroughgoing and complete an act of organized thievery and banditry had to have been done with the connivance of Philippine military authorities at the highest level.

My guide from the Clark Development Corporation (CDC), the agency in charge of converting the sprawling base into a mercantile and light industrial hub, did not downplay the extent of the damage. "Most of the sophisticated equipment, the computers, were carried out by the Americans before they left," said the guide as we surveyed the scene from atop FM Hill, the site of FM Tower, from which antennae once beamed music and news over the base and the region. In the background was the former base hospital, where severe casualties from the Vietnam War were flown aboard U.S. Air Force hospital planes. The rest, "lights, tables, chairs, were all looted," the guide had to admit. "The antennae on the air field were looted; the cables were chopped into pieces to get the copper. This was whole [*sic*] desolation."[1]

By the time the dust had settled and the CDC had stepped in as caretaker and developer of the base, still guarded by the Philippine Air Force, total losses were above half a billion dollars—nearly as much as the Americans had been offering to give the Philippines in annual aid money, as de facto "rent" for the privilege of using the bases another three years. The destruction, like the lahar on the slopes and valleys around Pinatubo, had to be seen to be believed or understood and comprehended in totality. What would a picture of a gaping hole in a building, or a missing toilet or shower, really tell?

The spectacle of building after building, gutted and stripped, laid bare the greed and rage of the hordes that had swarmed over the base. Methodically and efficiently ripping out anything and everything that might be of any value on the black markets beyond the fence, most of which was also stripped, the looters did as much damage as a conquering army. Over several months, with the knowledge if not complicity of every top-ranking officer in the Armed Forces of the Philippines, looters made off with hundreds of millions of dollars worth of some of the best facilities ever "voluntarily" bequeathed, if not surrendered, by any military establishment on earth.

The looting was already beginning when the Americans were ordered to flee on June 10, as Pinatubo was about to explode. A few daring Filipinos, willing to take their chances, were ripping off whatever they could see on the base through the ash and rainfall on June 15, after the American security force had fled for the night. Most of them, however, were as intimidated as anyone else by the potential holocaust descending upon them—and preferred to wait.

Colonel Corwin, the security chief, recorded losses and hazards: "Over 3,000 military unpacked households, $500M in recoverable resources, and a $2B base complex required protection by the remaining 1,200-man security force. The intruder problem escalated over tenfold and through final closure over 2,000 individuals were detected and driven off with 500 apprehensions."[2]

When the Americans returned before leaving for good, they were amazed by what had been stolen from their off-base homes—family scrapbooks, home videos, souvenirs, along with stereo sets, furniture, clothing and much else. "The looting began the day of the volcano," said Steven Campbell, former air force sergeant. "They had everything from GIs stealing from GIs to local nationals stealing. We weren't allowed to come back. I lost everything."

Campbell left Subic aboard the aircraft carrier Midway, while his wife and daughter returned to their home in nearby Arayat Province. When he got back several months later to reunite with his family and pick up what was left of their belongings, he discovered family heirlooms, scrapbooks and memorabilia all gone. "I'd been all over the world. I had Turkish mugs, German steins, Spanish ware, Philippine silverware—models of caribou drivers and nipa houses." He witnessed still more looting while he was there. "What I saw when I came packing out was a crime and a sin. GIs, some very high-ranking people, were paying local workers off with people's bicycles. They were selling so much stuff."[3]

To Campbell the lack of order—or routine name-checking—was shocking: "I could walk into the housing office and say I was packing out Joe Blow's house and take everything he had. When I walked into my own house on-base, I saw a GI in the house with a Filipino girl. Everything that wasn't heavy was gone." He believes that Filipinos stole most of it. "I'd say it was Filipinos because they were taking whatever they could carry."

He could not get over the lack of security: "There was enough air force security police in the daytime. At night there was nobody. Trucks, private vehicles were moving out loaded to the gills. These big pickup trucks would pay the guards at the gate, and away they went." His off-base house was a total loss. "It was completely collapsed by ash. It was all washed away. Everything was gone. There was nothing."

Whenever Americans revisited the base, they were amazed by what they saw—or didn't see. It was as if Philippine society, not content with abusing the American legacy, now wanted to abuse Filipinos, abuse their heritage, destroy what was theirs after nine decades of American domination. "When I came back in early 1992, they had pulled out the toilets," said John Cummings, a former air force major, seated at one of the tables in Margaritaville, his restaurant, bar and pool hall on the Fields Avenue strip opposite the main gate. "The water kept running—the base well went dry."[4]

Cummings was aghast as he witnessed the brazen display. "You could watch the army trucks. Everything in the world was going out the gates in government trucks, day time and night time." He was "sure some Americans took advantage of the situation, but 99 percent of the thievery was after the Americans left."

The *Philippine Flyer* offered a comforting assurance. "The fact is, rumors about rampant looting in homes and offices are exaggerated," said the paper, citing 296 break-ins—96 in government facilities, 200 in base housing. "Most household thefts occurred when we evacuated to the college. Fortunately, only two homes were ransacked. We found things missing in 76 more, and in the other 122, while forced entry may have occurred, there was no evidence that property had been stolen." ("We don't have good numbers on thefts in off-base homes," the paper noted dourly.)[5]

Homes off-base got hit first—and hardest. Landlords, servants, live-in girlfriends—they all began to rip off whatever they could haul. "The landlords opened up houses and started selling off the stuff," said Cummings. "They didn't think anyone was coming back. A lot of them were cleaned out 100 percent." It was, as a resident of an enclave of one-time American-officer homes put it, "open season." Or, as Colonel Ron Rand of the 13th Air Force admitted in bland understatement, "The people off base experienced much worse than those on base."[6]

Police Captain Edelberto "Bert" Ocampo, then a lieutenant, described what he saw: "When Pinatubo exploded, there was chaos. I was assigned to a place surrounded by residential subdivisions. All of these were being resided in by Americans. The Americans left in a convoy. They were told just to bring necessities. Just imagine all the houseboys and housegirls looting everything. Landlords too. Everybody." The cops divided household loot into two categories. "There were the 'browns' and the 'whites.' The browns were TVs, stereos; the whites were the ovens, refrigerators, washing machines. If they stopped by the checkpoint, we would stop them and confiscate"—but most followed other routes.[7]

Considering all that was stolen, Ocampo's men did not get much. "We confiscated 71 units in three months. By that time our station was surrounded by appliances. We were patrolling the streets, but we were not enough." He did not say what happened to the appliances that were confiscated. None of the Americans reported anything "returned" by authorities.[8]

If most Americans refrained from outright looting, many had their own ways of fleecing Uncle Sam. American service people quickly began filing claims through air force channels, sometimes selling cars, then claiming them as stolen, while resigning themselves to the loss of irreplaceable personal treasures. Local landlords responded to complaints by shrugging and blaming other Filipinos while the U.S. Air Force paid off. If anyone was arrested, the charges were soon dropped—a sure sign the local police were also deeply involved.

"Guys would collect insurance for their cars, then sell them on the black market," said Frank Hilliard, a navy veteran hired on as assistant base closure officer. More sophisticated Americans played a racket in buying cars from the base exchange at prices slashed to cover damages from Pinatubo, tore them apart to remove the ash, maybe replaced the bearings—and sold them at full price.

"A lot of Americans really made out big time," said Hilliard. "They were in the right place at the right time. They had all these buildings, chock-a-block with stuff. They were buying stuff worth thousands of dollars. You could buy a fridge for ten dollars." If nothing else, they were guilty of "insider trading since they were often the ones who were determining what could be sold."[9]

In a sense, the takeover of Clark by the Philippine Air Force was a triumph of nationalist militants in a war against foreign neocolonialists and imperialists. If that view appears farfetched, one need only wander into the headquarters complex of the base commander for a sobering perspective.

"In the '60s I read in the papers about Filipino scavengers," said a young Philippine Air Force captain, Allan Ballesteros. "The Americans treated

Filipinos like pigs. They shoot them, they tortured them"—a reference to incidents in which U.S. security guards in the 1960s had fired on looters. The captain leaned over his desk, warming to a key point in repeated efforts at shirking responsibility. "The looting was the attitude of the people."[10]

The looting of Clark was not exactly without precedent on American bases turned over to Philippine forces. Two decades earlier, in September 1971, the old U.S. Navy base at Sangley Point, at the southern tip of Manila Bay, was stripped after the Americans handed over the base to the Philippine Navy. "They took everything," said a local Filipino reporter. "Even the doorknobs were gone."[11] Sangley, much smaller than Clark or Subic, now serves as the major port for the Philippine Navy's pathetic fleet of 78-foot patrol boats and other small craft, including a few LSTs for landing troops and equipment for coastal defense, nothing more. The looting of Sangley, as Marcos was about to reach the apex of his rule under martial law, is sometimes cited as proof that ill-paid Filipinos looted only for personal profit, not for nationalist vengeance.

Much closer to the time of the eruption of Mount Pinatubo, Americans and Filipinos got another taste of what would happen to Clark once it fell into the hands of people who saw the bases as gold mines for personal profit if not as targets for subliminal revenge. After the turnover of Camp O'Donnell, a small but equipment-rich communications facility in the Zambales Mountains, "scavengers stripped the facility of all moveable objects, including copper wire from cables, a gas pump and a water pump," according to one aggrieved report in the *Philippine Daily Inquirer*.[12]

As a portent for the immediate future of Clark, perhaps the most significant aspect of the looting of O'Donnell was the manner in which Philippine Air Force officers managed to hide their crimes. A Philippine Air Force captain, Jose Sabijon, adopting the conventional explanation with which Philippine officers typically explain away the looting, said disingenuously that scavengers, otherwise unidentified, had to loot to live. Far be it from Captain Sabijon to interfere with poor people attempting to survive! "What they are digging makes enough for them to eat in a day," he explained. "I won't kill people just for that."[13]

Alas, the captain's noble sentiments did not impress anyone with the slightest knowledge of what was going on. "Sabijon could not have killed the scavengers because it was he who hired people to dismantle items of value in and out of the facility's holdings," said the *Inquirer*. "The items included telephone poles and buried cables"—all of which Sabijon's men trucked on down to "a junk shop" near Clark. One of the so-called scavengers, the article related sarcastically, was an official whose men "also dismantled everything they could get hold of." The authorities sanctimoniously promised the departing Americans that they would "salvage some valuable items" to "be donated to the Capas barangays [*sic*]"—none of which got "a single centavo from the proceeds."[14]

The precedents of Sangley and O'Donnell, and other lesser lootings, deepen the question: Why did Filipino authorities, from Cory Aquino and her advisers in Malacañang and her relatives in Tarlac, the seat of their power, fail to heed the lesson of recent history and defend Clark, as they would their own gated, guarded estates? The answer is that they had no interest in doing so—and they also had a number of reasons, ranging from nationalist sensitivities to bonds with those profiteering from the looting, to look the other way as they sped back and forth between Tarlac and Manila in black vans and limos along the highway only a few miles from the scene of the ongoing crime. The looting of Clark, then, was a climactic event in a continuum—one from which top Filipinos profited enormously.

Senior Americans presumably knew who did what, where and how but were reluctant to confront their Filipino "friends" while negotiating what they still foolishly believed would be an extension of the lease covering Clark and Subic. For all the official U.S. efforts at repairing public relations in the Philippines, the Americans understood how deeply ingrained was the subconscious image of the bullying American. Filipinos might revere General MacArthur as the hero who did return; they might welcome Americans in their homes with a charm seldom experienced by GIs in other countries. They might emulate American ways, but the hurt and anger go deep in the national psyche.

Such bitterness is not surprising. It has not been all that many years, in the long run of history, since Filipino nationalists, under Aguinaldo and others, waged an extended, bloody guerrilla war over the very region in which the Americans, often generous and easygoing and free-spending but also arrogant, patronizing and unexpectedly brutal at times, had lorded it over their "little brown brothers" for so long.

In that context, the rationales issued by Filipino officers for the military role in the looting appear as a deliberate if instinctive disinformation campaign rather than a cover for corruption. The easiest, first excuse for what happened is that the base was woefully undermanned after the Americans fled, before Pinatubo erupted. "From June to November only about 3,000 were here," said Ballesteros. "The Philippine Air Force had a little over 1,000 men on temporary duty. They had one helicopter. Most were here for support and security."[15] And they had to guard an area of 53,000 hectares—technically only 3,760 hectares, just 7 percent of it occupied by American facilities. All of it, however, was accessible through a 23-mile fence, broken up by eight gates opening on a 200-mile road network, bending and twisting among trees, around hills, past a rolling golf course buried, like the rest of the base, by six inches or more of ash.

Obviously, Clark was difficult to secure. When the Americans were at full strength—15,000 service people plus family members and 10,000 Filipinos—the base was losing astounding quantities of materiél to theft. According to Colonel Corwin, "The base experienced about 90 thefts totaling $50K per month prior to the eruption."[16] Unofficial estimates were much higher—about $20,000 worth of equipment was said to have gone astray *daily* because of systematic thievery before Pinatubo exploded and the situation got really out of hand.

The rate of theft post-Pinatubo increased to 400 reported incidents a month, precipitating an "uncalculated amount of losses," Corwin stated. "We weren't able to get back onto the base effectively because of the destruction. . . . We got clobbered that week in terms of thefts and losses on the base." How tough was his job compared to the others he had had? Of all his air force tours, including one as a commander in Vietnam, "the Clark tour was absolutely the toughest," Corwin averred without hesitation. After the volcano blew up, "It was just 18-hour days."[17]

Ceferina Yepez, who for years advised senior U.S. Air Force public affairs officers and was retained in much the same role, in her same book-lined office, for Filipino commanders, repeated the usual Philippine Air Force explanation for the looting. "There were a number of factors," she said. "The looting could have been because of the poverty of the people." Ballesteros elaborated on the theme. "After Pinatubo, people were living in poverty. When the Americans left, there was no more employment."[18]

That was an irrefutable truth, considering that U.S. forces at full throttle in the Philippines provided jobs for more than 23,000 full-time workers, nearly 23,000 contract workers, 22,000 hired and domestic helpers and hundreds more running concessions. Their annual payroll totalled almost $100 million, the country's second largest after that of the Philippine government, including its armed forces.[19] Such responses, however, skirted the issue of who organized the looting—and who profited. Yepez imagined that "there were people who know about it, but they aren't going to talk about it."

Philippine Air Force officers were glad to talk some more, while blaming Americans, not Filipinos, much less Philippine Air Force commanders. "Americans were the first ones who looted the base," Ballesteros charged when pressed for a fuller explanation of all I had seen and heard. "They spirited out cars, computers"—and, he claimed, much other valuable equipment before the Filipinos grabbed what was left.[20] As spokesman for the base, Ballesteros avoided more specific questions and answers by saying that he wasn't there at the time of the looting, but newspaper clippings reveal he was indeed the spokesman in late 1991 for the Clark Air Base Command under then-Brigadier General Leopoldo Acot.

One Philippine Air Force officer, willing to admit he *was* at Clark during the looting, gladly embellished on the popular rationale. "This intrusion, this looting was initiated by the Americans," he said, talking anonymously. "The trucks were all controlled by the Americans. All I know is the Americans did it." The officer turned indignant when reminded that much of the loot remained visible, years later, in the markets of Dau, reached by turning left from the main gate of Clark on Fields Avenue and left again up MacArthur Highway. It was the first town to the north, a transshipment point for buses and trucks bound for Manila.

"There is no such thing as looting at Clark because finders-keepers," the officer insisted, in all seriousness. Anyway, he claimed, the Americans never protested, at least officially, to Philippine authorities. "If you call [*sic*] somebody stealing from you, you should complain. The Americans never complained. After the eruption of Pinatubo, the Americans sold everything they cannot carry at a public auction"—the source, said the officer, of all those goods still stacked up in Dau.[21]

It was an old excuse for a market that had been a cornucopia of looted military plenty for decades. Long before the Americans left Clark, the black market at Dau was renowned as a source for anything a greedy warlord, a communist guerrilla, a gangster or entrepreneur might want. The looting, though, provided a touch of exotic variety. There, for all the world to buy, were night-vision goggles, smoke grenades, aircraft propeller blades, pilot's helmets, even, if you asked for them, hand grenades, bullets and rifles. "Some of it comes from the Philippine forces, some from the Americans, no one knows for sure," said a local editor.

The officer smiled when reminded of reports of hundreds of looters slashing through the fence, of goods stored in warehouses on-base for loading onto trucks, of cargo going out of the base through less-used side and back gates, of middlemen from Manila buying loot by the container load, without checking on the contents, of investigations, recriminations and rumors of enormous profits reaped by Philippine Air Force officers.

"The Americans abandoned it; we picked it up," said the officer. "Which is greater, looting or robbery? There's no syndicate or criminal plot. It just happened." Then too, besieged security guards "haven't got any cooperation from the outside," he pleaded. "The local police, the mayor, they don't care. Once the stuff goes out of the base, it passes through cities and towns"—where no law was there to stop it.

The officers' remarks were a cover-up—not for personal involvement, if any, but for the misdeeds of senior Philippine officers, politicians, bureaucrats and contractors who enriched themselves from the looting, were embarrassed by the aspersions cast upon them and now wanted to put it all behind them. The Americans were extremely reluctant to fight back with comments or revelations that might add to Filipinos' embarrassment.

A sign of Washington's public relations failure was the refusal of U.S. officials to talk about the court-martial at Andersen Air Force Base on Guam two years later, in November 1993, of an American officer purportedly involved in the looting—a case that Filipino officers love to cite. "Did you know a major was prosecuted in the States because of the systematic looting," Captain Ballesteros asked me, offering "proof" of the Americans' primary role.[22]

The defendant, U.S. Air Force Captain Chen Almacen, was a security liaison officer. The assignment seemed tailor-made for an American officer who actually had migrated from the Philippines. Although Americans saw Almacen simply as "Fil-American," he was the product of a much more distinctive background than the average Filipino immigrant to America. Unlike Almacen, most Filipino-Americans are members of one of the major lowland groups, ranging from the Ilocanos of northern Luzon to the Tagalogs of Metro Manila and much of central and southern Luzon, to the Cebuanos and Ilongos of the Visayan region, among many others.

Almacen is a "highlander," an Igorot, an often-oppressed minority of tough mountain people who inhabit the Gran Cordillera Central region covering much of the north. For centuries, the Igorots, in at least five distinctive tribes, have defied the efforts of the Spanish, the Americans and lowland Filipinos to subdue them, to force them to yield to central control and to exploit their lands, which are rich in gold and other minerals. They still defy authority even though the colonialists, both Spanish and American, eventually forced them into begrudging submission. Many of them now serve in key positions in local government and business.[23]

For Almacen, christened Reuben, nicknamed "Benny," eldest of five sons and two daughters of a school supervisor west of Baguio, the American-built center of the Cordillera, the American dream represented the way out of a middle-class existence with limits carefully defined by Philippine society. In his second year in college in Baguio he took the competitive test for enlistment in the U.S. Navy and, in 1972, signed on for a seven-year hitch. While in the navy Almacen showed off his karate skills so well that he got the nickname of Chen, the surname of a Hong Kong actor and karate expert. He legally changed his first name from Reuben to Chen when he was sworn in as a U.S. citizen in San Diego in May 1979, at the time of his discharge from the navy.

After two years as a local California cop, Almacen applied to become an officer in the U.S. Air Force. Commissioned a second lieutenant, he was assigned to the base security police group at Clark in 1980 and, by 1986, was a captain in charge of several hundred Filipino security guards. As an Igorot, however, he had complexes of which his American superiors were unaware—a need to show off his importance as an American officer *and* a member of a grouping looked down on by lowland Filipinos. Some of his superiors suspected the pressures he faced. "Almacen had an extremely sensitive job which not only placed him in constant physical danger but also exposed him to personal and political pressures from high ranking Philippine officials," said one American, Colonel William H. Dassler, suggesting that "we had kept Capt Almacen in-country too long—both for his own good and the good of the Air Force."[24]

Stories proliferated. Chen was said to go off-base in his civilian clothes with a weapon, an Israeli-made Uzi, bulging under a light jacket—against U.S. military regulations. Naturally, his *compadres* suggested that he do them a few favors—the kind that a man of means and influence does for friends in the Philippines. Still, to outward appearances, Almacen was doing well enough to have been selected for promotion to major. Then word spread that he was accepting bribes in return for signing passes enabling about six trucks a day to haul loot off the base. As anger rose over the looting by Filipinos, American authorities focused on Almacen to show "impartiality" in going after their own. Filipino authorities "cooperated"—that is, they diverted attention from their own glaring misdeeds.

General Acot, as base commander, cooperated so closely with the U.S. Air Force Office of Special Investigation (OSI) as to suggest a trade-off. The Americans criticized the Filipinos for rip-offs from the base. They were disgusted at the sight of trucks hauling out equipment from every corner of the base as soon as they had turned it over to the Filipinos. The Philippine Air Force countered with carefully placed claims that the Americans were the guilty ones—so why didn't they go after their own? Almacen was easy prey; as liaison officer he had signed numerous CABCOM 30 forms, issued by the Philippine Air Force's Clark Air Base Command, which permitted truckloads of scrap to leave the base as "donations."[25]

The authority to sign the CABCOM 30s exposed Almacen to criticism from all sides. For one thing, security at the gates, self-consciously divided between Americans and Filipinos, was absurdly weak. The U.S. Air Force guards had only loose control over all those entering the base, casually waving on empty trucks and vans as long as their drivers had a paper from Philippine or American authorities—sometimes including Almacen.

The Americans also stopped Americans when they were going out, looked at them and asked what they were doing, but they had no control over Filipinos other than the authority to issue CABCOM 30s, which Philippine Air Force officers could also issue. "The Filipinos would stop a

Filipino, and if he was so inclined the Filipino would slip some pesos to the guy and he'd wave them through," said an American officer who observed the process for nearly two years. "It was as corrupt as it could be. I could be waved through the gate by an American and waved out by a Filipino."

Under those circumstances, Filipino merchants did not see why they had to beg Almacen for his signature on the CABCOM 30s. "The story was people who I knew in the community came to me and complained, why did they have to get Chen's signature," said the American officer. "They didn't want to do that because they said Chen was asking them to pay him to approve their form. I know there were Filipinos who came to me and complained about that."[26]

Might such charges have been character assassination by people who resented Chen's questioning them? When an officer told Colonel Dassler, "'It appears to me there is the perception you have a problem by having Chen there,' he never agreed that Chen was part of the problem."[27] The stories spread, however, as Chen's enemies sharpened their knives.

Chen was more vulnerable than he realized. The Americans, if not overtly racist, may not have felt the same loyalty to this Philippine-born officer as they did to those whom they saw instinctively as true-blue Americans. For their part, Philippine officers, members of well-to-do, influential lowland families, saw Almacen as an upstart—a low-born tribesman who had wangled his way into many times the salary and perks of his Philippine Air Force counterparts. To the elite of the Philippine armed forces, Igorots hardly count as Filipino any more than Philippine-Americans count as "American-Americans" to the elite of the U.S. forces.

Among Almacen's worst enemies was a Philippine National Police major who, according to Corwin, "worked closely with OSI and had an office in the local OSI detachment." The PNP major made a point of calling Corwin and bad-mouthing Almacen in an effort at detracting from Almacen's credibility. He "directly lied to me," said Corwin.[28] The police major's contempt for Almacen as an Igorot was unstated, but there was no doubting his desire to get rid of him. In his reports to the OSI, the major was exaggerating the dangers of attack by communists—a menace as a guerrilla force capable of assassinations but never a threat as portrayed by him or, on the basis of his and other false information, as portrayed by the OSI to the Pentagon.

In the campaign against Almacen the PNP had an ally in Lieutenant Colonel Dale Luther, commander of the OSI at Clark. The OSI had reason to dislike Almacen's competing to provide intelligence: Almacen often contradicted OSI estimates and accused the OSI of fabricating information. OSI investigators "were trying to make a political statement," he said. Their reports "were sensationalized because the OSI wants Washington to think they know what they were doing. There was no warfare. The

NPA actions were systematic. The OSI reports were exaggerated. They look like John Wayne in the middle of a battlefield—to glorify their existence. Instead of training GIs on a common-sense approach, they exaggerated on everything."[29]

Almacen also offended people—some at the highest level—in other ways. For example: "The Philippine Air Force can authorize anyone to enter the base. They would drop off thieves at those gates and pick them up later, using military vehicles that the Americans provided for the joint equipment pool. Once we see any involvement, arrest a guy, we do a report. It goes up the PAF chain of command, from the security commander to the CABCOM chief of staff. Acot makes the decision. What do they do? They would tell us he was disciplined, then we see this guy working again. In my job, I cannot be too open. I identify a problem, relay a message. Acot didn't like it. A lot of times I see involvement of PAF personnel, nothing being done. Acot's anger showed when he gave the authorization to submit all the CABCOM 30s, about 50 of them."[30]

At Acot's behest, Philippine authorities were glad to hand over to the OSI all copies of CABCOM 30 forms signed by Almacen—and none of those signed by Filipinos for all the truckloads they had shipped off the base on their own. For the Filipinos, the investigation into Almacen was a welcome diversion from the international disgrace of their own looting. For the Americans, the Almacen case provided a chance to say, in effect, "Look, we're impartial, we're cracking down on an American officer." There had to be a fall guy; Almacen was it.

By "getting" Almacen, the Americans managed to draw some of the attention from a carefully contrived propaganda campaign featuring headlines in the Philippine press suggesting that the Americans were to blame for stripping the base. "US colonels linked to looting of Clark," was the startling headline that ran on the front page of the *Philippine Daily Inquirer* nearly a year after U.S. forces had pulled entirely from the base. "American military officers, led by the commander of the security group, systematically looted Clark Air Base," began the story, attributing the information to Reynaldo Sumawang, identified as a former civilian employee at Clark.[31]

The man whom Sumawang, an Aeta from Marcos Village, named as ringleader was none other than Colonel Corwin, the knowledgeable commander of the security police—and Almacen's boss. The article carried a list of other "suspects," including Colonel Dassler and Lieutenant Colonel James Baker, the chief of the civic actions office, three enlisted men—and Almacen. Not to be outdone, the *Philippine Star,* the *Inquirer*'s archrival for circulation, the next day ran an article headlined "'Systematic theft' at Clark exposed." The article opened with the flat assertion: "Long before the Americans turned over Clark Air Base in Pampanga to the Philippine government, 'systematic looting' by US officials had emptied most of it [*sic*] warehouses of millions of pesos worth of goods and equipment."[32]

Almacen, who said he himself paid Sumawang "a minimum" of 50 pesos (about $2.50) "out of my own pocket for any valuable tips of illegal activities on-base," believes that the OSI paid Sumawang more—enough to make sure he testified. At the same time, the OSI encouraged the theory of a cabal of colonels by making a show of "advising" Corwin and the others that charges were also contemplated against them. "They did it to intimidate them into not standing up for Chen," said Frank Spinner, the retired air force legal services officer who represented Almacen on his final appeal. "It was all a sham. They never seriously contemplated charges against Colonel Corwin"—or any of the others.[33]

Sumawang hyped up his story with claims of threats against his life. "I have received death threats," the *Philippine Daily Inquirer* quoted him as telling newsmen at the Clark Air Base Command. "Almacen's tentacles are all over the place." He claimed to be watched by people associated with Almacen—and warned against testifying in the United States. The *Philippine Star* story was still more revealing: it showed the link between the Philippine Air Force and Sumawang's testimony. The Clark Air Base Command chief, Brigadier General Benito Diamos, was reported to have said the American investigators had Sumawang under protective custody.[34]

The reports in the Philippine press, however, were clearly not to the liking of the Americans. They were after only one person, the one against whom they believed they had the tightest case, namely Almacen. Sumawang and the other Aeta witnesses were useful only if they supported the case that the American investigators were pursuing in earnest. The Philippine Air Force, having sponsored Sumawang's blanket charges against the American colonels, did not really press the point. There was, as PAF officers knew, no real point to press. Everyone knew the PAF was largely responsible.

The OSI did its best to impede Almacen's chances of a thorough defense. For one thing, the prosecution delayed the trial for two and a half years beyond the start of the investigation, which the record shows as having begun shortly *before* the eruption of Pinatubo. (Astonishingly, Almacen was never relieved of his duties at Clark—and was among those attending the closing ceremony.) For another, after his transfer to Los Angeles Air Force Base, Almacen was denied any chance of a thorough investigation of his own in which he could seriously try to track down relationships at the top level between General Acot and General Studer.

When Almacen was permitted to return to the Philippines, it was as a member of a U.S. Air Force contingent that included his air force defense lawyer, provided under military law, as well as OSI investigators and air force prosecutors. He stayed at the Oasis Hotel, a legendary watering hole for the local elite, but could not range around town on his own seeking out contacts and leads. Instead, the air force held a videotaped hearing in which prominent Filipinos, including Angeles Mayor Edgardo Pamintuan and Pampanga Governor Francisco Nepomuceno, testified to their friend's good character. Their empty words may have done him more harm than good by confirming how close he was to local notables, all of whom presumably were on the take from the base, directly or indirectly.

There were stories that Almacen might still have managed to avert the court-martial, which was to begin two weeks later in Guam, if he had gone along with a deal to resign his commission—and submit evidence against other officers. So sure was he of acquittal, however, that he was in no mood to compromise. He knew he had been set up—as much by Filipinos, including some who once appeared as friends, as by Americans.

The weekly *Angeles City Inquirer* got to the heart of the real case against him. "The U.S. Air Force had already spend [*sic*] one million dollars in this case alone," it reported. "Almacen is believed to be a 'fall guy' and heads will roll if he decides to tell the investigators what he really knows." The report linked the looting to the power structure behind it: "An [American] Air Force colonel, who works in the [U.S.] embassy said that the U.S. embassy has some dossiers on 'who's who' at Clark looting. If allegedly revealed, the Philippine Air Force hierarchy will be put in shambles and it's [*sic*] chief, Maj. Gen. Leopoldo Acot will be forced to 'sing' his 'accomplishments' of the former base, being its former commander."[35]

But why was Acot, after all the fuss over the looting of Clark, now a major general—on his way to the position of commander of the Philippine Air Force? The local paper had an answer to that too, though it was careful to attribute it to the unnamed American colonel. Cornered for questioning at a local fiesta, the colonel was reported as saying that "Acot 'holds some aces' among the high officials in the Philippine government that's why instead of prosecuting him they still promoted him."[36] In other words, Acot was in a position to know who else in the ruling structure was also profiteering—sharing the wealth.

The weekly also had the inside track when it came to understanding the dynamics of the fate that awaited Almacen when he got to Guam. The paper quoted Almacen as noting that "those people responsible for the release of the news reports about him came from the same people who were involved in the looting and are trying to turn the attention away from them."[37] No doubt, but everyone knew that kind of obvious insight would win no points for Almacen at the loaded court-martial on Guam.

With extraordinary prescience if not omniscience, the writer of the article concluded: "From what I gathered, Almacen will be definitely found guilty by the court martial. The U.S. Air Force has to find someone who will go to jail in order for them to satisfy their ego considering the looting was very rampant and nobody was prosecuted and put on trial." In other words, said the report, clearly based on more than guesswork and intuition, "Either Almacen starts revealing what he really knows about the looting or his career in the U.S. Air Force will be over."[38]

The Americans gladly paid all the expenses for a PNP captain, a PNP sergeant and six other Filipinos, most of them Aeta tribesmen who lived in a development called Marcos Village just beyond the northeastern perimeter of the base, to fly to Guam to testify at the trial. The word of Police Captain Bert Ocampo was crucial to the case—and reveals in microcosm how the looting was managed.

"There was a day in August 1991 when there were two truckloads of new beds and mattresses that passed by the police station which I was manning in Angeles," said Ocampo, relaxing in a corner of the Shanghai Restaurant on MacArthur Highway, rebuilt as Angeles City's largest eating establishment on the ashes of the one that had burned down while Pinatubo was erupting. "My men were at a checkpoint. They stopped these two trucks. When they asked for papers, they couldn't show any papers. All they knew was they were to deliver them to a 'Mr. Lao' in a nearby subdivision. I told my men to hold this truck. We locked up ten of them—including three who later testified in Guam."[39]

The next morning, said Ocampo, recounting what he had told the court, "one of my men, Sergeant Gaudencio 'Bong' Batan Jr., told me there was a call from Captain Chen Almacen, so I asked Bong what this captain needed from me, and my man said, 'He asked me why you are holding these trucks because these were donations for Marcos Village.'" There was, however, a damning flaw in the request. "My police station is on the southeastern part of Clark, so I told Bong to tell the captain, 'I don't work for him, he has no business telling me what to do.'"

Finally, Ocampo explained the crucial link in the organization of the looting—and in much else that happens in the Philippines. "That same morning I was called by a colonel to the Angeles police headquarters. One of the colonels there asked me why I was holding the trucks. I said I didn't have the documents. He told me to release the trucks. He showed me the documents signed by Captain Chen Almacen saying these were donations for the Aetas."

Ocampo was in no position to argue. "He told me not to ask questions, just release that, so I did that. He was a colonel, and I was a lieutenant. At the court martial, the prosecutors emphasized the direction the trucks were going. It was the opposite direction from Marcos Village." Ocampo also realized how close Almacen was to local officialdom. "I knew Chen Almacen because he used to rub elbows with all the high officials at Angeles."

Ocampo and the other witnesses had plenty of time to get to know one another—and compare notes. Ocampo guided, advised and shepherded the Aetas, who had never before been out of the country. He first realized how much they needed him when they were checking in at the Continental Airlines counter at Ninoy Aquino Airport. One of them tried to follow his suitcase onto the baggage conveyor belt, thinking that was the way to the plane. "I had to pull him off," said Ocampo, chortling over the memory.

During their two weeks on Guam, the witnesses stayed at a comfortable hotel on base, shopped at the base exchange and dined in military clubs and other facilities on sumptuous allowances of $25 a meal—enough for far more than any of them could eat. Evenings, they often went off-base for nights on the town, delighting in the American go-go dancers, who they happily observed were "more bold" (Fil-English for totally nude) than the Filipinas in the clubs at Angeles. Almacen flew in from Los Angeles Air Force Base, where he was assigned during the investigation. Not yet in custody while on trial, he stayed in quarters on base but, as the accused, received no meal allowance or per diem.

Witnesses were not allowed to attend court sessions except to testify, but back in the hotel they all talked about the trial. On the stand, Sergeant Batan and the Aetas corroborated Ocampo's story—and embellished it with tales of their own. "There were three of them who got computers from the dining hall," said Ocampo. "They got on their vehicle and said, 'We got them,' so Captain Almacen escorted them through the gate." The Aetas, most of whom had been picked up many times in the act of stealing from the base, were never charged—and were glad for the chance to implicate their former boss.

"I asked them why they were testifying against Chen Almacen since they were working with him," said Ocampo. "They said he didn't give them a big enough cut." All suspected that the Americans in the U.S. Air Force civic actions office, responsible for do-good activities with the community, were profiteering. One day, Ocampo encountered Lieutenant Colonel Baker, the former civic actions chief at Clark, also a prosecution witness, at the base exchange and asked him what he had against Chen. "I'm really mad at him," Ocampo quoted Baker. "He was giving donations when we were the only ones authorized to give away anything off base"—a reflection of a long-standing power game between civic actions staff and security police.

Were Almacen's detractors angry because his "donations" were depriving them of payoffs? Was another American officer jealous over "donations" that he believed he should control? Did he—and others—feel they were not getting a big enough cut when the "donations" left the base and were allegedly sold for profit? On a much higher level, was Almacen marked for reprisals by both Americans and Filipinos? "There were many people asking for 'donations,' chairs, desks, books," said Ocampo. "This was the cover of the Philippine Air Force. That was the time of General Acot"—Leopoldo Acot, the base commander.

The OSI had less luck with a local journalist, Robledo Sanchez, who said he would not testify for the prosecution since "there were other Americans, and you are not going after them." Sanchez' remarks, if credible, might have been among the most incriminating—against other Americans. "I took some pictures during the looting," said Sanchez. "I saw some American colonel. He took about three tons of meat. All the food was in storage in Clark. They sell it in Manila. The chief of civic action in Clark looted too"— a reference to Lieutenant Colonel Baker. When an OSI agent asked him "to pin down Almacen," said Sanchez, "I said, 'no way' because it was not only Almacen. It was not fair."[40]

The OSI did not want to know about the others, unless their remarks served to implicate Almacen. Rather than persuade Sanchez to join the side of the prosecution, the Americans had to accede to a defense request to fly Sanchez to Guam as a defense witness—required as a show of "impartiality" for the sake of a "fair trial." In the end, however, Almacen's defense lawyers never called Sanchez as a witness—his views were "hearsay" that might rebound against the defendant. In the milieu of a court-martial, testimony suggesting that others were "also guilty" would only antagonize the panel of military judge and military jurors.

Sanchez also might have introduced another element into the trial—that of racial prejudice. "It is this double standard of justice because he is a Filipino," he said when I interviewed him one evening in his home on an Angeles alley. Sanchez made his views known while enjoying himself at U.S. expense in Guam. "One of the colonels in Guam asked about Almacen. I said there's discrimination in the U.S. Air force. I said I don't know why they arrest him and not others. He said, 'Please don't write the story. If you can help the Department of the Air Force, they reward you.'" Sanchez does not exonerate the Filipinos. Philippine Air Force officers offered payoffs for cooperation, he said, while the PNP destroyed records of looting.

The question Almacen keeps asking is what happened to the cases of other Americans accused or suspected of looting. Why were they not tried, convicted and sentenced as well? What about the officer responsible for "civic actions," which put him in touch with local businessmen? Was he really the one whom Sanchez claimed to have seen pilfering the frozen meat? Who was it who arranged for a container loaded with $40,000 worth of meat to be stolen, as alleged by the OSI? Enlisted men were also investigated. One master sergeant tossing loot over the fence in broad daylight was caught on videotape by a military news team. The lens zoomed over his nametag and badges. Another was charged with giving away cooking ranges and washing machines from base housing. Were they punished? What about *their* court-martials?

Almacen "has been singled out for prosecution in this case either in bad faith or because of his race which is Filipino," said his defense attorneys, in a motion submitted at the start of the trial. The motion requested dismissal of all charges "because of this selective prosecution which appears to have been done either in bad faith or based on an impermissible consideration such as the accused's race." Both Colonel Dassler and Colonel Corwin had "implicated themselves in these charges," said the motion, by approving the movement of scrap material from the base.[41]

"Neither were prosecuted" after more than two years of investigation, observed the motion, because "neither is filipino [*sic*] like the accused." Both had "expressed their knowledge of alleged illegal activities and their own participation in the charges having to do with the scrapping operations." The presiding judge, an air force colonel, rejected the motion as unsupported by any evidence of "discriminatory prosecution."

Sanchez was not the only witness whom the defense attorneys, two junior air force officers, did not ask to testify. They did not call Almacen, either. Almacen wishes he had addressed the court—and believes the defense team was doing only a pro forma job on his behalf. "I didn't know better," he said, trying to figure out what went wrong at the trial, why he didn't testify, what points he might have raised. "I was relying on their case. They thought I would get tangled up by legal mumbo-jumbo." After hours, his attorneys were fraternizing at the officers' club with the prosecution when he wanted to talk to them about tactics and strategy for the next day in court—and the rest of the trial. "They didn't come to see me," he said. "I was alone."[42]

Long after it was all over, Almacen said he would have liked to have spoken out about why his name appeared at the bottom of all those CABCOM 30 forms authorizing truckloads of "scrap material" to go off the base. Without testifying, he had no chance to explain why trucks carrying "donations" for Marcos Village were going in the opposite direction, as alleged by PNP Captain Ocampo. "The road was cut off the other way," he said, charging that Ocampo's men stopped the trucks in order to get their own cut—a common practice.

"There was no criminal, no malicious intent," said Almacen, showing copies of the CABCOM 30s that he signed, all provided to the OSI by the Clark Air Base Command (CABCOM) as evidence—on Acot's orders. "Otherwise, why would I sign my name? Paid informants said, 'You need to go after Almacen because he's a millionaire, he's making all this money selling scrap.' That's what motivated the OSI. At the trial they were all embarrassed because it turned out they were all lies."[43]

The Americans, refusing to provide records of the Almacen case, did their best to hold publicity to a minimum. There were no articles in the local Guam newspaper, no American news agency coverage during the trial. There were no television cameras or hard-nosed reporters waiting outside the drab structure that housed the legal offices at Andersen Air Force base on the morning of November 7, 1993, when the court announced its verdict. "The air force did not want the world to know about a scandal in their own ranks," said an American on the base throughout the time of the looting. Only the witnesses were standing outside.

Suddenly, the doors opened. There was Almacen, found guilty on five of eleven charges, stripped of rank, sentenced to a year's hard labor and dishonorable discharge. "He had been free during the trial; he was not in custody," said Ocampo. "Now he was handcuffed. He was crying."[44] Grim-faced air force cops prodded Almacen, the sacrificial lamb being led to slaughter, to a van for the ride to the base stockade. It was the first stop on the way to the U.S. military prison at Fort Leavenworth, Kansas, several miles from the federal penitentiary at Leavenworth.

Around Angeles, no one believed Almacen was the only American on the take. "Chen works for the chief of security police and the chief of OSI, the office of special investigation," said Carlito Ganzon, a member of the Angeles City council. "They were not charged. Poor Chen. I think he was sacrificed. Probably a lot of stuff was missing before the investigation. He's got a lot of friends off-base. Many are high-ranking officials."[45]

Ocampo and Sanchez said they were not close personally, but both claimed that the collaboration between the Philippine Air Force and the PNP could not have happened without approval at top levels. Beyond that, however, Philippine and American authorities appear to have cooperated in a plan to "get" Almacen as the single scapegoat both of them had to have. The Filipinos needed the conviction of an American to show they were not "the only ones." The Americans needed to convict an American to show they were not just blaming Filipinos—and excusing other Americans for lack of evidence or letting them off with slaps on the wrist, "reprimands."

Out of Leavenworth after serving nine months of the one-year sentence, Almacen fought on for vindication, promising to battle to the U.S. Supreme Court for reversal of his conviction after the U.S. Court of Military Appeals, in early 1997, rejected his appeal without comment. He was technically on "appellate leave," which meant that he had no duties and received no compensation, other than medical and dental benefits. He was free to work elsewhere but spent a lot of his time in the apartment he shared with his wife and their two teen-age boys in Torrance, California, mulling over his strategy, his future, his chances for another professional position while attempting to erase the terrible blot of imprisonment, loss of rank and dishonorable discharge from his record.

"I was the victim of jealousy and discrimination," Almacen wrote a younger brother, Virgilio, who was living in the Almacen "family home," a sturdy cement structure with television and stereo on the main road through Sablan. Virgilio showed me the letter, typewritten, in good English, as we chatted in a setting of Chinese art and comfortable furniture, far above the level of most tribal people. The tone was one of rage—and revenge.

"When this is over it will be my turn to file criminal suits against those who set me up, including the Filipinos who told lies for money just to ruin my reputation," wrote Chen, signing off as "Manong" (elder brother), implying power and optimism too. "I will receive all the back pay that the U.S. government owes me. Even with what happened to me, our Almighty Father has been kind to us. We have our health, we're together."[46]

Virgilio and a sister, Judy, living in Baguio, talked about the case as a tragedy. "He was framed by some officers, American and Filipino," said Virgilio. "They want him to be down because of jealousy." Judy conveyed the agony of family disgrace. "It was very painful. People said my brother had a rich house. They said he had houses in Olongapo, Baguio, Manila. We are all very, very hurt. It was very, very painful, especially for my father. He has a good reputation. They ruined the family name, the family honor. Almost all the people in Sablan know each other. The father of my father was mayor of Sablan during the American time." To Judy, there was no doubt of the injustice of it all.[47]

Nobody defended Almacen more staunchly than his former boss, Colonel Corwin, who testified for Almacen at the trial. Before retiring, Corwin put down thousands of words in at least two sworn statements, praising Almacen's record, his character—even "his success in protecting American lives during the 1989 coup when he and several other attendees at the Balikatan 89 Exercises were trapped by rebels in a hotel during a gun battle in Makati, Metro Manila." He was, Corwin affirmed, "one of the very few security policemen asked to continually perform in risky situations."

Beyond all that, however, Corwin disputed the conduct of the case, the verdict and the sentence, if anything, more convincingly than does Almacen himself. He attacked as "simply gross" the failure of investigators to try to obtain all the forms signed by others for material to leave the base and charged that the refusal to permit Almacen to go back to Clark for a year and a half after the closure of the base "absolutely prevented any possibility of the defense" obtaining what it needed for the case.[48]

Corwin's defense of his subordinate was so detailed as to raise considerable doubt about the charges. He did not, however, touch on the most important issue in the case—that of whether or how the Americans and Filipinos cooperated to serve up one American officer on the altar of Philippine-American relations.

There was no mention of any relationship between General Acot and General Studer, no hint of Acot's crying need for Almacen's conviction as a device to deflect attention from the misdeeds of his command. There was no suggestion that Studer, equally desperate to pull American forces and ma-teriél from Clark as cleanly and expeditiously as possible, might have coop-erated with his conniving Filipino counterparts for the sake of goodwill in an extremely sensitive period in U.S.-Philippine relations. To the contrary, American officers defend Studer as a man of integrity.

If there had been no Studer-Acot "handshake," as Almacen suspects, was there a tacit understanding? Studer, in retirement in Florida, said he was aware of the investigation but had nothing to do with it, was never asked for a statement—and never discussed it with Acot. Nor does he believe that there was a "secret" deal on any level, with or without his knowledge. "I doubt if I would put a lot of merit to any of that, especially allegations of trade-offs," the general said flatly. "I have more faith in our system."[49]

Studer's old subordinates cite one instance when their general stood up to Acot. That was after Acot "ran up some ungodly bill in the ten or fifteen thousand dollars range at the officers' club," said an American colonel. "We wrestled with how to handle it. It's impolitic, impolite, it's unprofessional to go to him"—so what to do? "I watched General Studer making the decision. He decided, 'We're going to tell General Acot he's not going to use the club, he's going to pay the bill, or I am going to go to the mutual defense board [made up of Philippine and American officers convening regularly in Manila] and ask him to pay the money.'"

The result was swift and decisive. "The Phils came up with the money. I don't know where they got it, but they paid in full. Acot thought, 'This is the way it is, I'm the general, you pay the bill'"—but in this case Acot was wrong.[50]

Having tested the limits of American endurance on such a trivial mat-ter as an officers' club bill, Acot got along fine with Studer. "When we were getting ready to leave, General Acot had a nice dinner for General Studer in one of the hotels in Manila," said the American colonel. "He didn't have to do it. I don't think he did it for face or for show. He meant despite the things they disagreed on, General Acot still viewed General Studer as a professional and a guy he wanted to say good things about when he left." Acot had much for which to be grateful. The prosecution of Almacen was one of them. Studer might dun Acot for a club bill, but he was not about to call his Philippine comrade to account for the looting of Clark—or to undermine Acot's face-saving effort at blaming the upstart

Igorot American captain who, in his U.S. Air Force officer's uniform, had once so upset the lowlanders.

Studer himself refused to talk about the Filipinos with whom he had to deal—or to speculate about looting. He had more important things to think about. "I was aware, in the big scheme of things, that something like that had to be dealt with. I had other things on my mind like getting out the $200 million in assets," materiél the United States had to rescue from the base rather than donate to the Filipinos. "My priorities were on the people and their welfare and their safety," the general wanted to make clear. "I did not see any level of looting as being a showstopper." There were "a lot of parts—looting was just one of the parts."[51]

FOUR

Looting to Booming

Thievery at Clark had a long tradition. A saying among Americans was that "everything on Clark has been stolen, some of it just hasn't been picked up." One of the jokes while the Americans were there was that somehow they could never adequately protect the barrier cables they stretched across the runway, like the cables on the decks of aircraft carriers, to hook jet aircraft in case they failed to stop properly on landing. No sooner would a new cable be installed than Filipinos would sneak through security and chop it apart, extracting the copper wiring in sections.

"There were gangs and syndicates at every level," said a retired American colonel. "We had grandfathers who were caught stealing for 25 years. Anything that's not guarded, they stole"—including the lights and wiring from a lighting system set up for $5 million along the perimeter fence for the specific purpose of cutting down on theft. The Americans had a better chance of preserving the runway's landing lights, burning 24 hours a day, but these were also pilfered regularly.[1]

Within days after the eruption of Pinatubo, looters were plucking out the lights along both the old runway and the new one, opened in time for a final whirlwind of half a dozen transports ferrying supplies to the Persian Gulf during and after the Iraqi invasion of Kuwait on August 1, 1990. By the time the last Americans had left Clark in November 1991, every landing light was gone. For the Americans, loss of the lights and much else was no problem. They were pulling out in the summer of 1991 no matter how the Philippine Senate voted on the bases treaty. The runways, closed before the eruption, never reopened while they were there.

Much later, as Philippine authorities dreamed up a grand plan for turning Clark into an international airport, a substitute for Metro Manila's decrepit, less-than-safe-or-secure Ninoy Aquino Airport, one of their first problems was to replace the stolen lights and other missing equipment—and devise a security system strong enough to keep it all there. By that time, they had come up with a scheme, similar to the one for Subic, for converting Clark into a commercial center, featuring a new Holiday Inn plus gambling casinos, duty-free shopping and a new golf course in place of the old one, ruined by ash and mud.

Wistfully, some of the Philippine officers who love to blame the looting on the Americans also wish the same Americans had hung around longer to stop it. "Before November 26, 1991, we requested some American troops to stay," said a Philippine Air Force officer "They said yes, but nothing came. It's regrettable the bases agreement was turned down. If the Philippine Senate had extended it for three years, Clark would have been saved. If only the Americans had not pulled out, so much help could have been there. We could have taken advantage of the situation."[2]

The officer claimed, however, that the Philippine Air Force protected the flight line, base operations and the control tower. "All that equipment is still there"—a backhanded admission that the PAF could have saved much more if the airmen at the base, officers and enlisted men, were not sharing a fortune from the looting of less vital equipment. The failure of authorities to respond during the looting, their boldness in brushing off the thievery, in accusing Americans first and last, ranked as such a disgrace as to call into question their ability to do that much with the Clark Special Economic Zone—or to rule the country at all effectively.

The looting of the base picked up in earnest as soon as the U.S. Air Force began entrusting large portions of it to their Filipino allies. For posturing Philippine senators, it sufficed to shout a rhetorical "no" to the bases while negotiators haggled over the terms of a treaty that "nationalist" politicians were determined to reject. There was no equivalent oratorical rage in the Philippine Congress about the abuse of the bases by Filipino officers and colonels and generals looting their heritage with the impunity of an angry mob robbing a jewelry store in the midst of a riot.

"We divided the base into four or five sectors," said Colonel Rand, based at Clark for the last two years of the American tenure there. Instinctively, Rand defended the U.S. Air Force, which occupied most of a base theoretically under Philippine command. "There was no way to control it. Whenever we turned one over to Filipino control, reports showed that's where the looting was. Once the Philippine Air Force was done with the most rewarding looting, then your street looters would come in."[3]

Rand at least credits the looters with knowing what they were doing, often with downright consummate skill. "You're talking about people who for their whole lives have fended for themselves. The Filipinos would restore cars, build furniture, do wonderful glass and artwork and metal work"— skills they could also utilize in ripping the guts out of the base.

Word soon spread that senior Filipino officers were profiting along with the looters. Filipino reporters delighted in a play on the name of the base commander, Air Force Brigadier General Acot—his surname means "bring out" in the local Pampangan language and also comes close to the Tagalog "hakot" for "cart away." The Americans were to blame, countered a Philippine officer: "By virtue of the memorandum of agreement, everything should be turned over, but everybody forgot about it because when we went to do an inventory, everything was gone."[4]

The reason "everything was gone" was that most of it had already been looted. "There wasn't a real serious problem until they turned the base over to the Filipinos," said John Cummings, a veteran of three tours at Clark before presiding over Margaritaville. Each American unit "was directed to leave lists of what they left inside the building. They put an arbitrary value on the list. Everything they left behind was pretty much there."[5]

A former American official on the team responsible for handing over the American inventories remembers clearly the brouhaha over the discrepancy between the American and the Filipino counts. "They had a colonel, a civil engineer. He was the guy formally receiving all the facilities. We'd have my printout saying what was there. They'd sign documents." Then, ten days before the final turnover on November 22, 1991, Acot shocked the American team by demanding "new printouts," since so much was now missing. "We refused to give new printouts," said the ex-official. We gave the old printouts with statements signed by the legal officer saying the recipient refused to sign them, saying there were discrepancies."[6]

The former official vividly recalled the showdown with Acot and his staff. "I live here," he said. "I'm aware of the society and the culture. I know what happens. It was a total rip-off by the Armed Forces of the Philippines. It was managed and condoned by the Philippine Air Force. I was in meetings with Acot and his people. Right in the middle of a meeting, I'd see trucks going by with stuff piled up. Acot would say he didn't know what was happening, he'd 'look into it.'" The American doesn't know how high up the profit-sharing might have gone but observed, "President Ramos was secretary of defense at the time, Renato de Villa was armed forces chief of staff. They had to have known."

Stories of Acot's antics were common currency. The one my American informant liked best was about the efforts of a Philippine bishop in charge of refugee resettlement sites for people who had lost their homes after the eruption of Pinatubo. "This bishop asked for material to build community toilets. Acot told him to go to any building and pick out what he wanted and disassemble it—45 percent to go to the bishop for the resettlement sites, 55 percent to the Philippine Air Force."

Then there was the time the American was sitting in Acot's office complex working on a computer, entering data on the turnover, when suddenly he heard shots fired and hysterical screaming outside the window. "There were all these people coming out of the housing areas. I found out the Philippine Air Force had let them in the southwest gate and let them raid the whole housing area. There were hundreds of people. When they had all the stuff they could carry and were leaving, the PAF started shooting around them, over their heads. So then the people dropped the stuff by the road and ran, and the PAF picked it up and carted it away in trucks for themselves. You can still see the destroyed houses."

Frank Hilliard encountered crazy scenes as the Americans attempted to conduct an orderly handover and withdrawal amid all the looting and non-cooperation: "We basically closed the base with 2,000 men. The numbers went down. We were totally undermanned. All these hawkers came on the base trying to buy and sell stuff. We had people camped out on the base waiting to buy stuff. Some of it was legitimate. Some wasn't. You got total chaos."[7]

The Americans were frantic. "We had 60 days to let Congress know what we were turning over," said Hilliard. "We sent a 280-page document of what we knew we still controlled. We couldn't turn over anything without congressional approval. Suddenly, one congressional committee said, 'Let's get that fuel out of here via the pipeline from Clark to Subic.' The pipeline was already breached by the Pinatubo eruption and sealed off at Subic and Clark. It was a prime target for salvage. A lot of it was gone. We contracted every fuel truck in northern Luzon and shipped it to the port at Manila. We still left 750,000 barrels of JP4 jet fuel. Presumably it was sold to Philippine Airlines. It's not there now, and they only had about five F-5s that could use it. We left 1,200 running vehicles, more than there were PAF assigned to the base, plus all the POVs [privately owned vehicles] were left."

Hilliard was the last American off Clark. "I drove the Mazda pickup with the computer records. I drove out two days before Thanksgiving 1991. The whole thing was to shut it down and get the last two aircraft with people from Clark out of Subic in time for Thanksgiving. We hauled out the big red fire truck the last day and took it to Subic." After all the thievery he had seen, Hilliard considered himself lucky to have denied one final costly piece of equipment to the looters and gotten out before the deadline.

Colonel Rand backed up the overall impression of a concentrated Philippine Air Force attempt to pass the buck: "They tried to blame us while we were there. The preponderance was done by Filipinos. Some members of the Philippine Air Force were taking kickbacks, were turning the other way."[8]

A local businessman, Ener Lumanlan, organized a group to discuss the looting with the Philippine Air Force commander, General Loven Abadia. "I told him what's going on, but most of his men were involved in the looting. Later on utensils from the officers' club, including tables and plates, turned up in Cebu," said Lumanlan.[9] The story is legend. "Utensils, desks and office equipment, they're all over," my guide from the Clark Development Corporation told me during my tour. "You can find plates at a restaurant in Cebu that say, 'Clark Field'"—or CAB for Clark Air Base, the distinct imprint on kitchen and dining regalia.[10]

Senator John "Sonny" Osmeña, of the Osmeña family from Cebu, did some on-scene investigating. He visited a restaurant in Mactan, near Cebu, where furniture and kitchenware from Clark was plain to see, and cited such evidence as reason not to approve Acot's promotion to air force commander in 1993. Oddly enough, the restaurant was said to be owned by—who else?—an air force commander, Major General Loven Abadia, who was pushing Acot as his successor. Acot "should explain why this happened," was Osmeña's plaintive, futile lament.[11]

The generals may have grown a little restive while a panel made up of members of both houses of the Philippine Congress balked at approving Acot's appointment. One senator, Alberto Romulo, made a show of observing that Acot hardly deserved to move up since he had failed to "protect" Clark. Acot said nothing. His career scarcely blemished by the looting, much less the hearings, he easily got his promotion and served a full tour as air force commander.

The Abadia family flourished, too. Loven's elder brother, Lisandro Abadia, was already an army commander—and soon to become the armed forces chief of staff, Acot's superior. All three retired with honor, dignity and wealth—Acot to a mansion near the golf course at Villamor Air Base, by Ninoy Aquino Airport, where he may be seen swinging the clubs almost daily.

Filipino officials are geared to shield the generals even in retirement. Lulu Ilustre, assistant secretary of defense for public affairs, a long-time Ramos favorite also named by him as chairman of the government television station, flew into a rage when I asked to see Acot. "Who have you interviewed," she demanded. "Get out, get out," she shouted when I refused to tell her my sources. On Fields Avenue, a foreign barkeep observed, "They are outraged there should be any consequences for their actions."

Acot need make no excuses. He counts on his friends to come up with explanations, ranging from flimsy to false. "He said when the Americans were here, there were 1,200 security police with dogs, jeeps, horses and here we are, we have only 400 security police covering almost 10,000 acres," said Lumanlan. "These are groups from neighboring *barangay*. The way it is done, nobody is watching this area. There was no official list of what is left on the base. There were only 800 Filipino personnel. When the Americans left, only 400 Filipinos were guarding the base."[12]

Such talk, however, is misleading. The Americans did leave lists. Lumanlan's estimate of the size of the security force is far too low. Nor has anyone explained why Acot, if he was so worried, did not urgently call for reinforcements to cope with what amounted to a hostile invasion. "It was not General Acot alone who was doing the looting," Lumanlan responded lamely. "He was a gentleman." Someone, admittedly, had to have commanded the thievery, for everybody's benefit but that of the people. Lumanlan preferred not to name names.

Until the departure of the Americans, the thievery was relatively amateurish. The large-scale professional stripdown went on through all of 1992 and into 1993 while Philippine authorities deflected attention by inciting the Americans to go after Captain Almacen. The looting operation was by then thoroughgoing and systematic—the job of skilled craftsmen under tight control. Most had once worked on the base for the Americans and had learned not only where to go but also what to do when they got there. Not a few of them had made virtual careers of stealing from the base.

"That's Wagner Elementary School on the left," said the tour guide as our van roared by. "They took out everything. They had a place where they kept all these items—refrigerators, washer-dryers, everything."[13] The looting of the high school, more than any other example, proves the role of the Philippine Air Force command.

An American, fearful of releasing his name "because they have ways of getting people," painted a horrifying picture of the conspiracy as he witnessed it. "I was the only one here," said the American. "I was ramrodding the clean-up crew. I was salvaging as much material as I could from the school. We were going to turn the school over to the Philippines. A lot of stuff was to remain there. The Philippine Air Force gave me a date to have everything out of the school, but politics got into it. They found out a lot of material was there. This was a $6-$7 million school. We had a business lab, a chemical lab, a geology lab. The school was one of the most modern in the world. There was an intercom system, a gorgeous auditorium."[14]

The original date for the Americans to hand the school over was October 15, shortly before the last of the Americans were to leave Clark, but Philippine Air Force officers repeatedly advanced the date so that the Americans would not have time to remove hundreds of new computers and IBM Selectric typewriters. "They say October 15, then they say October 1, then September. Then one day in August a Philippine Air Force colonel came in and said, 'You have to be out of there now, this Friday.'" The American accused American officials—military, diplomatic, civilian—of coddling the Filipinos, hoping to appease them during final negotiations on the bases treaty, which the Philippine Senate had yet to vote down.

"This was a political thing," he said. "Politics was it. The Filipinos said, 'We need access to the base,' and wanted to 'secure all the schools.' We were trying to get out everything. It was August 20, 1991. They just said, 'As of this weekend, you're not welcome in this base any more.' We lost about 120 computer systems." It was what he saw after leaving the school for the last time, however, that conclusively proved the role of the Philippine Air Force. "I tried to get into the school the following Monday. There was barbed wire around the building and Philippine Air Force people with M16s pointing at me."

When the American returned much later, after the Filipinos evidently figured they had nothing else to guard, he found a scene of total destruction. "Not only was all the materiel stolen, they ripped the walls out so they could get the wiring and the switches. They ripped the flooring so they could get the PVC plastic piping. There was new expensive carpeting. It was gone."

Colonel Rand described the pillaging at Wagner as he saw it around the same time: "The high school was really discouraging when I walked in. It looked like someone had put a bomb in. Whoever did the looting did it without regard to being neat or without any care or regard for what was left. They would find a wire somewhere, they would rip it right out. If there was anything, copper wire, aluminum, all that stuff had a premium."[15]

Rand waxed philosophical. "You look at the whole moral climate of the country, the little people see big people doing it, and for a thousand pesos, about $40, everybody can get 'salvaged,'" he said, using the Fil-English term from the post-war period, when the Americans tossed what they no longer needed into salvage dumps outside bases and encampments. "It was a thousand pesos that one guy paid a Filipino to salvage his wife"—while Rand was there.

The higher the official, in the American view, the bigger the crook. Rand believes "there probably was a godfather" lording it over the looting of Clark. "If we believe in the godfather concept, you grab the low-hanging fruit. If I were the godfather, I would get all the easy big-ticket items. Then I would move to the next sector and do the same thing. I would know that cash cow would not be pumping out that kind of milk forever."

Ultimately, the Americans blame the top Filipino commander. "Acot at that time was brigadier general," said one of them. "He made enough money so he could afford to be a major general. He says nothing happened. He says he never saw one tractor-trailer going off that base or any trucks being hauled off that base. Acot had to be aware of it. There was no possible way he was not aware. You had IBM Selectric 3 self-correcting typewriters for sale all the way to Manila. You saw those trucks. They were loaded. You had anything from ten-wheelers up to 18-wheelers. It was pitiful."[16]

My guided tour of the new Clark passed by still more scenes of destruction. "These were the enlisted homes"—houses for enlisted men and women and their families, said my guide. "The houses were collapsing under the ash from Pinatubo. Some of them were still stacked up with appliances after the evacuation. They stripped the wire and got the copper. There were buyers on the outside."

Where heavy-duty equipment was needed to haul out the loot, heavy-duty equipment was found—and used. "At the commissary they had these big freezers," the guide explained. "They needed a crane to lift them up." Who got the vaunted ice-cream maker, beloved by a generation of sweet-toothed American GIs? "RFC bought one to make ice cream," he replied, not hesitating to name the country's biggest food-processing conglomerate, the Republic Food Corporation, as an unabashed recipient of stolen goods.

The looting of the base hospital exemplified the skill of the looters, military and civilian, in covering their tracks. Ostensibly, the facility was stripped after local authorities said they needed equipment for city clinics damaged by lahar. The Angeles City Hospital was in such poor condition that foreign charities shipped in donations. Why not expect help from the base hospital, too? Equipment from the Clark facility wound up in a storehouse before going elsewhere, mainly to private clinics at enormous profits. When U.S. investigators looked for evidence, they were shown the gleaming gifts from overseas and were told, "Look, we got all these donations from Clark, just like we told you."

Not all structures, however, were gutted. "Some buildings occupied by the Philippine military were preserved," the tour guide interjected defensively. "The officers' houses are better. These are preserved. They didn't loot these houses." Did the looters menace *any* of the quarters of Philippine officers and airmen? "The commander was here," the guide replied. "His people were here. What do you think?" Rand put it this way: "When the Philippine Air Force put people in all the houses we had just turned over, when the Phils lived in them, they took care of them."

By the time of the closing ceremony on November 26, 1991, about 200 Americans were left on the base. General Studer, Colonel Rand—and Captain Almacen—were all there to see the U.S. Pacific Air Force commander, General Jimmy Adams, present "the symbolic key" to the base to General Lisandro Abadia. "It was very, very, very emotional," said Rand. "The most dramatic point was the impact on the people that final day. I don't think there was a dry eye there when we took the flag down after being there for 90 years—Filipinos for four or five generations who had worked on that base and Americans who had raised their families there, the impact on both sides was terrible."

Moving though it was, the ceremony was the last word in face-saving. Members of the Philippine Air Force, whatever their rank, savored the spoils as would the victors in pitched battle. Generosity depended on rank, but all those assigned to Clark got to move, along with wives, children and extended families, into rent-free houses far superior to the shacks and shanties in which enlisted men typically live off-base or in civilian life. "They have the knack of choosing the best houses," said the tour guide with a grimace. "The commander has the best one"—a mansion remodeled at least twice since the Americans left.

Rand observed the contrasts whenever he accompanied his next commanding general from his base on Guam on return visits for meetings of the Philippine-U.S. Mutual Defense Board at Camp Aguinaldo. "Each time I came back the only thing I was surprised at was how much taller the grass was. Every place that stayed vacant a while, where nobody was living, was up for grabs. My first house was on the backside of the base. The flow of lava was about a quarter of a mile from my house. I went to my old house more than once. Each time I left there was less in it. Anything that had metal in it, doors, windows, anything that had metal was gone." A second house to which he had moved after the eruption of Pinatubo survived intact, thanks to the Philippine colonel who moved in after him. "It was a new home just up the hill, the first house across the street from General Acot," said Rand. How did it look? "Pretty good," the colonel surmised.[17]

As the Philippine Air Force made itself at home, settling in or stealing depending on the level of need and greed, Philippine authorities occasionally tut-tutted but never viewed the looting as an emergency. There was no sense in Aquino's government, much less at the top echelons of the armed forces, that anything was amiss. A few months after the last Americans were gone, the Department of National Defense, stung by publicity, dispatched several hundred Philippine marines to stop the looting, but the operation was a notorious failure. "The word was the marines and air force had a gun battle over who got to steal what parts of the base," said an American living off base. "They had to adjust the payoffs."[18]

So effective was the Filipinos' disinformation campaign that American officials also forgot about the disaster at Clark—and they profess no knowledge of it. Diplomats at the American embassy and officers at the Joint U.S. Military Assistance Group, a shadow of the old U.S. Military Assistance and Advisory Group that preceded it, are fonts of ignorance. Washington, having gotten out in an atmosphere of face-losing propaganda, decided to cut its losses, forget about the destruction and move on—to improved economic ties, a low-key aid program and military contacts in the form of joint exercises, training and port visits.

Around the offices of the Clark Development Authority, in one of the old U.S. Air Force headquarters buildings, the emphasis is also on the future. There, a retired Philippine Air Force major general, Romeo David, president of the CDC and the Clark International Airport Corporation, in charge of repairing the damage, bringing in investment and turning Clark into a symbol of the new Philippines, talked about Clark's prospects as a regional hub with air freight and civilian flights.

Some day, a railroad is to link Clark to Ninoy Aquino Airport, providing a kind of shuttle service. A Spanish company has been toiling away at the Manila-Clark Rapid Railway System, dubbed Northrail—a $900 million, 100-kilometer line to Manila. Some day, Northrail is to run on the right-of-way that was first laid under Spanish rule but was abandoned several months before the eruption of Pinatubo and is now covered with squatters' shanties and garbage. Some day, there is also to be a six-lane highway linking the zone to a new highway to Olongapo and Subic.

The revived airport and rail and road connections were all to be ready by National Day, June 12, 1998—the one hundredth anniversary of the date on which General Aguinaldo, in Cavite, had declared the short-lived Philippine Republic. A century after the revolution, Clark was preening for a gala celebration featuring Spanish, American and Japanese exhibitions—"all the countries that conquered us"—as a prelude to bidding for Clark to become the site for the World Expo in the year 2002. (The British occupation, 1762–1764, evidently did not count.) Ramos himself, as a regular visitor, General David told me, "would want the infrastructure in place at the soonest time possible."[19]

More to the point, said David, "We have a lot of light and medium industry plans." Already, approximately 50 factories were putting together television sets, spinning out textiles and finished clothing and whipping up food products—light industry that he hoped would lead to much bigger development. If nothing else, Clark was already a mecca for gambling, a budding Las Vegas of the East, luring big spenders on special flights from Taiwan, Hong Kong and other havens of wealthy Chinese with millions to spare and spend. A Vegas-style floor show, featuring sequined foreign dancers and a raspy singer, performed in a club below the biggest casino.

Still, the base had a sadly seedy look. Huge stretches of once-pristine grass were growing high, running to weed and jungle, while dilapidated vehicles, cannibalized by the looters, filled garages. Old barracks were still shorn of windows, with doors and siding rising ghostlike from seas of undergrowth. Vegetables grew in one-time flower gardens, and chickens scratched away on the front lawns of officers' homes. David, who was base commander for two years in the 1980s, well before the Americans left, admitted that the zone "could stand a lot of improvement" but saw Clark as soon flourishing again at the heart of the local economy.

By 1996 the base had more than 15,000 people working there—a figure supposed to triple in five years—and investment of about $400 million. That figure, equal to the spent-or-missing lahar fund, was also elusive. No one was certain how much was in hand, or just "pledged" or "committed," and whether those factories now in business were the precursors of substantial investment. Duty-free shops offered perhaps the best hope after Ramos gave local people duty-free privileges up to $200 a month while banning duty-free for those from outside the area—a concession to Manila department store tycoons angered by the competition.

David countered the negativism, citing signs of a comeback off-base. "Even in the neighboring community, I understand 75 percent of the community is back. Things are perking up."[20]

Local entrepreneurs agreed. "Business is going up more than 200 percent because of duty-free," said William Kwong, owner of the Shanghai Restaurant, born again as the city's leading place for fine dining and meeting, with function rooms capable of seating 3,500 people. "Now it's very hard to find a house to rent. You have to buy one. Before a house was 500,000 pesos, about $20,000. Now it goes up to 2.5 million pesos. They have put up the Holiday Inn in Clark. They are building a Hyatt. They are building a 54-hole golf course, three 18-hole courses. Before the course opened, a share was 200,000 pesos. Now it is 1.5 million. There will be five casinos inside the base. They are putting up a movie studio."[21]

The formula for success was a new one in official Philippine strategy, a trinity of three Gs—golf, gambling and girls. The gambling might be expensive, but the big players, the Japanese and the Chinese from Hong Kong, Taiwan, Malaysia and Singapore, were sure to save on both the golf and the girls. Japanese in particular liked the price of golf—it was a fifth or a tenth of what they paid in fees in Japan. And the girls, if not all that available inside Clark, were as visible now on the other side of the fence as they had been in the GI days. Indeed, they were staging a comeback as the twin magnets of golf and gambling inside "the base," as it's still called, attracted high rollers prowling for cheap sex in between other forms of game playing.

One reason for the revival along blocks still pocked and pitted by boarded-up fronts of one-time GI nightclubs was another Filipino campaign—another anti-foreigner drive, a follow-up to the antibases campaign. Manila Mayor Alfredo Lim's morality drive in the fleshpots of Ermita had an immediate impact on Angeles.

Foreign visitors, notably Australians and Germans, the two most conspicuous national stereotypes in the Ermita district, migrated to Angeles in search of the remnants of the sex industry that once catered to GIs. Foreign managers and investors in nightclubs that were shuttered or severely restricted by Mayor Lim quickly followed. By the mid-1990s, Fields Avenue and surrounding side streets were booming again—not quite as they were when the GIs were turning the scene into a carnival of sex but enough to attract ever more foreign visitors.

For Filipinos, and not a few visitors from foreign countries, the Australians were a strange breed. They looked and often acted like the American GIs and military retirees who found the living, the women, the prices and the lifestyle far easier in Angeles or Olongapo than "back in the world," the GI expression for back in the USA. They were, however, definitely different. These Aussies, unlike the relatively cultured academics, businesspeople, diplomats and journalists from down under who were most likely to surface elsewhere, were of the tradition of the legendary swagman, the name of an Australian hotel chain in Manila, Angeles, Baguio and elsewhere. They spoke in incomprehensible accents, were quick to insult the next man at the bar or to respond with anger on their own behalf or that of their "mates." They looked with racist contempt on Filipinos—and didn't much like Americans, either.

Some of these tough-talking, hard-drinking Australian tourists engaged in sailing and scuba-diving, but for most the quarry was women. Frustrated by Mayor Lim in Manila, they were doing very well in Angeles, where a number of them ran bars featuring dancers available for the night for the 500-peso or $20 bar fine, split between girl and bar.

The fun hardly ended but was temporarily dampened in mid-1995 when a group of 15 Australian women, led by Meredith Burgmann, a member of the New South Wales state parliament, descended on Angeles to investigate reports that 50,000 Australian men were visiting the Philippines annually on sex tours. They blamed not only "dirty old men" in search of underage partners but also squads of "footies," Aussie-speak for rugby, football and soccer players, on team outings. Burgmann charged that Australian travel agencies, hotels and resorts were collaborating on sex tours and called on the Australian government to enforce its Child Sex Tourism Act, under which Australians are liable for prosecution in Australia for underage sex overseas.[22]

The Aussies of Angeles were not exactly hospitable, much less cooperative, with their countrywomen. At the outset, they made public relations errors that played into the women's hands—and guaranteed a storm of publicity in both Australia and the Philippines. An Australian hotel manager refused to honor their room reservations, claiming the ladies failed to show their passports. Next, Australian barkeeps posted signs saying "No un-escorted ladies"—and refused to serve them.

The ladies, on getting back to Manila, held a press conference in which they claimed that 83 percent of the hotels and 80 percent of the bars in Angeles were owned by Australians.[23] (Actually, Aussies were involved in 17 percent of the hotels and 23 percent of the bars, according to a local busi-nessperson's group.)[24]

The furor prompted Ramos to proclaim the need to protect Filipino women and children "from this social menace and to curb the sexual traf-ficking of foreigners in this country." It was "imperative," he said, "to strengthen the ethical and spiritual values of victims of said sex tours and to devise viable economic alternative [sic] to wean them away from prostitu-tion."[25] Angeles Mayor Pamintuan formed Task Force Magdalena and or-dered unannounced "visitations" in which plain-clothes police inspectors harassed bar owners over violations of building and sanitary codes—and the dress, demeanor and ages of hostesses. The cops raided ten clubs, mostly Filipino, closing them down while prodding bikini-clad girls into waiting vans—all lavishly featured on the television news and the front pages of the Manila press.

The comparison between the response to a brief publicity flare-up abroad and reports of the looting suggested underlying concerns and priorities. The government was far more alarmed by embarrassing international publicity over the scourge of foreigners undermining local morals than by the loss of hundreds of millions of dollars worth of property. The difference was that the foreigners, on this as on other levels, made easy targets in the national media, while the culprits in the looting remained pillars of the armed forces, of business, of a political structure that had bravely "said no" to Americans on the bases.

The attack on the fun and games of foreigners was a follow-up to earlier attacks by antibases forces. Through the crusade to get rid of the bases ran a steady stream of invective against GIs for compromising the morals not only of Filipino women but also of an entire community of thousands of restau-rant and nightclub workers, suppliers and family members.

These attacks were intertwined, in the years before the American with-drawal, with much more serious leftist pressure. On October 27, 1987, four Americans were unfortunate enough to stray into the sights of New People's Army (NPA) gunmen seeking "targets of opportunity" for random shooting. Two of the targets were GIs, another an American of Filipino ancestry, the fourth an American retiree. One of them died in the same Dau market, in front of a McDonald's, where the loot from Clark was to go on sale.

A year later, guerrillas in a dump truck shot and killed two American civilian technicians in a car outside Camp O'Donnell, the air force and navy communications and monitoring "spy" facility near the Crow Valley firing range on the slopes of the Zambales Mountains. (There was bitter historical irony—O'Donnell is in Capas, in Tarlac Province, where the infamous Bataan Death March of American POWs wound to its brutally sad ending after the American surrender to the Japanese on the Bataan Peninsula in 1942.)

The most notorious episode was the "execution" on the morning of April 21, 1989, of Colonel James "Nick" Rowe, who had escaped the Viet Cong after five years' captivity in the Mekong River delta. Rowe was shot and killed in the back seat of his car within 200 meters of the gate of the compound of the Joint U.S. Military Assistance and Advisory Group in Quezon City. NPA leaders had ordered his death for his activities as a "counter-insurgency expert"—he had advised Philippine forces in their war against NPA guerrillas. The assassins got close enough to ambush him after his newly hired driver, wounded in the attack, had made the fatal error of failing to change the route to work every day.

All told, at least nine Americans were assassinated in the final four years of the American military era in the Philippines. The last victims were two GIs, maintenance technicians with an air wing based in South Korea, who were taking part in one of the Cope Thunder exercises. The two were shot inside a trike, a motorcycle with a canopied seat attached to the side, outside the Holiday Lodge in Dau on May 13, 1990. The killers claimed to have been members of NPA "sparrow units." Often the units were attached to what the NPA called "the Mariano Garcia Brigade," named for an NPA commander, a veteran of the old Huk revolt of the 1950s, who had died in a clash near Clark.

To some extent, the NPA accomplished what it was after. "As a result of the two killings we changed the scope of Cope Thunder," said Colonel Rand. "We reduced it so we could put everyone from Cope Thunder into quarters on the base. We said we're not going to make it easy for them." The operation, which once involved 100 planes and 1,000 airmen, was cut in half. Others felt the impact. "The result of the killings was tough on the civilian community," Rand claimed. "We stopped letting people have free reign on the downtown. All the merchants suffered as a result. If that was the objective of the people doing the killing, then they succeeded."[26]

The sense of insecurity afflicted those at the top the most. "The fact was I was one of the prime targets for assassination in my tour," said General Studer. "I couldn't go anywhere except by bulletproof car—when I was off the base I was constantly surrounded by close-in security."[27]

Beyond a few isolated killings, was the threat all that serious? "I certainly respected it," Studer replied without hesitation. "It was always there. but I respected it even more after they shot two of my airmen." He believes that the intelligence reports he was getting justified strong measures even though such killings were rare. "Our intelligence was pretty good. There were those times when maybe it could have been a situation that could have resulted in someone's being hurt. We could maybe avoid it by security measures. We would periodically curfew, lock down the base"—keep the troops inside and all visitors outside the gates.

The mood of the Americans at the time was approaching desperation. "Clark AB had been in Threatcon Charlie since late 1989 as a result of the [abortive] Dec 89 coup against the Aquino regime, threats of further coups, the May 90 assassination of two airmen in Dau outside Clark AB, and further threatened NPA activity," according to Colonel Corwin, who used the military term denoting a serious threat condition around the base. "Base personnel were restricted to the base, sometimes a small liberty zone near the base, and sometimes a few safe areas/recreation areas in various parts of Luzon."[28]

Corwin perceived "a 'Fortress Clark' mentality" in which restrictions, modified periodically "by increased/decreased threat levels continued through base closure in Nov. 91." Senior officers, seeing themselves as automatic targets like the ill-fated Colonel Rowe, had more to fear than junior officers and enlisted men. They "rarely ventured off-base and contact with Philippine military and civilian officials . . . was limited and normally on-base." Corwin's conclusion, underlined in his report: *It was far from a normal environment.*[29]

The killing, in retrospect, could have been worse. One day in 1990 a team of guerrillas was all set to ambush a truckload of GIs on their way to a firing range. They had wire stretched across the road, linked to a huge mine ready to go off, when a farmer literally stumbled upon it. He touched it too lightly to set it off, traced it to its source—and notified the Philippine Air Force, which removed it. Guerrillas also had plans for rocketing the airstrip—a task that might have seemed simple considering its proximity to shantytowns near the base. Another plan they considered was to attack officers living off-base with their families. They never quite nerved themselves for expanded operations, however, perhaps because the Americans had elaborate intelligence services and were ready with such basic precautions as retreating to the sanctuary of the base.

As the Americans ordered GI families back on base, banned GIs from going out on the town and set curfews, businessmen and bargirls alike protested vehemently. Bar owners staged "pro-American" rallies while bargirls pressed against the camp's wire fence, urging GIs to come on out and see them, and Philippine and American negotiators debated solutions. One device that seemed to work was "the quad patrol," in which a U.S. Air Force military policeman rode in a jeep with three Filipinos, including a local policeman, a member of the Philippine Constabulary, and a member of the Philippine Air Force. As attacks on Americans dwindled, leftist and rightist Filipinos battled each other. If a guerrilla killed a Filipino cop, rightist vigilantes, members of the Angelino Simbulon Brigade, named for a slain San Fernando police chief, would turn against the leftists. Salvagings were everyday occurrences.

In those days, Americans at Clark were suspicious of everyone, including local reporters competing for scoops on the slaughter. Two U.S. agents, a young man and woman, would linger in the Shanghai Restaurant, a favorite hangout of journalists, hoping to overhear tidbits—and track the hacks' comings and goings. "They acted like they're on a date," said one of them, Cesar "Bong" Lacson of the tabloid *People's Journal*. "Everyone knew who they were." (The reporters pronounced them "CIA," but most likely they were OSI.) "A Filipino-American inside the base was helping us. There were photos of nine of us in the Office of Special Investigation." When a U.S. public affairs officer denied entry to the officers' club for obstreperous hacks covering a ceremony, they passed a mock resolution declaring him "persona non grata."[30]

The ongoing campaign against the hostess bars, then, was not about law, order, decency or morals. It was a legacy of an old crusade, one that Filipino politicians and bureaucrats love to carry on while ignoring rampant prostitution in every city and town. There was and is, however, one crucial difference between the foreign and the Filipino clubs. The latter pay off the police, who are among their favorite customers and, sometimes, their owners and protectors. The foreigners offer drinks to visiting cops and ply them with gifts now and then but are less likely to bribe them so blatantly and regularly.

Either way, with or without American troops, no matter who is paying off whom, this city of angels is not about to live up to its name. Authorities may stage periodic clean-ups, but they need the bars for economic well-being. The number of registered, licensed "entertainers" went down by less than 10 percent, from 5,642 in 1990, the year before the Americans pulled out, to 5,100 in 1994. Three times as many women are believed to work as "entertainers," full or part-time. Prostitution also spawns a terrific traffic in drugs, with about 5,000 drug users treated annually in government clinics— again probably far fewer than actually are addicted.[31]

"There was no clear alternative livelihood for the displaced 'entertainers,'" said one study. "With the withdrawal of the bases, prostituted women had the greatest difficulty in gaining entry into the social and economic mainstream." Thus "Angeles still welcomes entertainment bars as a means of pumping investment into the city."[32] Foreign bar managers smolder under what they complain is the hypocrisy of the campaign against them. Since foreigners cannot legally own bars in the Philippines, they have to operate through Filipino partners or by investing in local corporations, which own the bars run by the foreigners. Such precarious arrangements, say foreign investors, leave them at the mercy of dubious partners in cahoots with equally dubious arms of the law.

All the foreigners, whether banded together in the Australian mafia or on their own, claim that they are scrupulously following the rules by refusing to hire girls below 18, the legal age of consent. They make all the girls display their licenses, hanging from their hips as they gyrate above the bar, certifying weekly medical checks and all-too-infrequent blood tests, legally required for women "entertaining" customers. Foreign barkeeps—convivial businessmen, some retired from the U.S. Air Force or Navy, often married or living with ex-bargirls—rationalize the profits they mine from the golden bodies on display in their raucous joints by portraying themselves as society's benefactors.

One of the most curious of the lot: a former Canadian journalist, Bryan Johnson, author of a book on the fall of Marcos.[33] No ordinary hack, Johnson for years was correspondent for the Toronto *Globe and Mail,* Canada's leading national newspaper, working out of Beijing and Manila. He had enjoyed extraordinary access at Malacañang—and also had a dream dual role as a sports columnist covering Toronto's baseball team, the Blue Jays. He threw it all over, however, to open a club in Ermita called Brown Sugar, then migrated to Angeles after Mayor Lim banned the bikini-dancing and bar fines that had given Brown Sugar its name. Soon he and a partner, an American physician with the bucks to invest in ministering to fleshly needs of a nonmedical kind, were rebuilding a one-time GI bar on Fields Avenue. Proudly, Johnson dubbed it "LaBamba" in tribute to his favorite music.

Among the liveliest hostess bars on Fields Avenue, LaBamba featured nachos, as befit its Latin name, along with some of the prettiest girls on the strip. That figured, since Johnson, a man of intelligence and taste, preferred to do most of the hiring himself from among the out-of-work, poverty-stricken teens flocking to his door—and to the doors of the other clubs as well.

The girls, about 20 of them, were prancing about on a stage in the middle of a rectangular central bar, to the deafening sound of one of Johnson's favorite tapes, when I happened by. The crackdown had been less than an overwhelming success. In concession to the morals squad, the dancers now wore cut-offs and T-shirts, not quite as fetching as skimpy bikinis no matter how hard they worked at it. Off-stage, however, they were as available as ever, as evidenced by their persistence in planting themselves beside customers and suggesting they buy them drinks at inflated prices—all in anticipation of the bar fine and the trek to a nearby hotel.

"The base closed in conjunction with a cataclysmic event, the explosion of Pinatubo," Johnson, ever the journalistic analyst, told me the next day over lunch up the street, at Margaritaville. "It wasn't just one stressful event. It was as if a marriage broke up, the parents lost their jobs and their kids got arrested all at once. This is why Ramos is having such a hard time closing the bars. Without the bars, there would be no hotels, nothing." Johnson portrayed himself as a community-minded sort who wouldn't mind a crackdown if only the president and mayor weren't so darn phony about it. "If I thought it was sincerely motivated by anything other than cynical motives, if this were a Buddhist monk elected as president, I would applaud it, but in the Philippines, these are the most cynical, opportunistic people."[34]

As for his own business, Johnson pleaded, "Don't identify me as a bar owner since, under Philippine law, I cannot have any part of any Philippine business." That said, he defended LaBamba as "the best bar on the street" and contrasted the ambience with that of the city's numerous "Philippine" bars. "If you went to a Philippine bar, the atmosphere would be sleazy. The customers would expect a strip show. Filipino bars are extremely bold"—a reference to the "boldshows" featuring total nudity in some Philippine hostess clubs.

The way Johnson described it, he was running a dating service. "Essentially, foreign bars are places to meet Philippine girls. Nothing happens. The only objection anyone could have was they foster prostitution, but from the bar owners' perspective it doesn't matter what the girls do"—once the customers pay the bar fines, the bars get their cut and the girls satisfy the customers, without which the bars would not get too many more bar fines.

On the theory that talking to visiting journalists would deflect gossip and criticism, Johnson had long since propounded his philosophy to visitors who approached him with a morbid fascination in his career change. "A lot of people say to me, 'Don't get involved in this, it's not reality,'" he once told a Canadian reporter. "To me, this is reality. Other journalists used to talk to me at dinner parties in accusatory tones. Morality? What morality? I can't be bothered talking to them about the morality of the bar. Why should I explain anything to them? They don't know a thing about how these girls live or where they come from. And now they never will know because they don't care."[35]

In his conversation with me, Johnson warmed to one of the foreign barkeeps' favorite themes as he reviewed some of the facts of life in a class-ridden, socially sick society where sleeping with foreigners is not merely acceptable but an enviable way out for many otherwise desperate people. "There's a ludicrous surplus of high school graduates who can't get any jobs. Most of these girls in the bar are non-high school grads. They can't even go abroad to work as maids. High school teachers and librarians in this country are paid so low that they go overseas as maids. Most of these girls don't speak English very well."[36]

Johnson completed the argument with a few demographics. "About 50 percent of the population of the country is under 20, 70 percent under 30. In Angeles, a city of 200,000, 60 to 70 percent is under 20. These girls usually come from broken families. The father is essentially a trike driver"—roaming the streets on a three-wheeled motorcycle taxi. Johnson harked back to a time when he was living with two girls, one of them a girlfriend, the other her sister, aged 14. "Her auntie said, 'You can work soon.' The way they look at it, maybe she'll get lucky and marry a foreigner." Not a few foreigners, he observed, do marry girls they meet in bars. "Intrinsically, there's no difference between these girls and anybody else. They just haven't had the opportunities."

Ah, the freedom to choose! That was what Dave Carlson professed to advocate as he presided over the Fire Station, once the Firehouse, one of Ermita's swingingest, noisiest, best-known clubs, now an echo of its former self on a back street off Fields Avenue. "They're selfish; they want everything for themselves," was Carlson's first remark when I asked why authorities were making life so tough for him and his girls. "I'm supporting 500 people here," Carlson estimated, throwing in the innumerable relatives and friends, members of extended families, dependent on each girl's earnings. "Every girl is over 18 and licensed."[37]

Plying me with rum-and-cokes, Carlson tugged at my sleeve, asking loudly, "Do you see any prostitutes in here?" Were it not for his large presence at my side, the answer would have been, sure do, but discretion dictated listening. "I was forced out of Manila by Mayor Lim," he went on. "He's a complete crook." The picture of Carlson as a Don Quixote tilting at the windmill of a corrupt bureaucracy faded, however, on considering how well he'd done off a business that relied, first and last, directly or indirectly, on sex for sale. He reputedly made a fortune from the old Firehouse before dumping it for a fire-sale price, about $500,000, more than it cost but less than its pre-crackdown value.

Against a backdrop of raucous music, flashing lights and young bodies, Carlson painted himself as a hero, a do-gooder—anything but a flesh merchant. "I took this place four months ago," he boasted. "I cleaned it up. I'll pull out if I'm hassled." That said, he grinned at a girl at the end of a line of six or seven twisting about in disco-style unison to an oldie-but-goodie rock number. "When I got her, she was nothing but trouble. She was on drugs. I made her clean up. Otherwise I wouldn't have her. Now she's great." Oh yeah, he added, "These girls can select their customers; they don't have to go out if they don't want to." He eyed me warily. "Are you going to hammer me," he asked as I smiled into another rum-and-coke. "You're going to hammer me, aren't you?"

For a Western journalist to "hammer" Carlson would, by any standard, be an act of utmost hypocrisy. Nobody had enjoyed his old Firehouse in Ermita more than the journalistic hordes who gravitated there in the midst of the People Power revolution. Carlson was still going with the times. A fire-equipment engineer from Chicago, he had arrived in Manila 20 years earlier to work as a consultant—and named his first bar "Firehouse" as a whimsical reminder of his profession. Now he had designs on resuming his original career. "They need fire equipment for the new airport. They don't have anything." Would Clark really make it as an international airport? He replied in mixed metaphor. "This place is a gold mine. It's going to explode." But can it work? "It'll work if they make it work. Right now they don't have any fire trucks."

The authorities were treading a fine line in which they aimed to have it both ways. Yes, they wanted the foreigners' clubs to keep humming as long as they drew money and visitors—and did not embarrass the country by their scandalous doings. Among the greatest concerns: child sex. There was no doubt that children, real children, not just teen-age girls painting their faces like big girls in the blinding lights of the clubs, were available on Fields Avenue. Kids begging for food and money were easy fodder there, as they were in the park in front of the historic Malate Church in Manila, in Olongapo and elsewhere.

Goaded by the same nationalism that drove out the American forces, influential Filipinos want the foreigners to go, on whatever pretext. They envision a strip of luxury hotels, financed possibly by Japanese or Taiwanese or Hong Kong or Singapore or Malaysian money, on the same blocks where the glittering lights of hostess bars beckon pleasure-hunting men from around the world.

The foreigners who are there wonder, however, about a certain paradox in official thinking. "We think it's ironic," said Max Ross, a retired U.S. Navy petty officer, president of the Angeles City Tourism and Businessperson's Association, including most of the foreign businessmen on the strip. "The president of the Philippines says, 'Invest in the Philippines,' so when a Philippine wife comes here with a foreign husband and invests in a hotel, then he's accused of operating through a dummy, so the president asks the mayor to shut the bars."[38]

Offering his views from his stool at the end of his 24-hour open-air counter down Fields Avenue, Ross saw the city as having "suffered a series of setbacks" in the raids. "We needed cleaning up, we had some boldshows," he conceded, but they were marginal. "Some of these guys have invested $100,000–$200,000 in sound systems, lights. They're not going to jeopardize their licenses. Most of these clubs operate as legitimate operations."

Expansively, Ross portrayed Angeles as a boon to the nation. "The economy has picked up mostly because of tourism in places like Angeles.

Last year, tourists pumped 1.9 billion pesos into Angeles, about $73 million. We have 120 western-style bars, restaurants and clubs. About 2,000 tourists come here every day. About 1,500 retired U.S. military live here. We have a Veterans of Foreign Wars Post, two American Legion Posts and RUMPL, Retired Uniformed Military Personnel, the Disabled American Veterans Association."

Ross wasn't the only foreigner eager to boast of the marvels of Angeles in the face of Filipino nationalist disapproval. John Cummings' Margaritaville menu featured a chart, "Relative Bang for Your Buck," comparing average daily expenses in Angeles with those in such legendary watering holes as Soi Cowboy and Patpong Road in Bangkok, Thailand, in Seoul's Itaewon and Pusan's Texas Town in South Korea and, more than 20 years after the fall of the American-backed regime in Saigon, in the new Saigon under loose communist rule.

No doubt about it, prices for such categories as "transport," "lady drink," "drinks," "barfine" and, last, "hotel" are typically a third or a quarter those of the competition. Japan and Hong Kong are so far off the chart as not to be worth mentioning—all the more reason for the big spenders from booming Asia's money pots to exploit the local talent, as do the tourists from Australia, Europe and the States, as did the GIs for generations before.[39]

FIVE

Free Port or Hacienda?

Oh, we won't go back to Subic any more
Oh we won't go back to Subic
Where they mix our wine with Tubic
Oh, we won't go back to Subic any more[1]

U.S. Navy bands played the song accompanied by the lusty voices of sailors and marines whenever they boarded ships for the return home after hard duty at the naval base conveniently tucked around the Bataan Peninsula north of Manila. Sailors and marines also sang it in the dance halls in Olongapo, a thriving base town ever since American forces had driven out the Spanish and then some diehard Philippine guerrillas and had run up the American flag on December 10, 1899. A standard around the time of World War I, the song faded into obscurity after the Americans evacuated the base in the face of the Japanese invaders on Christmas Day, 1941.

The song was never revived, which was unfortunate. It would have been an appropriate reminder of a storied past. When the last Americans were piped aboard and the helicopter carrier *Belleau Wood* hoisted anchor on November 24, 1992, the song of the day was "Auld Lang Syne," sung by thousands of townspeople. The local mayor, Richard Gordon, and the last American base commander, Rear Admiral Thomas Mercer, linked arms at the head of a parade from city hall to the main gate of the base. "Thanks Americans for Everything" and "Philippine-American Friendship Forever" read slogans on placards held aloft by cheering marchers, many of them fearful of uncertain futures without the 42,000 jobs provided by the base and the hundreds of millions of dollars pumped yearly into the economy by the free-spending Americans.

The Americans were going, leaving behind a bloodline that endures among thousands of Amerasian children, some of them still living in a special area of the sprawling base, about to become a "free port" in a "special zone," many thousands more scattered among a community that now totals half a million people. Most notable among those with American forebears are the area's two best-known, most aggressive and dynamic leaders, the Gordons, Richard and Katherine, co-bosses of a transformation they dream will turn them into the first couple of the entire nation.

Anxious to show off the new Subic as the crucible of the new Philippines, a commercial giant and worthy member of a booming Southeast Asian complex of fast-growing national economies, they soon embarked on a self-righteous campaign to rid the town of the sleaze and scum associated with the American era. Together, Dick as chairman of the Subic Bay Metropolitan Authority (SBMA) and Kate as mayor of Olongapo, they collaborated on getting their inspectors to close down the once-roaring bars outside the main gate, on Magsaysay Street. They also ordered their minions to harass the aging Americans, Australians and other foreigners still running bars along several miles of roads running around the bay in Barrio Barretto, a beachfront strip envisioned as a luxury resort area for rich and powerful investors lured into both the base and the town.

There was a personal paradox in the Gordons' drive to get rid of the Americans. The first Gordon to arrive in Olongapo was a marine named John Jacob Gordon, the offspring of Russian Jewish parents who settled into the restaurant business in Kingston, New York, in the late nineteenth century. Young John Jacob, named for the American tycoon John Jacob Astor, served in an American army infantry unit in the war against Spain in Cuba in 1898. Switching to the Marines, he was on one of the nine ships of Admiral Dewey's fleet when it defeated the Spanish in Manila Bay in 1898. Storming ashore, he and other marines established a base at Sangley Point, which juts into Manila Bay like a sentinel from Cavite. He was at Sangley when U.S. forces in late 1899 vanquished the defenders from Aguinaldo's army who had driven the Spanish from Subic Bay and then had had the temerity to fire on U.S. gunboats.

Gordon did not join the battle for Subic but was ordered there later as a member of an expanding occupation force. Unlike the vast majority of American serviceman, the young marine chose not to go home again. Instead, he accepted his discharge where he was when President Theodore Roosevelt declared Subic an American naval reservation in 1904. Seeing a fortune to be made right around him, he bought some farmland and opened a saloon beyond the limits of the American reservation. His rivals were a Filipino dance hall operator with a three-piece combo and a Chinese restaurateur offering ham, eggs and "flied [*sic*] fish."

All of them had a keen sense of the future. Thirsty sailors and marines on passes marched first to Gordon's saloon, where he was free to offer alcohol and other amenities uninhibited by naval regulations. Named Gordon's Farm, it was known to Americans as "Gordon's Chicken Farm"—an allusion to the ladies on the premises. To its credit, the establishment also won a reputation that placed it in a class above its rivals when cholera swept Subic Bay in 1907. "The clean water and healthy atmosphere at Gordon's place made it popular and was credited with saving many lives," according to one account.[2]

John Jacob Gordon married a Filipina named Paula Martin, of mixed or *mestizo* Spanish ancestry, and had to work hard to support their growing family. He and Paula, whom he had met while at Sangley, had five children before her tragic death in 1916 as she delivered still-born twins. The same year, he married another Spanish *mestizo*, Veronica Tagle. The daughter of a revolutionary colonel who had fought with Aguinaldo in Cavite against the Spanish, Veronica bore him one son, James Leonard Gordon. John Jacob's four surviving sons by his first marriage all migrated to America; three of them set up restaurants and the fourth played the saxophone in Dallas. James was the only one of his offspring to stay where he was.

John Jacob went into hiding during World War II, then was captured and interned by the Japanese. Son James fought on as a guerrilla. Gordon's Farm was burned down in the war, but James more than compensated for his father's loss. With the approval of his father, who lived on for nine years after the war, James invested in a movie theater, radio station, hotel and cabaret and opened a popular restaurant, Jimmy's Little Kitchen, enriching himself, like his father, from the foreign servicemen. He also married well—his bride was Amelia Juico, from a Chinese and Spanish *mestizo* family with real estate and other holdings. He and Amelia had five children: Richard, the eldest, three daughters and a younger brother, James "Bong" Gordon Jr.

The Gordon name remains a constant in the evolution of Olongapo, at every stage reflecting and refracting the history of a community that sees itself near the end of the twentieth century as epitomizing the Philippines' economic revolution. The family—not merely Dick Gordon but also his forebears, along with a complex web of in-laws and other relatives—has strived, ever since the original John Jacob Gordon set up his saloon on the fringes of the American military holdings, to work with the Americans even while asserting independence from them.

Ironically, Dick Gordon faced much the same challenge in dealing with his mother. Wealthy and getting richer, owner of prime beachfront and downtown real estate, Amelia Juico Gordon did not like her son's choice of the aggressive young woman whom he had known from school days. The future mother-in-law looked down on Katherine Howell for what she was, the illegitimate daughter of an American sailor and a woman who had come to manage and then own a nightclub featuring bikini-clad dancers and hostesses for hire. Richard Gordon saw Kate for what she also was—an ambitious partner who shared his dreams of glory. His will prevailed over that of his mother, but the two women remained hostile toward each other, often on nonspeaking terms, for years.

If the future Katherine Gordon had a less illustrious past than her husband, her origins say as much about the Philippine-American experience—and about American and Filipino attitudes toward each other. There are, however, differences between her background and that of the typical Amerasian child left behind by a less-than-caring GI. For one thing, Kate's father, Clement Howell, although he shrank from marriage, did not completely hide. Kate's mother knew where to reach him in the States. For another, her mother was from a better background than that of most of the girls picked up by wandering sailors in the local nightclubs. She was an Esteban—a well-known local family—and made certain that Kate not only finished high school but went to a Catholic college.

Still, years later, Kate longed to link up with her father, who was teaching school in the Midwest, by then married and the father of another family. Finally, in 1993, he agreed to fly to San Diego, where James Gordon Jr.'s wife had lived and worked for five years, for a week-long reunion with his long-lost daughter.

For all their moral posturing, the Gordons are true products of the era of American colonialism—progeny of American servicemen and inheritors of wealth earned in part from catering to their pleasures. The Gordons' arrival as nouveau riche members of the nation's elite, virtually all boasting Chinese and Spanish ancestors, places them in an unusual category. Although the Gordons have Chinese and Spanish forebears, they are the first descendants of full-blooded Americans, members of the armed forces of the occupying colonial power, to aspire to become top leaders and policymakers of the Philippines' ruling class.

Could the Gordon name some day rank along with those of the other first families—Cojuangco and Aquino, among others, along with Osmeña, Zobel, Elizalde, Soriano, Lopez et al.—all of mixed blood, some Chinese, some Spanish, none originally American? (Family members were known to marry the occasional American, but only after their dynasties were well established.) Might the Gordon family, with tentacles reaching into law, politics and business in Olongapo and Manila, make it among the mythical, mystical "first 40 families," displacing well-entrenched but less ambitious rivals?

Dick Gordon knows he faces many enemies. For him, salvaging is no paranoid fantasy. His father, James, was elected in November 1963 as the first mayor of Olongapo, which had been entirely governed by the Americans as part of the U.S. Naval Reservation area until August 1959. He remained in office after Olongapo's designation as a chartered city in June 1966. Deeply enmeshed in cutthroat politics and payoffs, James might have gone on to greater things but for an assassin's bullet that killed him on the morning of February 20, 1967, as he stopped to talk to a woman in the treasury department of City Hall while he was walking to his office upstairs.

Intuitively, James Gordon looked to the day when Olongapo, like the country, would be truly free. He saw the city as launched on a proud new era—one, that is, in which it no longer had to suffer what its politicians, local as well as national, perceived as the humiliating pressure of the bases. The town, an obscure fishing village when the Spanish built a naval station there in 1884, in the twilight of their rule, owed its growth and prosperity to the arrival of the Americans. These same Americans, however, could also be a liability—if not a menace—if the Gordons, now established, wealthy pillars of the community, were to realize their full potential, for themselves and their country.

Anti-American pressure rose quickly when the Americans, bolstered by a bases agreement signed in 1947 with the fledgling government of a newly independent Philippines, showed no signs of relinquishing their rule over Olongapo, bursting with 60,000 people, most of whom owed their survival to jobs on the base. A journalist, Jose C. Balein, crusaded against a system in which the U.S. "reservation administration" imposed taxes in addition to the taxes people paid their own country. President Ramon Magsaysay, who was from neighboring Zambales Province, ordered inquiries into what a local observer called the "deplorable and despicable conditions affecting the Filipino civilian residents"—and urged the talks that led to turnover of the town two and a half years after his death in a plane crash in March 1957.[3]

James Gordon had no notion of getting rid of the base in his glory days as mayor before his assassination. Nor did his sons imagine such a denouement. During this period, the family solidified its power in the style that characterizes Philippine rule everywhere—by expanding its holdings while spreading its political grip through a proliferation of relatives in high places. Dick Gordon, in law school at Ateneo at the time of his father's assassination, known around campus for his glib talk and cheerleading, was deemed too young to replace his father. The solution, however, was simple. After a brief interregnum, the widow Amelia ran for mayor in the next election in November 1967 and won handily.

In 1971, the year before Marcos declared martial law, James and Amelia's son Richard, at 26, debuted in national politics as the youngest delegate at a constitutional convention that Marcos intended to use as a pretext for prolonging and extending his power by any means. In 1979, when Marcos was still ruling by martial law, Richard, now 34, was ready to run for mayor and to lay the cornerstone of his own dynasty in a city that, as he made increasingly clear, would be his personal domain.

Elected as Olongapo's youngest mayor in 1980, Gordon was now an accomplished political figure. His skill as a talkative opportunist was matched only by that of Marcos, with whom Gordon had comfortably allied himself in the period when Benigno Aquino and hundreds of others were arrested and held for years under martial law. Gordon's campaign priority was law and order and cleaning up the city—for all of which Marcos professed to be fighting nationally.

The idealism behind the change in the town's management from American to Filipino governance was marred, however, by an underlying reality: the real beneficiaries would be the Gordons and a few other leading families. How much most people really cared—or trusted in the judgement of the activists—was far from clear. Everybody knew that Olongapo was a single-industry community, that 40,000 people streamed on and off the base every day and that many more counted on the base for their livelihoods and the survival of many, many more dependents. The statistics on the number of prostitutes alone were overwhelming. By 1985, more than ten years after the end of the Vietnam War and the flurry of military activity that accompanied it, there were about 4,500 of them working out of about 600 bars.[4]

For Richard Gordon, the ultimate slogan was "Aim High Olongapo"—words he compelled jeepney owners to paint on the sides of their vehicles whether they wanted to or not. So little did he care about the abuses of martial law that he readily espoused Marcos' cause when Cory Aquino challenged Marcos for power in 1985, just two years after the death of the martyred Ninoy.

Gordon, who may not have imagined that Aquino could ever drive Marcos from power, did not hesitate in those days to tell anyone who asked that he was supporting Marcos, who knew how to repay a friend in such a key city. For Gordon, the status quo meant security for the financial and political interests of a family that was by now, through inheritance and marriage, the most important in the city though not necessarily in the province or in the region.

Gordon attempted to have it both ways during the years when pressure was mounting to send the Americans home. He assiduously courted the American commanders, who were much impressed by his efforts at making the streets safer for American sailors. So successful was his campaign against petty thievery and drug-dealing that the admiral in command of the base, citing "close cooperation and coordination between base authorities and city administration," deemed the atmosphere safe enough at one stage to lift the curfew.[5] Just as Gordon had seen a future for himself with Marcos, he saw the future with the Americans—or perceived that the future lay in not appearing overtly anti-American while the vast majority of the people of the city counted on the Americans for a living.

The mayor displayed all his powers as a political opportunist by emerging at the top in what might have been a difficult transition—first from Marcos to Ramos via Aquino, then from American to Philippine control of the bases. His success was all the more remarkable considering that he had opposed both changes, initially regarding them as undermining his power. Dumped as mayor in the reform movement in which Cory appointed officers-in-charge of administration of city halls in place of the old, corrupt Marcos elements, Gordon reviled the leader responsible for temporarily derailing him.

"You Americans like Cory because she speaks nice English, she was educated in the States, and this is a Cinderella story," he remarked with considerable truth less than a year after Aquino's ascent to power. He grew more emotional as he talked on. "I've been taking pills lately. I have nightmares. I see a situation where troops wearing uniforms, not Philippine Army troops, are running around with firearms. I've got two letters telling me that I'm on the hit list of the NPA [New People's Army]." Out of office, he still hinted at his ambitions. "If I had it my way I don't know who should be president. Right now I have a few ideas. But one of these days, I'm going to take a crack at it myself."[6]

Gordon bounced right back, getting himself elected in 1988 when Aquino approved a new round of mayoralty elections. Safely re-ensconced in City Hall, he resumed his close relationship with the American base commanders, appearing to cooperate with them on local security and drug control while nightclub owners showered him with the usual gifts, in accordance with long-established custom.

Gordon had no problem rationalizing conduct that he later pretended to loathe. "Any place there's a military base, there's going to be crime, there's going to be prostitution," he told an interviewer, echoing the arguments of the most ardent defenders of the American bases. "But there's a lot of people who are making a lot of money, who are able to send their kids to school. Is that a rationalization? Perhaps. But is that reality? Yes. Some of these girls send their brothers, send their children to school."[7]

Sometimes, to show off his independence, the mayor staged calculated acts of defiance. Once, when U.S. Navy cops at the gate of the base refused to let his security guards carry their weapons onto the base, he angrily turned back, screaming in protest at this arrogant American affront to national sovereignty, and to his dignity, rights and honor as a Philippine government official. In the end, however, the mayor was not all that hard-nosed. "Nobody can give me something better than this base," he said. "Don't tell me about alternatives. . . . The base has its negatives; it has its positives. All that we have to do is minimize its disadvantages and maximize its advantages."[8]

After the eruption of Pinatubo, Gordon was back jousting with the American admiral in another gratuitous effort at showing off his power vis-à-vis the Americans. This time his ego was deflated by the admiral's refusal to authorize the use of a back road through Subic to the Bataan Peninsula for the evacuation of as many as 300,000 people from Olongapo. "Gordon was angered mainly on principle," wrote Kelvin Rodolfo, who was with the mayor in Olongapo as Pinatubo was erupting. Rodolfo paraphrased the questions Gordon was raising in rhetorical rage: "How dare an American deny Filipinos a route to safety through their own land? Does Philippine sovereignty not ultimately transcend the conditions of lease when Filipino lives are threatened? Does a homeowner in dire emergency not have the ultimate right of access to a room he has rented out?"[9]

At his blustering best, Gordon warned the admiral "he would make the passage if he decided to do so, by force of arms if necessary."[10] Luckily, however, Gordon's display was nothing more than that—an oration for the benefit of whoever was listening, in this case Rodolfo and a few others. For one thing, there was not going to be any evacuation. While the roads were deep in tephra, the fury of the eruption was abating.

In any case, the admiral had an excuse that no one had at Clark: the Philippine marines "were responsible for issuing passes into the base," but the Filipino marine general was conveniently "nowhere to be found."[11] For the American admiral, or the Filipino general, to have opened the base would have been to invite the same kind of looting then beginning at Clark. If Gordon could later brag about keeping out looters, he had the U.S. Navy to thank for shutting the door at the outset.

Gordon's rage matched only his oratorical opportunism. For all his wrath, he was never so concerned about Philippine sovereignty as to oppose the bases agreement. He fully supported Aquino's ill-fated call for renewal of the treaty while viewing her as incompetent, not least because she acted so tardily and ineptly in the bases debate. Just to prove his contempt for the woman who had replaced Marcos, his ally, he endorsed her hated first cousin, "Danding" Cojuangco, in the 1992 presidential election.

Aquino, whose hostility to Danding goes back to an ancient dispute over wealth and power in their native Tarlac Province, could not succeed herself under the "Aquino constitution" adopted in 1987 while she was president, but Gordon was not enthusiastic about her favorite, Defense Secretary Ramos. Had not Ramos, once a Marcos protector as chief of the Philippine Constabulary, betrayed his boss by taking on leadership of the People Power revolution that thrust Aquino into power and temporarily placed Danding, one of the country's richest men, under a cloud?

Danding Cojuangco might have won had not Imelda Marcos waged her own quixotic campaign and picked up 10.32 percent of the votes. As it was, Danding finished third with 18.17 percent, behind Ramos, who had 23.58 percent, and Miriam Defensor Santiago, who had 19.72 percent. (Salonga finished next to last with 10.16 percent, an indication of the grassroots unpopularity of his antibases crusade.) Gordon would seem to have made a terrible miscalculation by betting on the wrong candidate. With the imminent departure of the Americans whom he had so assiduously befriended, however, Gordon saw a chance to expand his power on a nationally visible scale, and he set about doing so by parlaying rejection of the bases treaty into his biggest triumph.

Gordon sought the affection of Ramos as shamelessly as he had that of Marcos, courting the new president as passionately as he had ever pursued the disgraced, deposed and now deceased dictator. At the outset Gordon had to sell himself as the only one qualified to take charge of Subic. The job had the potential for absolute power over a facility with an infrastructure that included, among other things, a full-scale international airport, berthing facilities for large vessels, repair shops and factory sites, hotels, clubs and restaurants—altogether unmatched in their totality and proximity by any other Asian port, worth $8 billion and still more if built from scratch.

Control over all that treasure, Gordon figured, would provide the means to vault into the presidency in the 1998 election—assuming that Ramos did not ram through an amendment enabling him to succeed himself. For Gordon, the challenge was to convince Ramos to name him chairman of the Subic Bay Metropolitan Authority, responsible for converting the military facility into a free port after the Senate said "no." There was a trade-off, however. The easy part was to promise full support for Ramos, whom Gordon flattered endlessly in speech after speech. Gordon had a long history of currying favor. He had no trouble switching allegiance and was duly rewarded for his new loyalty when Ramos named him SBMA chairman, for political as well as economic reasons, before the Americans pulled out in 1992.

Ramos, however, had one stipulation—that Gordon fill only one job at a time rather than cling to two or more posts at once, as powerful Filipinos often do. In other words, Gordon had to give up City Hall if he wanted to retain SBMA.[12] The solution to that dilemma exposed the extent to which "the chairman," as he now liked to be called, had gone to convert Olongapo, on-base and off, into his reservation—the precise area that had once been the American naval reservation before the Americans reverted most of the town to Filipino authority in 1959. He would turn City Hall over to Kate, then serving in the lower house of the Congress, representing their interests in Manila. Sure enough, after an interregnum in which a cousin filled in as mayor, Kate was duly elected in May 1995.

Now, throughout the city, on- or off-base, sprouted the signs of the Gordons' omnipotence. Kate, right after her election, had her name painted on police patrol cars and the vans of *barangay* captains, sometimes with a heart and the slogan, "Kate Cares for You." Dick was proud enough of his wisdom to post quotations from his speeches on billboards around the base. "What this country needs is not just a change of men but a change in men," was one of his most self-quoted quotations, intended to show the shift in attitudes that he personally was bringing about. "From a bastion of security to a bastion of economic prosperity," said another.

There was very little Dick and Kate would not do for publicity. The walls of the twin centers of their power, City Hall, on Rizal Avenue, the main street through town, and SBMA headquarters, whence U.S. admirals had once gazed out on Subic Bay, were lined with adulatory clippings from magazines and newspapers. Outside the main gate, a billboard hailed the selection of Dick along with Lea Salonga, star of the Broadway show *Miss Saigon,* as "Two Filipinos Out of 20 Great Asians for the Future Honored by *Asiaweek* Magazine, June 22, 1995 issue."[13]

For a visitor, the publicity blitz might begin with a video, *Rising Above the Storm,* a paean to Subic's emergence as a free port after the ash spewed by Pinatubo—not as heavy as the downfall on Clark but enough to cover the grounds and collapse the roofs of numerous buildings—had been cleared.[14]

The video was a masterpiece of one of Subic's more intriguing entrepreneurs, a former American CIA officer named Michael Sellers. It was not clear, from conversations with Sellers and Gordon, just who was co-opting whom. Sellers brought to Subic a career resumé even more diverse than that implied by his CIA past. Tall, heavyset, he had been a lineman on the University of Delaware's football team in college and had tried out with the Washington, D.C. Redskins, a background that left a permanent imprint on him in the form of an irreparably split upper lip. Abandoning football, he received a master's degree from New York University's film school—all before joining the CIA for 12 years, including tours in Manila and Moscow. Married for a time to a Filipina, he had formed a production company called the Pacific Hollywood Corporation and gravitated to Subic "in search of a good movie location" for tales of derring-do in jungle settings.

Gordon, however, exacted a high price from Sellers for the right to operate so freely and profitably. While pursuing a dual career as producer and restaurateur, Sellers and his British director, Bob Couttie, had to double as Gordon's public relations consultants, speechwriters and all-around flacks. They wrote many of Gordon's perorations, often staying up through the night on behalf of a boss who liked to yak away into the early hours in his office or in one of the fancy restaurants in nearby former American officers' clubs.

As if that were not enough, Sellers and Couttie produced a weekly television show, *Subic Patrol,* a 30-minute potpourri of flattering publicity, and edited a weekly page of press agentry entitled "Spirit of Subic," run as advertising in the *Philippine Daily Inquirer.* Both efforts were textbook examples of sycophantic journalism that featured remarks about or by Gordon and the SBMA.

Gordon described Sellers as "a good friend." In turn, Sellers did not appear embarrassed by the compromises he had to make. Instead, he spoke enthusiastically of the free port and his role in its success. "We're growing frighteningly fast," he said. "It's hard to keep up. You have these major companies moving in. It's a field day for entrepreneurs. We went from eight to 140 employees in a year and a half. I just got sucked into some of the other things. They kept landing in our laps."[15]

The video Sellers produced for the SBMA reflects his own enthusiasm as well as that of the chairman. "A city that has risen from its own ashes, a modern day Phoenix," notes the voiceover. Although 30 U.S. Navy ships rescued 17,000 American sailors and their dependents after Pinatubo erupted, the video observes, "For the citizens of Olongapo there is no escape—60 people died." Into the breach, heroically, stepped the figure of Richard Gordon, who credits himself with having called his aides and ordered them to "get aboard and put the fight back into Olongapo."[16]

For Gordon, the challenge was to persuade the Americans, embittered by the final gasping death of their reign of sovereignty, that you can't take it with you. "A steady outflow of personnel and equipment was begun," drones the video. "There was a lot of pettiness on both sides, the bowling lanes were taken out," says Gordon, on screen. "I said, 'Stop this foolishness.'"[17] As far as Gordon was concerned, whatever the Americans built on Subic Bay belonged to the Philippines. He was even upset when U.S. Navy vessels tugged off three drydocks, worth a few hundred million dollars, that he dearly coveted, along with all the other assets, most of which could not be moved.

If Gordon wanted it all for his political/economic machine, however, there was a significant difference between his approach and the misconduct of the Philippine Air Force at Clark. After protesting the closure of the base by the Americans to a stream of would-be evacuees, he saw the advantage of making certain no one looted the place. There was far more to be earned by building on the riches before him, he realized, than by destroying them. "I was afraid there might be looting," says Gordon on camera. "I was really scared"—a sense he failed to convey while loudly protesting the refusal of the Americans to open the base post-Pinatubo.

The chairman affects an air of open innocence in the video as he describes what he wants viewers to believe were his emotions as he contemplated the greatest single windfall ever to befall a political leader in the Philippines, possibly anywhere on earth. The windfall was even more incredible considering that the Filipinos had fired nary a shot for it—and could still hoot the Americans off their soil as if they had defeated them in armed conflict. Gordon neglected to say that Subic was much easier to defend from looters than Clark; much of it fronts on water, not land, and the portions that might have been worth looting were more concentrated, easier to guard and accessible only by three or four gates. More important, neither Clark nor Angeles City had a political family of the Gordons' stature, background and vision to ensure protection.

For Gordon, the rationale for anything he did was the success of the Subic Bay Freeport, which like Clark is still called "the base" in local vernacular. "What had worked for the United States Navy would not be sufficient for the demands of the growing city," says the video. "Improvements would have to be made"—ranging from the vast "duty-free" shopping centers to reconstructed factories on the sites of old U.S. Navy repair shops to new facilities at Cubi Point, the modern airport built into the bay by the Americans.

Cubi was the point of greatest pride. An acronym for Construction Unit Battalion One, the Seabee unit that built it in the 1950s, Cubi ranks as an engineering wonder. (The Seabees said the acronym also meant, "Can You Build It?") Seabees excavated the dirt for the base and extended it into the bay in the shape of an aircraft carrier with a 10,000-foot strip for the largest military planes. Gordon scored a personal triumph when Federal Express picked Cubi as its regional hub and Japan, after balking at giving FedEx "beyond" rights for loading and unloading in Japan on the way, relented under pressure from Washington and Manila in mid-1995.

It was a measure of Gordon's control over the community that he dared, while the Americans were pulling out, to institute a program for "volunteer" labor on the base, to guard it from intrusion while preserving it for development, and actually got away with it. "The volunteers kept the place intact," says the chairman on the video. According to the anonymous narrator, "While the volunteers held the fort, Gordon told investors of the attractions." The great industrial sites, the five-star Subic International Hotel and the Subic Resort and Casino, all in former American facilities, led the list. "Volunteers cut grass," the voice carries on, portraying the draft of "volunteers" as "part of the social experiment."

There was, however, no real "social experiment." The reality was that Gordon, for all the wealth already accumulated by him and his wife, each related by blood and marriage to still more wealth, did not want to pay from his own pocket the paltry salaries he might offer the large, unemployed labor force suddenly made available by the Americans' departure. His grip on the levers of local government and his political resources enabled him to compel thousands to volunteer on the promise that some day, if they did well and the base prospered in its reincarnation as a free port and industrial zone, they would all be offered paying jobs.

Gordon's volunteer program was a powerful lure. In the first months, college graduates, some of them with degrees from prestigious universities, joined laid-off clerks and typists, grass-cutters and weed-pullers, in working for nothing. The college graduates and office workers—those with the connections and loyalty—were assured of paying jobs within a year or so.

Political loyalty, not professional qualification, was the litmus test. No one associated with the political opposition had a chance. The Gordons' intelligence system was pervasive. There were stories of dismissals of those who had got on the payroll—and then were reported to be of dubious loyalty. Volunteers identified with foes were either frustrated in getting regular jobs or dropped altogether from whatever they were doing. Better not to keep even a volunteer who did not seem sufficiently respectful of the man whose aides called him "the boss," if not "Mr. Chairman."

Originally presented as a stopgap, emergency measure, the volunteer program survived long after the American departure, though on a reduced basis. Most of the volunteers performed menial chores—rows of pathetic figures labored listlessly in the sun, like prisoners, weeding or picking up trash, bereft of hope or even enough food to sustain themselves. Gordon himself was sensitive to charges that he might be promoting something very close to slave labor or indentured servitude. "Is volunteerism dead in America?" he countered, defensively, when I asked about the criticism. "They don't have to work if they don't want to." Anyway, most of the volunteers were "older people who like something to do."[18]

Volunteers gave a different story. "You have to work maybe a few months before you can apply for a job," said one. "Then you don't know if you get anything." The program was especially cruel to the elderly. They didn't have a prayer of getting jobs since by policy the SBMA hired no one over 35 except under special circumstances, meaning personal connections with "the boss." Still, they toiled on in hopes that their servitude would ensure work for younger members of the family—and guarantee that relatives on the payroll might cling to the jobs they already had.[19]

One volunteer, putting her index finger to her lips, asked me to refrain from too much talk as we sat in a bus transporting SBMA workers, volunteers as well as those on salaries. "People can hear," she said. "Then it's no good. They throw us out if we say something bad." She whispered that volunteers got no rice or bus fare, even for SBMA buses, which charged two pesos (about eight cents) for a ride, but the work was not always as onerous as it might seem. "You pick up some garbage or cut the grass a little and sit around. Then you go home."

The video nears its close on a high note, with President Clinton very nearly giving a personal endorsement for Gordon, saying, "We want Subic Bay to be a vast economic resource" and "we are very pleased and supportive of the agreement signed by Fedex and SBMA." The chairman, however, has the last word: "I see a lot of peace, a lot of prosperity and a lot of pride." Gordon showed his pride in a tireless round of speech-making and hand-shaking as befits a politician on the rise—though not necessarily a businessman with a serious understanding of what it takes to turn the base into a long-term success.

One day, in August 1995, he was in a former repair facility at a party marking the first anniversary of the local assembly of armored cars by the British-invested Asian Armored Vehicle Technology Corporation. "We have a work ethic in Subic," said the chairman. "It is an ethic based on discipline." He recounted how he drove in one of the first armored cars "to give inspiration, to show that we are indeed working for a new Philippines against pessimistic prognostications of people around the world." The Philippines, he said, has "the skill, the talent to put together our armed forces"—or at least to assemble the armored car, called a Simba, an African word for lion, now a status symbol for national police and soldiers on internal peacekeeping duties.[20]

Gordon warmed to his theme as he talked on, though skeptics wondered how connected were all his comments by logic or syntax. "All of us ought to behave in the highest professional performance that you can undertake," he said. "Look at the quality of the work that you turn out. Make sure, when it says, 'Made in the Philippines,' that you can compete with the best of the rest in Asia. We give them a special rate here so we can give jobs and give them a special push. Today you're on your way. All of us hope for a tremendous leap in faith."

Then there were the statistics. "Two years and seven months ago, it was a dream. Today you have 170 companies. We have secured $1 billion and $29 million investment here today. In July we expect to export $38 million."

Always, there were comparisons with Hong Kong—a special figment of the dream as the colony approached the end of British rule in mid-1997. Gordon saw an influx of Hong Kong and Taiwan investment—a flight of capital that would be enough to turn Subic into another Hong Kong with high-rise apartments, towering banks and regional corporate headquarters, factories upon factories, ships loading and unloading at piers dominated by huge gantry cranes, rail networks and highways. "We will be beyond Hong Kong," he told the Filipino workers and foreign engineers in the shadows of the armored cars. "The best is yet to come."

That evening, the chairman found himself before a different type of audience—a group of British executives gathered for dinner in Seafront, the prime dining facility. Suddenly, he recalled a conversation with Chris Patten, then Hong Kong's governor. "I do not believe we should raid Hong Kong," he was saying, reversing the implications of his earlier remarks. "We would like to advise modest investment in Subic. The British believe in spreading investments. We speak very good English. We have a very good harbor, deeper than Hong Kong. We are close to losing space. We are seriously considering reclamation. Look across Subic Bay. It looks like Hong Kong island before the British took over in 1842."[21]

It was far from clear from such flights of oratory, however, how much substance the chairman brought to his work. Would-be investors complained that members of his staff were amateurs, that they often did not get responses. Nor was it certain how much of the money invested in Subic was pledged—or in the bank. Some of the great names on the list of investors were clearly pro forma, represented by small offices as gestures, not real commitments.

Similarly, no one knew what to make of the exhibits of the Subic of tomorrow, of the year 2000 or the year 2020. A walk-around gave as much an impression of decline as of progress. Paint was peeling, roads were sprouting grass and gardens were running to seed, perhaps for lack of volunteers to do the mundane chores that Gordon did not consider worth paying for. There was a sense of the fragility of the Subic adventure, of the vacuity of some of Gordon's claims.

It is customary in the Philippine ruling structure for contractors and other interests to pay, under the table, at least 10 percent of profits to the person who doles out the contracts, the space, the permission and the means to make money. Foreigners might frown, rail and criticize, but the system remains the system. The Philippines, moreover, is no different from its ASEAN neighbors, Indonesia, Malaysia, Thailand, Brunei (fiefdom of the world's richest man), not to mention communist Vietnam, latecomer to the group, admitted in 1995, 20 years after victory over a far more corrupt, U.S.-supported Saigon regime. (The tight little island city-state of Singapore, under iron-fisted Senior Minister Lee Kuan Yew, may be an exception among ASEAN nations.)

Gordon pursued a dual track. He was the prototypical political boss in arrangements with Filipinos but a more or less straight-talking "honest businessman" to the Americans and the Europeans and possibly the

Japanese and overseas Chinese, whom the free port needed to achieve the aims suggested in the chairman's pronouncements. The lines were blurred—what Gordon exacted from Chinese investors, unburdened by scruples about greasing the way in business deals, was far from clear. Gordon also had the power to reward bureaucrats, politicos, columnists and the like with easy investment terms, along with discount housing in former American officers' quarters.

What was clear was that both Gordons, Mr. and Mrs., had most of the townspeople fairly well intimidated. "People here in Olongapo are afraid of the Gordons," said a local politician who dared oppose Kate in the 1995 mayoralty campaign. "They're being harassed by these people."[22] Another local official privately described Gordon as "the man who never forgets." Those who crossed him, who seriously disagreed with him, said the official, "are dismissed or never get promoted" or, if they cannot be fired outright, "are transferred."

The chairman's face darkens when he feels challenged. At public functions, his expression may change suddenly as he scans the room and spots someone who has displeased him, whom he perceives as less than loyal. Around town, shopkeepers, restaurateurs and businesspeople smile when asked what they think of the first couple. "Nobody can talk," said one. "They're the boss."

The message came through loudest in their efforts to clean up the town, to rid it of its international image as a garbage heap of evil and present it as a desirable center in which to conduct international business. "I'm being very, very strict," said Kate, talking in her office in City Hall. "Things have really changed. No longer are we going to cater to the animal basic instincts of man and woman." She betrayed a sense of revulsion over the indignities of the American era. "When the Americans are here, you end up being a domestic helper. Times have changed. We have decided we are going to make a difference. We have gotten our act together."[23]

Kate saw the city, that is, the rest of Olongapo outside the free port, as catching up with the port area in terms of appearance and facilities and drawing in business just like the free port. "We have to be able to approximate the peace and order, the beauty in the SBMA," she said. "I am doing a little beautification. I am going to fix up the parks, the landmarks. I am dialoguing with all the sectors. We envision the downtown as a commercial area and the condos in the mountains." Most of all, "I will never again give licenses to the saunas, nightclubs, bars, that sort of business."

She was enforcing those rules with a vengeance. From the foreign-run bars of Barrio Barretto all the way to the downtown nightclub district, there were no more bar fines, no more rows of girls dancing in bikinis. So serious was Kate in her mission that some of her critics wondered if she was reacting against her mother, who had profited immensely from her own hostess nightclub/restaurant.

Another theory was that the mayor was only play-acting—and wouldn't object if the clubs adjusted their rules and otherwise cooperated. Bar owners soon learned to circumvent the law by charging customers for six drinks, equal in price to the bar fine, for the privilege of getting a girl off the premises, and the girls charged as much as ever for an hour or a night.

Whatever Kate's vision for her city, there was a flaw in the program: 60 percent of the work force of Olongapo, population 250,000, remained unemployed. Kate believed she had the answers. "They lack skills," she said. "We're setting up a school of arts and trades in an old hospital. We are setting up schools of nursing. I am talking to people. We need engineers and technicians. When the bases pulled out, these people had families to feed. A lot of technicians and skilled people left for abroad."[24] Now, she suggested, it's time they came back—and worked for the new companies pouring in. She was not deterred by the reality that few new companies were investing in town or that rows of shops and clubs remained shuttered four years after the Americans had left.

Kate demonstrated her toughness publicly in what she called "dialogues," sessions in which she gave orders and answered a few questions about how to carry them out. At one, in the old base movie theater, whose rows of fading, tattered brown seats were infested with tiny bugs that bit and stung through thin layers of clothing, she kept an audience of several hundred representatives of all the town's nightclubs, bars and restaurants waiting more than an hour, then threatened those who were too busy to show up for a performance that was definitely déjà vu to all of them.

"I want to know the names of all the business establishments that did not come today," said Kate, sounding like a tough school teacher talking to a group of recalcitrant troublemakers. "I want them on my desk by tomorrow morning." The purpose of the meeting was to let everyone know how determined she was about a new rule against the sale of bottled liquor outside supermarkets. The mayor linked a crackdown on liquor to the future of the community.[25]

"This is not a whim," Kate was saying. "It is necessary to ban hard liquor in order to save lives in this city. I have been consulting with the whole of Olongapo. I have consulted with store owners. I am now consulting with you." Her voice assumed a menacing tone. "You can take my word for it, I am no longer allowing the opening of new business establishments like nightclubs, bars, saunas, massage parlors and the like. We don't need that any more. That is in our past. That's why I have made a point always to dialogue with the citizens of Olongapo." For those who didn't quite get it, she added for good measure, "I also want you to know I am a woman of conviction—and you can take my word for that again."

Her lecture began to sound like a campaign speech. "Last Saturday President Ramos visited the city of Olongapo and praised the spirit of all the Filipinos of Olongapo [scattered applause]. I am very proud. I am really very proud. We would not have been able to fulfil our duties without the cooperation, the dedication of the Filipinos of Olongapo City." Then she was boasting, quoting a columnist who had written that Ramos "pointed out Olongapo as a model" and "Mayor Kate Gordon and husband Dick should take a bow." After more self-praise, she announced, "I am ready to listen to you." No one, however, seriously questioned anything.

Such firmness and toughness might come across more as a veneer for absolute control than as a real attempt at a clean-up. For many members of the community, the response was to treat the first couple as cult figures, lord and lady who dispensed benefits in return for unswerving fealty. The cult of personality emerged at Dick Gordon's annual birthday parties, at which all members of the community were invited to participate. Gordon pretended the parties were spontaneous, that he knew nothing about the plans to honor him in such style, but there was nothing spontaneous about the *asalto* (surprise party) thrown for his fiftieth birthday on August 5, 1995.[26]

Around midnight, the captains of each of Olongapo's 17 *barangay* drove by SBMA headquarters in a torchlight parade, the words "Kate H. Gordon" painted on the doors of their vans. Behind them, crowds marched in unison bearing banners proclaiming, "We Are Proud to Have You as a Leader." There were hundreds of balloons and more signs reading "Happy Birthday." Then the vans stopped, the *barangay* captains stepped out, showing off T-shirts inscribed, in red letters, "Happy Birthday, Chairman Gordon, we [heart symbol] you." The backs of their warm-up jackets displayed, "Go for the Gold, Go for Gordon, Happy Golden Birthday to a Great Leader." A few T-shirts read simply, "Flash Gordon."

With the air of a patronizing prince at a tribal rite, Gordon stepped down from SBMA headquarters, shaking hands and saluting firemen on a convoy of fire trucks flying balloons from their roofs. Then he led the parade on the short walk to the posh Seafront Restaurant as firecrackers popped and the skies lit up in a fireworks display. Conspicuous among the crowd walking near him was one sign, signed "Port Operators," reading, "Happy Birthday, Sir Dick, Without You, Today Is Yesterday, But With You Hero of Men & Country, Today Is Tomorrow, We Luv U!!!"

Once inside, everyone dug into a buffet supper. The chairman, wearing a warm-up jacket inscribed "Subic Patrol," the name of Sellers' weekly TV show, was all false modesty as he grabbed the mike and thanked his fans and family.

"I don't know why you keep coming back on my birthday, on Kate's birthday, on my mother's birthday, on my father's birthday," he said. "Today is a special day indeed. I have never seen so many getting happy at somebody getting old. [Laughter.] One is always measured in this country by the amount of money he has in banks, the clothes that he wears, but one can never imagine the wealth of friends. Look around you here tonight, here you see investors, former bargirls, senior citizens and young people, rich and poor. Here you see international investors. We have become an international community."

It was vintage Gordon. The drinks flowed freely while a team of disco dancers up from Manila performed in cut-off jeans, the kind that Kate banned from local nightclubs. Dick was in his element, pressing his programs and pretexts for extending his power from Olongapo to the country. "We shattered the myth of many Americans who left here with a heavy heart, a cynical heart. They saw what we could do. They shook the hand of the chairman and said, 'Congratulations.'" Who could be "so fortunate," he asked, "as to see a Federal Express plane land?"

The hyperbole reached a climax on November 24, the third anniversary of the handover of the base, a year before the gathering of the 18 leaders of APEC that Gordon anticipated as his crowning moment. Gordon evoked the image of John Kennedy as he reworked JFK's historic pledge to put a man on the moon. "If the Philippines cannot go to the moon, we will go to the world," he told a cheering crowd that included American diplomats and several American navy officers from a deep-sea salvage ship, the *Beaufort*, visiting Subic on a training mission.[27]

The chairman offered more statistics: "Consider that in the last three years Subic has signed 190 companies. The Japanese are going to develop 150 hectares. The Filipinos of Subic Bay have developed a Philippine face, combining all the tribes of the Philippines. Subic is for everyone. We have 36,000 Filipinos employed gainfully."

After Gordon, there was Ramos. "Three years ago, when the American flag that flew over the base was finally lowered, it had been 450 years when the first foreign soldier landed on Philippine soil," Ramos reminded the crowd. "There was not a single day when there was not a foreign soldier." He, Ramos and Gordon, "lowered the American flag and raised this big Philippine flag, which is still waving proudly." By now, he declaimed, "Subic has become synonymous with success."

Around the main gate, however, workers complained that they were paid much less than when the Americans were around. Gordon and the foreign investors, notably those from Taiwan, they said, were conspiring to hold them to pay scales equal to less than five dollars a day. "If you complain, you are fired," said one. "There is no defense"—and certainly no talk of a labor movement. In any case, Gordon's claim of the number of jobs was exaggerated. Scarcely more than 11,000 were reporting full-time. Employers dismissed workers to keep wages low—or when orders were down.[28]

Businessmen also had their complaints. Japanese bankers in Manila were reluctant to invest heavily in the free port "when the future is so insecure." Shippers said the port was charging too much and were reluctant to put in for short visits—or even minor repairs. Investors had horror tales of encounters with the young and inexperienced bureaucracy that Gordon had put together, many from among his following of friends and hangers-on. The chairman, it was said, was too often out politicking or partying with his cronies.

"There are a lot of stories," said one foreigner, talking over lunch at Mike Sellers' Hollywood Steakhouse. "It can take a long time to get anything done." Part of the problem was Gordon's passion for control. "He has to make all final decisions. Nobody gets in without his approval." Gordon might keep applications on his desk for weeks, weighing the pros and cons of topics and proposals about which he had no grasp, no qualifications—and little really good advice.[29]

Uncertainty about the SBMA was accentuated by a bitter controversy over a contract that Gordon awarded in 1996 to Hutchison Port Philippines, an offshoot of the venerable Hong Kong conglomerate Hutchison Whampoa and Hong Kong's Guoco Group, to develop the port. A Manila company, International Container Terminal Services (ICTS), loudly protested that it had submitted the winning bid—a plan calling for shippers to pay nearly three times as much in royalties as Hutchison had proposed. Gordon argued that ICTS wanted high royalties for Subic in hopes of diverting business to its own facilities in Manila and Batangas, where royalties are far lower. Moreover, ICTS had promised to invest only $20 million rather than the $60 million pledged by Hutchison, which runs much of Hong Kong harbor as well as port facilities in southern China.[30]

The battle cut deep into clan feuding. Skeptics asked what was the quid pro quo for Gordon's support of the bid by Hutchison, nothing if not experienced in winning lucrative contracts. Then there was the influence of the Andres Soriano family, one of the country's richest clans and partner with ICTS Chairman Enrique Razon, doyen of another wealthy family. Was old-line power and money squeezing out the upstart Gordon? Ramos, fearful of offending established wealth as well as nationalist sensitivities by favoring a foreign company, ordered rebidding—a switch that raised further doubts about the Philippines' reliability and Ramos' motives.[31]

The Hutchison case was not the first to arise from bidding at Subic. The government's commission on audit offered what was seen as "striking evidence of honest employees doing their duty in uncovering the anomalies and financial wrong-doing of other government officials." An introduction to excerpts from the report urged readers to "see the danger posed by those who use their public office to plunder and loot public funds and remember how similar kleptomania of the past regime brought the country to the edge of bankruptcy and economic decline." There were "questionable contracts approved by the SBMA," including one for air navigational equipment "to the highest bidder for $7.5 million when the lower bid was $2.5 million for the same equipment."[32]

Subic faced another problem when jealous Filipino merchants demanded that Subic and Clark lose the duty-free status that attracts Filipinos looking for prices 20 to 30 percent below those in Manila. Subic was harder hit than Clark. The crowds at Subic's duty-free shops, less than half the norm when lahar blocked the main road to Manila in the rainy season, were likely to go down still more. "It will be disastrous," said Bong Gordon. The Subic page in the *Philippine Daily Inquirer*—financed by Tony Trillo, owner of the PX Club, one of the duty-free stores—joined the fray. Richard Gordon "takes a lot of interest," said editor Couttie. "He tells Tony what he wants, and Tony tells us."[33]

The government responded with carefully calculated compromise. Everyone lost the right to duty-free shopping *except* for the 350,000 residents aged 18 and above in Angeles and environs and another 350,000 from in and around Olongapo. Each of them could spend $100 a month on duty-free products at the base closest to home. As the shopping crowds declined precipitously, the new rule threatened a free-for-all in which the locals exported their newly bought goods through middlemen to the rest of the country.

Each base now had to prove it could make it as a commercial center, not a shopper's paradise. There was no question, though, that Subic symbolized the Philippines' role in a new Asia. Less clear was who was profiting. The Dick-and-Kate phenomenon had unsettling implications, likely to grow more so as they heated up their drive to become the first couple of the nation, if not in 1998, then in 2004. For the Gordons, the one-time navy base was a private reservation, in the tradition of the great Cojuangco hacienda, Luisita, and other great spreads of a landed elite that had acquired their property from the sell-off by the American colonialists early in the century of great estates acquired from the infamous Spanish friars.

Unlike the owners of other great estates, Gordon would never content himself with nurturing the SBMA gradually. He was far more interested in Subic as a political stepping stone than as an end in itself—an ambition that angered jealous rivals. One disturbing nightmare was that Gordon, if he went on to higher office, might get Kate appointed as SBMA chairman. Investors trembled at the thought. "She's really bad news," said a foreign businessman. "She's much more dictatorial [than her husband]."[34]

The real danger: the emergence of a Third World-style autocracy in Olongapo whenever the chairman fulfilled his dream of including the whole community in a zone covering the same area as that under American military control before the Americans handed over the portions outside the base itself in 1959. Referring to the fenced-in base as just the "security area," the confines of the old U.S. Navy port, Gordon said he wanted the SBMA to extend its writ over the old American reservation area, four times as large as the base.[35]

"The dictatorial tendencies of Gordon will eventually deter the full development of the Subic Freeport," predicted Leonardo Roman, the governor of neighboring Bataan Province, who was outraged over Gordon's bid for the SBMA to annex a former refugee processing center in Bataan. The governor promised to ask Ramos to dismiss Gordon not only for his "lack of perception of the needs of multinationals" but also for being "too politicized."[36]

For all his rising power, Gordon saw shadowy forces arrayed against him. "The culture of envy applies to politicians who are jealous," he told me in his office overlooking the expanse of Subic Bay as he prepared to host the APEC forum. "I believe the powerful, the economically abundant will always be worried when another power comes in that could threaten their hold."[37] Finance Secretary Roberto de Ocampo, also a presidential hopeful, one of those responsible for undermining the Hutchison deal, undercut Gordon still more by refusing extra tax incentives for foreign investors—a measure Gordon wanted to lure companies from Hong Kong. The message was clear: Gordon could not count on Ramos to back him against wealthier, entrenched family interests in league with politicians, such as his neighbor in Bataan.

SIX

"Priestly Defender"

The leaders of the 18 Pacific Rim "economies" were meeting for a few symbolic hours at pristine facilities inside the base near the glistening waters of Subic Bay. Several hundred reporters were banging away on deadline inside a modern press center, rewriting statements, monitoring events on TV screens, sifting through "pool" reports. The final hours of APEC '96, the Asia Pacific Economic Cooperation group, were perfectly scripted and flawlessly executed. For Richard and Katherine Gordon, APEC was their finest hour—a chance to shine as the genial, efficient host and hostess of the notables gathered right there in their own backyard. For more than a year, they had planned, rehearsed and psyched themselves and the town for the moment.

Only one thing could go wrong. What if the thousands of malcontents, dissidents, old-line revolutionaries and young radicals managed to slip around or through the net of thousands of soldiers and national police, get into the town, scramble to the gates of the base—and demonstrate their hostility to the whole show? It was a nightmare for which the Gordons—and Ramos—were fully prepared. Police roadblocks, fortified by heavy trucks, repeatedly blocked a caravan of protesters wending their way from Metro Manila after a series of anti-APEC conferences staged by at least three groups ranging from moderate-left to radical.

Ramos had said the critics were free to express their views, even to demonstrate, but by the time they reached the outskirts of Olongapo, it was clear his words were meaningless. On a bridge over a ravine where the road descended from the mountains, a dozen huge tractor-trailer trucks were so tightly massed as to almost blockade the way for pedestrians, much less vehicles. Olongapo, on APEC Day, November 25, 1996, was inaccessible by land.

Gordon, however, was taking no chances. Inside the town, hundreds of stick-wielding young men, "volunteers," patrolled the streets. Kate's *barangay* cars were seen at strategic points supervising the volunteers. City Hall workers talked excitedly into walkie-talkies, then denied they were working. "We are all volunteers," said a woman on Kate's staff who recognized me as I left the establishment of the Reverend Shay Cullen, an inveterate critic of the Gordons and of the Americans who had preceded them on the base.[1]

Cullen, who had come to the country about 30 years before as a Columban father fresh out of Dalgan Park seminary in Dublin, was in his element. He had turned his mission into a meeting place for a conference staged by the radical Bayan organization Bagong Alyansang Makabayan (New Patriotic Alliance) and was happily playing host to a few enthusiastic protesters, including an activist couple from Canada and several American women. The day before, a few dozen of them had marched down the road that courses around the bay, stopping at a bridge where they lit a bonfire and hoisted a banner reading, "No to APEC!"—quickly removed by "volunteers"—that they had hoped would be visible from the base across the water.

They were painting "No to APEC" signs on the porch of Cullen's mission when I dropped by, but it was clear that they weren't going to get outside Cullen's front gate, down a rather steep driveway leading to the main road. Already Kate's people were calling in reinforcements, more young men with sticks, who would block the way and not hesitate to crack heads.

On down in the center of town, the volunteers brandished baseball bats as well as sticks. A mob of them swarmed Rizal Avenue, 200 meters from City Hall, as a group of anti-APEC protesters burst out of an office building across a side street from the public market. "You see what is happening in Olongapo," one of the protesters shouted. "We are under Olongapo dictatorship," shouted another. "They have goons everywhere. They are Gordon loyalists—they want to kill the Olongapo people who are against them."

Uniformed policemen on the scene made little more than a pretense of breaking up the fracas. Under the eyes of the police, I saw one volunteer, his head bloodied by a blow from a stick wielded by a protester, standing with a baseball bat at the corner of the market facing City Hall. Quietly, he crept up behind the protester, slammed the bat on his head and ran. The protester slowly crumpled to the pavement, gravely injured, the worst casualty of the day. More volunteers ran down a back street chasing the remnants of the ralliers, grabbing two as the police descended on them. The protest was safely over, just two miles from the base where the leaders and journalists were winding up whatever they were doing at APEC. The Gordons could breathe easy.

"The goons of Gordon are all over the city," said the leader of the rally, a woman named Ameth Concepcion, president of the local chapter of a federation of cause-oriented groups allied with SLAM APEC (Solidary of Labor Against APEC) run by a noted radical figure, R. C. Constantino Jr. "They are paid about 200 or 300 pesos for the day," eight to twelve dollars.

How much democracy had to do with her protest, however, was very much open to doubt. Both Concepcion and Constantino came from elitist backgrounds, she the daughter of a local judge and attorney who had opposed Gordon politically, he the son of Renato Constantino, one of the country's best-known leftist writers. While the APEC conference was going on, R. C. staged his own anti-APEC summit. In an abandoned tire factory in Quezon City, he hosted labor union officials, farmers' representatives and spokespeople for "the urban poor," all holding appropriately radical positions.

Concepcion and her cohorts had not had to run a gauntlet of police barricades. They already had rooms in the office building, courtesy of the building's owner, a local tycoon named Conrado Tiu. "The protest is about Gordon, the way he's dictating the lives of the people," said Tiu, receiving me in his elaborate office suite. "There are violations of human rights. Houses are demolished. People are salvaged. Nobody can make a move because we are monitored. Our telephone lines are being bugged. How can you survive?" Tiu's immediate complaints had to do with money. "They have the highest business license fee in the country," he said. "When they are bidding, they do not award to the lowest bidder."[2]

The interests of Tiu and the dissidents under his roof made him a friend of Father Cullen, whose crusade might otherwise have been of little interest if not altogether alien to the wealthy son of Chinese immigrants. Tiu viewed Cullen as an ally or at least an antidote to his enemy, Gordon. As hosts of protest groups, they shared common cause—one that had everything to do with power and money rather than ideology or religion or justice.

For Shay Cullen, the key to the donations he needs for his mission is public relations and sensation. He has become a master of both. One evening, crusading against the exploitation of Filipino children, he led a German television crew and local policemen into a bar named Alpenblick. The police arrested the two Swiss partners after one of the girls said she was 16, below the age of consent. Later an ID card showed she was 18, and she admitted that the TV people had paid her to say she was a minor. A prosecutor still pressed charges on the grounds that the partners were offering the girl for a fee; one of the TV types had paid the bar fine with marked money as part of Cullen's scheme to ensure the arrest would stand up in court.[3]

The episode was one of a series earning worldwide publicity for Cullen. He has been a complainant in a dozen cases in which foreigners are charged with having had sex with teenagers and children, both boys and girls. In one of his most notorious conquests, the priest snared a retired Australian engineer, Victor Fitzgerald, on whose yacht he had found three young girls. He filed a complaint against the yachtsman, but there were no witnesses and they recanted their "confessions."

I saw Fitzgerald in the local detention center in Barrio Barretto, 100 yards from nightclubs habituated by retired American servicemen, on the fringes of the city, up a winding road from the base and the heart of the town. Outside the cell, where he was being held without bail, the girls' mothers, one of whom had worked for him as a maid, were offering him food and sympathy. "Cullen offered the kids 50,000 pesos [$2,000]," Fitzgerald shouted at me, clutching the cell bars. "This man has made an enormous business ruining people. It's a very big business."[4]

Actually, Fitzgerald could easily have avoided imprisonment. He'd been out on bail, cruising in his yacht, when Cullen, claiming that he might flee the country, persuaded the court to revoke his bail and jail him while awaiting trial. So why hadn't Fitzgerald, whose yacht was stripped by vandals, then destroyed within days after his arrest, sailed away when he had the chance? "I didn't leave because I didn't want to run away from something I didn't do. I had my yacht, my passport. I could have gone any time."[5]

Fitzgerald's pathetic protests did not impress the judge, who found him guilty, on May 7, 1996, of sexual abuse of a 13-year-old girl whom he had lured onto his yacht and molested over a period of ten days in exchange for gifts, including money. The judge said that "clearly" Fitzgerald was "a pedophile," sentenced him to 8 to 17 years in prison—and ordered him to give the girl 50,000 pesos. It was an enormous sum by local standards and, coincidentally or not, the amount that Fitzgerald said Cullen had offered the girls to testify against him.

The case, however, was fragile. The judge chose to believe the girl was pressured "not to divulge the sexual abuses" against her when she took back her confession. The girl's brother was said to have chained her while her mother told her to sign papers clearing Fitzgerald. It was unclear, however, who was paying off or influencing whom. There was no doubt that the girl had been manipulated by Cullen and his Preda Human Resource Development Foundation. (The priest stopped publicizing what Preda stands for—Prevent and Rehabilitate Drug Abusers—after dropping a drug program that never got the publicity showered on him by his child abuse campaign.) What made the case all the more bizarre was that another judge had acquitted Fitzgerald of a rape charge against a second girl after she recanted. All the so-called evidence was circumstantial.

An exultant Cullen called the verdict "really a landmark decision for the struggle in the Philippines against child prostitution." He added to the sensation with more wild attacks. One of his favorite themes was the evil of the American armed forces, which he blamed for fostering the conditions under which child abuse flourishes. "The society is reeling from the impact," he said with a satisfied look in an interview for ABS-CBN, the leading Philippine television network, after the court had issued its verdict on Fitzgerald.

"Maybe it will be like this forever." The report showed footage of Cullen striding toward Fitzgerald's yacht to arrest him—footage thoughtfully arranged by Preda.[6]

Fitzgerald, a tragic figure in handcuffs, old beyond his 66 years, was heard to say, "I am a scapegoat, and that is exactly the situation." Later, he was too shocked by the verdict to receive anyone in prison. Through a guard he sent me the message, "It's a frame-up." As he contemplated spending possibly the rest of his life in a Philippine prison, he saw no point in talking to anyone since "none of you did me any good when I talked to you before." Four weeks later, he blurted through the bars of his cell: "They've got their sacrificial lamb. If I have served some useful purpose in saving some children from getting molested, then I'm happy."

An Australian legislator, Meredith Burgmann, said she hoped the Philippines was "at last taking the issue seriously" but feared the case "was probably just a show trial."[7] As a show, the impact was dramatic. Hours after the court issued its verdict, the lower house of the Philippine Congress approved a bill setting the death penalty or life imprisonment for anyone found guilty of pedophilia, defined as sexually explicit conduct with a male or female below the age of 14.

Cullen had another case going against an Englishman named Michael Clarke, who had promoted a sex tour to the Philippines. A young man from Christian Aid in London, Martin Cottingham, came out with a crew from Britain's Independent Television Network (ITN), linked up with Cullen, and caught the travel agent on film saying that he could supply anything they wanted. There were no witnesses, however, and only one blurred tape. In the yard outside his cell, next to that of Fitzgerald in Barrio Barretto, Clarke, unable to raise bail of 20,000 pesos, or about $800, railed against the injustice that was keeping him behind bars.

It seemed that Cottingham had spotted Clarke's ad in a British magazine, *Exchange & Mart,* dated March 30, 1995, promising "the ultimate holiday for adventurous men." Cottingham made it his mission to see if Clarke was selling underage girls or boys to the middle-age men who flock to Southeast Asia, notably Thailand and the Philippines, in search of any kind of sex they want. Clarke fell into the trap, faxing, "We have a [*sic*] extra special girls here" and "welcome to bring your own girls, no problem." With that, Cottingham and ITN correspondent Adam Holloway booked tickets through Clarke and, on April 29, flew out with an ITN crew to catch him in the act.[8]

The videotape showed Clarke, unaware he was being recorded, saying, "I could provide younger girls, young girls 12 years old, a Filipino"—in a voice that Clarke claimed was not his. "But the children do have protectors like this Irish priest," said ITN reporter Adam Holloway, homing in on Cullen talking about "the abusers who are coming out here and sexually abusing these children for a pittance, buying and selling them like animals in the market—and we want to put an end into [sic] that."[9]

Then it was off to the beach where Holloway, at last identifying himself to Clarke, said, "Why, you just said to me that there are a lot of young chickens here." Clarke replied, "But there are young chickens—beautiful girls, and they are professionals, and we are trying to encourage tourism." When Holloway asked about children, Clarke backed off. "Nothing for the children," he said. "I have family. My family here is a Filipino"—an allusion to Clarke's Filipina girlfriend.[10]

Clarke might not have been in trouble had not an influential Philippine senator, Ernesto Herrera, happened to see the ITN report on CNN, carried in the Philippines by cable. The senator, like Richard Gordon, had opposed the withdrawal of U.S. forces from the bases and voted in favor of the bases treaty. By now he supported Gordon's efforts to turn Subic into a major mercantile center but also found a soulmate in Cullen, who had once made drug and child abuse the basis for his campaign against the U.S. troop presence.

Cullen marshaled Herrera's nephew and public relations chief, Joselito Herrera, to journey to Olongapo and add his testimony as evidence at Clarke's trial. "You can't be overzealous when it comes to issues like child prostitution," said the younger Herrera, whose uncle was the prime force behind the bill calling for the death penalty for pedophiles.[11] It didn't matter that a National Bureau of Investigation (NBI) agent had also journeyed to Olongapo, testifying for Clarke, claiming that the NBI did not find enough evidence to warrant charges. Cullen, videotaping the testimony in hopes of embarrassing the agent, murmured later that he was taking "bribes"—but from whom, or why, was not clear.

Riding a wave of publicity surrounding a Yorkshire Television hagiography on his crusade, Cullen got the court to postpone cross-questioning by Clarke's court-appointed counsel for a month while he visited Europe and America in November 1995. The trip was a smash-hit, five-star success—and elicited great black headlines in the London tabloids. "WE'LL NAIL PERVERTS ON CHILD SEX JAUNTS," blared the *Sun* over a three-column picture of Cullen with the caption, "Determined . . . Fr Cullen has devoted his life to rooting out evil child perverts."[12] *The Star* story was much the same. "END EVIL CHILD SEX ABUSE HOLIDAYS," shouted the headline over a full-page feature written without the slightest pro forma effort at seeing through the self-publicity blitz.[13]

As his trial dragged on, at the rate of one session every month or two, Clarke whipped up his own propaganda attack, firing off anti-Cullen letters to the *Foreign Post,* a weekly paper for foreigners, and to Kate Gordon. "The authorities are being hoodwinked, lulled into believing that the high moral ground he [Cullen] holds is being used for the benefit of children and the Filipino family," Clarke wrote, "So behind the visage, he presents a more sinister purpose, one of the seven deadly sins, GREED."[14]

To the mayor, Clarke charged that Cullen "has been using Preda for years to accumulate millions of dollars"—and suggested it was "common knowledge" that Irish priests "such as Cullen are sent to every corner of the earth using the umberella [*sic*] of our dear Lord in Heaven to accumulate monies, which after a careful laundry process is filtered back to the 'Rebel Army's Armory' the I.R.A."[15] (Cullen was furious when I relayed Clarke's suggestion of laundering money for the Irish Republican Army. Giving me a first-hand taste of the methods of intimidation and innuendo with which he attacks his foes, he suggested I was "a CIA agent"—and threatened to have me "investigated in Washington.")

On his final day in court, in early June 1996, Clarke attempted to read a statement, but the judge cut him off. Clearly the court had chosen to accept the testimony of Cottingham, flown in from London for one hearing. "On four separate occasions the Christian Aid guy had asked Clarke if he could supply girls," said a British diplomat. "The American police would have been accused of entrapment." It mattered not that no child was offered by Clarke, that there was no victim, that the case was based on the flimsiest of evidence. The judge found him guilty of offering child prostitution and inciting to commit child prostitution and imposed a maximum 16-year sentence. "Clarke could have had Perry Mason working for him," said the diplomat. "He wouldn't have had a chance."[16]

At about the same time, in Angeles City, Cullen had a retired British Royal Navy officer on trial on charges of fondling neighborhood boys who came to swim in his pool. Michael Douglas Slade, who had risen to lieutenant commander in supply and catering and had once served on the royal yacht *Britannia,* had left his wife and children before gravitating to a relaxing life in the Philippines—and steady work in Angeles City as a caterer and maker of gourmet pies.

After being held for eight months by immigration authorities, he came up with money for bail—nearly $3,000—while awaiting the outcome of trials on three charges of child molestation. "It's a waste of the court's time," said Slade in his home with a swimming pool, once the luxurious off-base quarters of an American Air Force officer. "Cullen stirred it up. The children had no complaint. If he thinks he can make this stick, he's a fool."[17]

Slade claimed that Cullen not only offered money to the boys to charge him but also sought to get one of his employees to testify against him. The neighborhood boys couldn't understand. One showed up during our conversation with a bolo knife, begging Slade to let him cut down some coconuts and go for a swim, but Slade shooed him away. Cullen returned to

Slade the charge of compromising witnesses, protesting that the court's decision to free Slade on bail would give him a chance to suborn the boys.

It didn't help Slade's case, from the viewpoint of publicity, that a British tabloid in 1975 had caught him as he left a meeting of a group called "Paedophile [*sic*] Action for Liberation" (PAL) in London.[18] Slade said he was there as a member of the National Council of Civil Liberties and had no idea what the meeting was about. "I didn't know what a pedophile was," he said. "I thought it was someone who rode a bicycle. I was horrified." The explanation was good enough for the royal navy, where he remained on active duty for another three years before resigning for a high-paying job in Saudi Arabia. Settling in the Philippines a few years later, he said that he never thought of fleeing to avoid trial. "I'm very happy here," he told me. "I'm innocent. I want the thing disposed of."[19] The British press loved the case, dubbing Slade "the pork pie pervert"—an allusion to his catering business that including baking and selling pies of all sorts to local expatriates.[20]

Back in Olongapo, the priest liked to show off the tape of the Yorkshire TV special portraying himself as the "priestly defender"—and Slade and Fitzgerald as sex criminals. One high point was a conversation in which Slade said "the lawyer does the deals" and one witness "could be bought" if he "gave her a couple of thousand dollars."[21] What the tape didn't show was that Slade, anxious to prove his innocence, said he would not deal with anyone on that basis. He added that he had no idea the reporter was secretly filming the interview, which he was assured was not for quotation but for background understanding, to fill in the reporter on what everyone knows is the way the system works.

The Yorkshire special purported to expose what have long been well-known, oft-publicized scenes of Filipinos soliciting for child prostitution, of the children themselves talking on camera, but the result was a disgraceful piece of journalism. In Cullen's zeal to show how he caught these middle-aged wanderers in his net, in the reporter's lust for lurid footage, the accused were made to appear not only guilty as charged but like silly, evil old fools, even though the charges would not have stood up for a moment in a British, American, Australian or Irish court.

The whole show was quite offensive to Filipino sensitivities, a response that reflected as badly on some Filipinos as it did on Cullen. An old Marcos lieutenant, J. V. Cruz, once the late president's glib spokesman, then his ambassador to the Court of St. James, now the London-based columnist for Manila newspapers, attacked the Yorkshire production in one of his columns as "a terrific ego trip" in which Cullen "is Sir Galahad, Superman and Mother Teresa combined, apparently the only person in a country of 67 million people who cares about Filipino boys and girls who sell their bodies for money."[22]

Cruz berated Yorkshire TV for giving "the impression that all Philippine government officials and functionaries (except for one stalwart woman prosecutor) were accomplices in this business" while failing to give "the slightest suggestion that the Filipino people and the Philippine government were totally outraged by the depredations inflicted on Filipino boys and girls." The priest "doesn't care, of course, if the Philippines is depicted in the rest of the world as a barbaric country whose fathers and mothers sell their children to foreigners for less than would buy a decent *merienda*"—the word for snack, borrowed from the Spanish and widely used in the Philippines.

True enough, but until recently Philippine authorities had been notoriously unresponsive to the entire problem. Like most influential Filipinos, Cruz appeared far more upset by the negative publicity than by the underlying issue. The country did not have a law against pedophilia, believed endemic in Philippine society, especially among family members, until 1992.

Since then, the police have distinguished themselves more for using the law as a tool for extracting bribes than for prosecuting offenders. "The anti-pedophile campaign may yet be given a bad name by law enforcers who are over-enthusiastic in getting arrests as prosecutors are in getting convictions," reported a weekly for foreigners. The paper claimed it was "'common knowledge' that some police officers in Manila's tourist belt are known to extort money from tourists and hotel guests on some trumped-up charges, including entrapment in pedophile cases."[23]

If there was any real dividend from the publicity, it was in the form of cooperation between British and Philippine police after the British parliament passed a sex offender act effective September 1, 1997, under which British citizens were liable for prosecution in Britain for sex crimes against children outside the United Kingdom. British Foreign Secretary Robin Cook, in Manila in August 1997, signed a memorandum pledging cooperation in combating child abuse and agreeing to provide women and children's "protection training" for the PNP to battle "this awful problem." A British child abuse expert, Tony Butler, chief of the Gloucestershire Constabulary, visited Manila the next month to advise the NBI about its anti-child abuse division, formed after two Scotland Yard detectives led the first child protection course in Manila in 1996.[24] The emphasis was on what Filipinos could do about Filipinos.

Cullen was not impressed. In his relentless pursuit of foreign offenders, he charged that the NBI had been deliberately slow. In interviews and letters to newspapers, he claimed that NBI officials ignored blatant crimes, leaving it to him to bring charges on his own. NBI officials had quite a different response. "There is no case," said an NBI lawyer in Olongapo. "They have no proof against these people. We look into them and find nothing. We feel very hurt. He is abusing these people."[25] Cullen countered with claims about the motives of the NBI people, implying they responded only when paid or, similarly, were paid for silence.

The reality was the priestly defender needed to "get" the foreigners for the sensational publicity on which he thrives for donations, fame and whatever he wants for himself and his foundation. Far from being a priestly defender, he emerges from his crusade against pedophiles as a priestly pretender, reaping donations from the publicity but doing little to solve the seemingly intractable problem of rampant child abuse in a country in which 60,000 children are forced into prostitution. By the time the Yorkshire special was broadcast, the priest was getting so much publicity that he reminded a visitor of no one so much as Chairman Gordon and Mayor Kate. Like them, he loves the newspaper and magazine clippings that he photocopies for visitors, posts on the walls and shows off at seminars.

In that spirit, Cullen was quick to jump on a case, any case, even when he was not involved and the government was clearly doing its job. When an investigator from the Bureau of Immigration and Deportation called in search of help in tracking down one James Peifer, a former U.S. Navy lieutenant wanted for nine sex offenses in Pennsylvania, Cullen ordered a young member of his staff to ask U.S. Navy retirees if they had seen the man. When NBI agents discovered from other sources that Peifer was working at the children's zoo inside Subic and arrested him in his rented home, Cullen fired off a press release saying that Preda investigators "assisted in the hunt for Peifer"—and got his own name mentioned in news agency reports.[26]

Child abuse, according to Cullen, was far more widespread than anyone wanted to believe—a view that no one disputed. The Manila press was full of revelations of the extent of exploitation of juveniles not only in the Philippines but in countries around the world. They reported at length on a UN study estimating that 400,000 to 500,000 children and teenagers in India were forced to sell themselves—a number followed by the United States with 300,000 child prostitutes and Thailand with 100,000. The Philippines' 60,000 child prostitutes ranked fourth—ahead of Sri Lanka, whose 30,000 child prostitutes were mostly boys.[27]

Foreign tourists, notably from Germany and Australia, were widely known to descend on these countries in search of sex with underage boys or girls, but the figures did not cover the much more widespread phenomenon of child abuse, including pedophilia among family members, by fathers, uncles, in-laws, caretakers. If child abuse among Filipinos occasionally made headlines, it was far more likely to go unnoted, if not condoned. ("For Filipinos to abuse children is bad," said a foreign volunteer who had been working on behalf of abused children, quietly, without publicity, for 12 years. "For a foreigner to abuse children is much worse.")[28]

Unconcerned about such details, the priest accused American military retirees in Barrio Barretto, up the road from his large mission high above the bay on the way to town, of sinful motives for living in the Philippines. "A lot of these people use their Filipino wives to cover their activities with children. They hide here for that reason."[29]

That's a claim that retired servicemen—and foreign tourists—loudly dispute as the sun slips down on their old way of life. They say they're in Barrio Barretto because they like it, and it's no crime if they have Filipino wives or girlfriends. Many cite the second families they support as proof of their good intentions and question Cullen's motives and the uses of the donations with which he conducts his activities.

The sea breezes blew in across the calm expanse of Subic Bay, rustling the palm and coconut fronds on the roof and sides of Les and Tess's open-air bar while two or three one-time American sailors and a couple of middle-aged Europeans sipped bottles of beer and contemplated the easy life half a world from home. For them, the days slip by listlessly, uneventfully; some of them time each bottle of San Miguel beer by the hour. A bottle at ten, another at eleven, a third at noon, pause for lunch, and on into the afternoon and evening. Martin Tubbs, a retired navy warrant officer, confessed that he did little but take care of a few chickens that he sells on the local market. After 29 years in the navy, he figures he'll enjoy life free of hassles and intrusions.

It's that way for several thousand retired American service people hanging on in the Philippines, about 1,500 of them in and around Olongapo. The good old times and memories linger on in Barrio Barretto. Jeepneys run by on the national highway, carrying people to the center of town and the base, but most of the foreigners prefer to hang out in "the barrio." For them, a day consists of venturing from ramshackle homes and going to any of the 20 or 30 bars that have survived the departure of the American navy—and the crackdown on the hostess bars and go-go dancing.

Old-timers still say Olongapo is the best place in the world. Where else, they ask, can one live on retirement pay with a new wife or girlfriend, free from the daily worries about money and family that inhibit the good life back home? They may proudly acknowledge the existence of a former wife and a few kids "back in the world," as GIs call the United States, but most haven't seen them in years—and communicate rarely if at all. Time, however, is catching up with the easy existence of not only the Americans but also the Europeans and Australians who followed them in search of a lotus land of low prices, cheap and available sex and, for those who cared, most of the conveniences of home.

The good old boys at Les and Tess's—and the other bars along the highway through Barrio Barretto—like to say it's all politics, an opportunistic drive to turn the place into a first-class tourist resort, one that will make money for the politicians but not the people. Les Wagner, who runs the bar with Tess, a Filipino woman and the owner of record in a country where foreigners are banned from owning such a business, agrees. He believes there won't be any changes very quickly, even if the politicians have some grand ideas and know how to make it tough on those who break the rules.[30]

These days, Tess complained, inspectors drop by several times a week demanding to see liquor licenses, restaurant licenses and other pieces of paper. They were always checking on the electricity, the toilet facilities and everything else, looking for any excuse to issue a summons, a threat, or maybe even close the place down. The Swiss-Italian owner of a vaguely Tyrolean joint named Swiss Taverne said that he too was embarrassed by inspectors interrupting him while he was with customers. His wife, a Filipina and the owner of record, said there was nothing going on but feared that the inspectors discouraged customers. One day her husband threatened to fight an American suspected of gossiping about underage girls in the bar.[31]

Around Barrio Barretto, the impact of the campaign has been devastating. No longer does a visitor see lines of bikini-clad girls on makeshift stages behind bars while customers idly ogle them, sometimes choosing one or two to rent for the night by paying the bar fine of about $20. Plenty still goes on, but by banning bikini-dancing and bar fines, authorities are spreading the message that foreigners are not welcome unless they come as businessmen to work or invest in the SBMA.

Some of the SBMA facilities are visible right across the bay from the back of Les and Tess's place. There, shimmering in the sun, are the hangars, the tower and the 10,000-foot airstrip of Cubi Point. The streets leading to the base—once among the most raucous and raunchy of any navy liberty port in the world—are still lined with shuttered windows and doors, many of them bearing the faded, peeling names of the legendary bars that were haunts to generations of sailors and marines.

A reminder of the American military tradition lives on in American Legion Post number four, downtown near the main gate of the base. A three-inch cannon from the Japanese "hell ship" *Oryoku Maru* points menacingly from in front of the door. The ship, a bronze plaque explains, was sunk by American planes in December 1944 in Subic Bay with 1,619 American prisoners in the hold. Inside the legion hall, retirees dine on old-time SOS—chipped beef on toast—while playing bingo and watching sports on ESPN.

Back in Barrio Barretto, still more veterans crowd the bar and tables of VFW Post 11447, playing pool and dining on breakfasts and lunches reputed as the best in the town. Clay Strode, a one-time navy technician, believes the inspectors who come to find fault don't have much to complain about. The VFW post runs about the cleanest restaurant in town. Still, officials don't care for the allusion to "foreign wars" in the name, so the sign on the wall says only "Veterans Post 11447."

To the Americans hanging on ever since closure of the bases, Barrio Barretto is a second home. They're not sure, though, how long the easy living will last after the old salts who are there have faded away. The message, "Clean up your act," comes through loud and clear—not just to violators of minor rules but to anyone thinking of exploiting the presence of thousands of girls willing to sell themselves for survival and escape from poverty in a society where economic progress hardly trickles down.

Father Cullen knows that his dream of embarrassing the establishment, first the Americans, then the Filipinos, would excite little notice, much less serious consideration, were it not for the publicity he generates from the crusade against child abuse. In pursuit of publicity, he sees nothing less than evil in the motives of the Gordons and their followers. Remind him that Mayor Gordon is closing down nightclubs, forcing curfews and banning bar fines, and he's got a ready rejoinder. "That's what she's saying now, but that's all a cover-up. They are telling complainants not to pursue cases."[32]

The priest advised me to go to the nightclub district near the main bus station linking Olongapo to Manila. Owners and managers said business was off, the girls were barred from dancing in bikinis, the customers were staying away. The girls, however, were still available for a price, no longer a "bar fine" but a fee "to be negotiated with the hostess," as a mamasan explained. Certain customs are likely to endure regardless of crusading priests or politicians, whether they work with or against each other. Nightclub habitués predict the clubs will be back, as they are in every other city and town in the country, though never as they were in "the American days."

After visiting the Gigolo, a club featuring a "cultural show" of sultry but long-skirted dancers from Manila in place of the near-naked ladies of yore, I walked a couple of blocks to a decaying hotel, the Admiral, a once-flourishing hostelry that fell on hard times after the Americans had left.

The Admiral had both a past and a present; there were no paying guests, but it remained the exclusive preserve of Dick Gordon's younger brother, Bong, who was using it as his political headquarters, and their mother, Amelia Juico Gordon, who owned the place and also was residing there. Now in her seventies, she was the matriarch of a dynasty that also includes three daughters—one living near Washington, D.C., married to a retired American navy officer; another the wealthy owner of the White Rock Hotel; the third the owner of a posh restaurant and catering business in Intramuros, the historic walled city of Manila.

Waving my way past a few guards at the entrance, I strolled into what was once a coffee and souvenir shop and found it deserted except for an elderly woman seated at a small table, beside a crib with a sleeping baby. A guard told me, "There is Mrs. Gordon." I asked her about the baby. "It's mine," she said simply. She saw my amazement. "I've been adopting babies since 1962. I've taken in more than 200 babies." A couple of small girls ran up and sat beside her. "Good night, mama," said one of them while the other clutched a cookie.[33]

Amelia Juico Gordon spoke proudly of the records of some of the kids she'd raised after their parents abandoned them, occasionally just by leaving them on the doorstep, more often tearfully pleading they had no money. "Most of them finish high school," she said. "Some others go to college. I have a nurse and a pastor"—though she, as a Catholic, was not sure where or how the pastor, a Protestant, came by his religion. Next to the coffee shop was a once-spacious lobby now filled with rows of chairs facing an altar. "Twice a week we have our prayers," she said. "We have no bible. We study in the church."[34]

The former mayor, who owns much of the town, was also proud of the clean-up of the city. It's a crusade that goes back many years to when Cullen was still teaching at Columban College, the town's leading educational institution. "I started the clean-up during the time when I was mayor," said Amelia. "That's why people are already disciplined in a tradition of a city." As mayor, she used to get letters from parents of sailors who read in the papers about her clean-up efforts, futile though they seemed. "They were very glad."

Were the people of Olongapo happy to see the Americans go? "As much as possible, people would like them to stay here," she responded without hesitation. Did son Dick ever come around? "He has no time," she replied, with a trace of bitterness. How about Kate? She said nothing about the daughter-in-law of whom she never approved, with whom she has never come to terms.

The conversation returned to her other "children," some of them the offspring of American sailors and local bar hostesses. "I have plenty of Amerasians; my mother used to take care of them also. I have four or five half-breed American blacks." Clearly not up on politically correct phrasing, she smiled contentedly. "I have triplets whose parents want to get them back—two boys and one girl." The boys are at Boys' Town, a community she's set up in the mountains to the west. It occurred to me that she might have actually done more for more lost and hungry local children than Father Cullen. Why hadn't I read or heard of her efforts? The old lady kissed a little girl on the forehead, told her to go to bed, then focused, briefly, on my question.

"Oh no," she said. "I do not want people to know. It is not necessary. It is for the children." That's a lesson the Reverend Cullen might do well to absorb from the mother of the dynasty that he reviles. It's advice he is not likely to follow, however, in his own special program of exploiting kids for his own purposes.

In a monumental clash of wills between the chairman, Richard Gordon, and the priest, Shay Cullen, it is difficult to tell who has the bigger ego, who is the more unscrupulous. Either way, the children remain the victims, tools in a greater struggle, for ideology, power, prestige, gifts, whatever the priestly defender/pretender thinks he needs to sustain and expand on his mission, his cause, holy or not.

SEVEN

Rebels Divided

Whatever the threat from China, from Chinese pirates, even from distant foreign powers ranging from Russia and Japan to the United States, in some unimaginable neo-imperialist outburst, the Philippines' worst enemies are indigenous. They range from gangs of killers and kidnappers, many of them with military or police backgrounds, paid poverty-level wages by an elite that prefers to rely on private security guards and entire private armies, to full-fledged uprisings by organized rebel groups. From hardy mountain tribesmen battling for "lost land," from "loyalists" loyal only to the Marcos legacy, from radical idealists who style themselves "nationalists" to impoverished shanty-dwellers, farmers and fishermen, the nation seethes with unrest.

Curiously, the best-known leaders of the Philippines' two most troublesome revolts, however different in membership, ideology, goals, almost any standard one can name, have a lot in common. One is Muslim, the other communist, born to a Christian family, but they were close allies in the '60s. It was a decade of rising rebellion and heady hope in a nation then falling under the rule of Marcos as its American ally, benefactor and former colonizer plunged into an unpopular war across the South China Sea in Vietnam.

More than 30 years later, both these leaders were "chairman," one the chairman of the Moro National Liberation Front, the other the chairman of the Communist Party of the Philippines. Those august titles, however, were not exactly the rewards of triumph. Rather, they symbolized the power and prestige, sometimes an almost mystical charm, that both men held among relatively small bands of fanatic if frustrated followers.

In middle age, moreover, these men shared yet another common attribute. In the struggle for ultimate victory, they both had to live abroad, in exile. They operated from bases half a world from home, enjoying the perks and sometimes the riches offered by foreigners, all on the theory they could do more for "the people" while overseas than in the urban slums and rice paddies and jungles where most of their followers fought on for a better life.

If victory appeared elusive, both saw themselves as historic figures, cast by fate and their own dedication and resolve as inheritors of fights to right all the wrongs heaped upon their followers for centuries. Together, Nur Misuari, the Islamic scholar from Sulu, in the Sulu archipelago off the southwestern coast of Mindanao, and Jose Maria Sison, radical campus politician, talked for hours during their days at the University of the Philippines about their common struggle, their mutual determination to defeat the arrogant authoritarian forces ranged against them, their dream of a new country, a new social order.

The common denominator was their sacrifice for the masses—"Joma" Sison for oppressed Filipinos everywhere but mainly for the predominantly Christian populace, Misuari the progressive Muslim battling for the citizens of Bangsamoro, the nation of the Moro. (Muslim rebels refer to themselves as "Moros" even though the name was bequeathed by the hated Spanish colonialists, who got it from their own wars to drive the "Moors" from Spanish soil. To the Spanish, the Muslims in their far-off Asian empire were the same infidels as those of Arab origin who had migrated to the Iberian peninsula from northern Africa.)

Old-timers at the University of the Philippines recalled vividly the campus relationship between Nur and Joma. "We were involved in the founding congress of Kabataang Makabayan, the Patriotic Youth," said a lecturer at the university's Institute of Islamic Studies. "Nur was very close to Joma at the time. They used to conduct teach-ins under the trees. They were good friends." Samuel Tan, a Muslim from Sulu, director of the institute's Mindanao studies program, remembered Misuari. "He was in Asian studies. He got a master's and was teaching political science when he left in 1968. I did not expect him to be a revolutionary. He seldom articulated the Muslim cause. He was nurturing the thought." By internationalizing the Bangsamoro program, "Misuari has redefined radical revolt to accommodate the Islamic paradigm."[1]

In waging their "revolutions," Misuari and Sison shared themes of poverty and exploitation. "The so-called 'Moro problem' should not be viewed simply as a Moro-Christian conflict, but a war against oppression and exploitation brought about by our continuing colonial history," said a leftist commentary. "It is necessary to transcend ethnic and religious biases in seeking to end the age-old war. We must recognize the common problems and work toward the common goal of genuine development where the masses— Moro or non-Moro—are the primary actors and major beneficiaries."[2]

Beyond the campus relationship, however, the evolution of these causes reveals more differences than similarities. In the five provinces where the majority of Muslims live, 83 percent of families eke out an existence below a poverty line of $2,000 a year in pesos.[3] Despite the poverty, the most influential among the Muslim community, 6 million by government count, 12 million by their own claims, are far more concerned with the Koran than with atheist socialist ideology.

The Moro advocate the creation of a breakaway state, an independent Muslim nation torn from an "imperial" Manila regime, just as the Muslim nations of Central Asia broke loose from Moscow after the demise of the Soviet Union or, for that matter, the Palestinians formed a nation of sorts on land previously held by Israeli forces. Wealthy Muslim traders and landowners would dominate any Moro nation, as they do other Islamic states. They remain the biggest donors to the rebel cause and to the mosques where rich and poor flock to worship.

Joma might countenance a Muslim region in an opportunistic compromise but viewed his party as embracing all Filipinos—even if virtually no Muslims saw fit to join and NPA guerrillas did not challenge Muslim rebels on their own territory. In the years after their days of youthful optimism, Misuari and Sison went separate ways, abandoning brilliant careers as academic stars at the nation's most prestigious university, hounded by authorities, especially after Marcos imposed martial law in 1972.

Any rift between the nation's top communist and top Moro rebel was secondary compared to much more serious fissures within their movements—fissures that did little to solve problems or attain goals while weakening their organizations as crusaders for change. Theoretically, communists and Muslims might some day battle one another in Mindanao, as they did in the anticommunist slaughter that followed the abortive communist coup of September 30, 1965, in largely Islamic Indonesia, covering most of the sprawling archipelago to the south. Now, however, the most glaring divisions among Filipino rebels were not between Muslims and communists en masse but among rivals within their movements and among followers once unified behind the banners of their causes.

You sense the tensions among Muslims in visits to their base areas on Mindanao, an island of vast jungles and agricultural estates fought over for centuries. Technically, you are in the Philippines, but really you are in the heart of Bangsamoro, the Moro nation, homeland of the Islamic people whose leaders ruled the region by "the swish of the kris"—the dreaded sword with long curved blade—before the Spanish tried but failed to subdue them beginning more than 400 years ago.

The fighters for this land of sweeping low mountains and valleys covered with triple-canopied forest fire American-made weapons that come from all over—including the Armed Forces of the Philippines, the "enemy" they vow to fend from their homeland as fiercely as they fought the Spanish or Americans.

They get the hardware from middlemen, who buy it from corrupt officers, as well as from suppliers in Indonesia, Malaysia and Brunei, nations of Muslims once bound to local sultans and rajahs by blood and religious ties. They never run short of money, it seems, thanks to distant benefactors in Saudi Arabia and other Islamic countries, who pour in the funds needed to keep alive the spirit of Islam in Mindanao against waves of Christian intruders.

The shooting has largely stopped around the base of the Moro Islamic Liberation Front (MILF), known as Camp Abubakar, a complex of seven districts covering 15,000 hectares about 40 miles northeast of the city of Cotabato, across the broad sweep of the Moro Gulf from Zamboanga. Visitors are warned nonetheless not to venture anywhere alone for fear of kidnappers and thieves who also claim to be fighting in the name of Islam. Across the mountains, soldiers from an Islamic "lost command" pillage churches and markets and homes when villagers appear reluctant to give them the requisite donations. There are reports of skirmishes, and bombs go off—sometimes set by one side disguised as another to sabotage peace talks.

At Camp Abubakar, central staging area for the MILF, the troops are primed for more serious matters, for war, as they have been for centuries. After years of training sessions largely unmolested and unchallenged by Filipino troops, the Bangsamoro forces may be more primed, more ready for action than ever, at least to judge from two days I spent walking around with them and visiting their training facility. The soldiers at the base camp of the MILF, not to be confused with Misuari's Moro National Liberation Front (MNLF), talk about *jihad* or holy war as if they were on the front lines of an ongoing shooting conflict as fierce as any in the world. That's partly because many of their leaders were trained in Afghanistan, where *jihad* remains the rallying cry of leaders of warring groups, notably the Taleban fanatics currently in power in Kabul.

In reality, however, there was not that much of a bloody *jihad* going on around Abubakar's rickety outposts, campground, training facility and Islamic university in a faded cement building when I visited the camp in desolate farmland surrounded by jungle-covered, low-lying mountains. Rather, there was a stalemate, an armed truce, in which young guerrillas, many of them armed to the teeth with American infantry equipment, notably M16 rifles and M60 machine guns, M79 grenade launchers and a few antiaircraft artillery pieces, held their own against Philippine forces down the road toward Cotabato, a focal point of both Moro revolt and government efforts at combating it.

The truce reflected efforts at achieving a lasting peace in keeping with an agreement signed at Tripoli under the watchful eye of Libyan leader

Moammar Khadafy on December 23, 1976, between the Philippines and Misuari's MNLF. The leaders of the MILF swore to abide by the truce even though they were not a party to the talks that culminated in the follow-up agreement negotiated in the Indonesian capital of Jakarta nearly 20 years later.

The MILF's standoffish attitude is a symptom of more than its absence from "the peace process," as it's called here, as in efforts at resolving other protracted conflicts ranging from Ireland to Bosnia to Israel and Palestine. The MILF leader, Hashim Salamat, broke off from Misuari and the MNLF soon after the signing of the Tripoli agreement—but not because he disagreed with it.

Indeed, the new MILF position was for absolutely strict adherence to the terms reached at Tripoli calling for "autonomous" Islamic rule over 13 (now 14) provinces in Mindanao and the Sulu archipelago, plus nine cities. Like Misuari, they were especially adamant in their opposition to a "plebiscite" among local residents to see if they favored autonomous Islamic rule.

The vote, as everyone knew, would be a resounding "no" in well over half the cities and provinces. The reason was that for most of the twentieth century, non-Muslim, Christian Filipinos have been migrating to Mindanao under a series of promotional efforts that go back to the Spanish colonial era, got fresh impetus under American rule after 1900 and intensified when the Philippines gained independence in 1946. All Islamic leaders—MNLF, MILF, extremists, moderates—claim that a plebiscite would be utterly unfair given the "invasion" of their turf by "outsiders," non-Muslims streaming down from Luzon, the large northern island, and the Visayas, the central islands just above Mindanao.

The "new" arrivals, a majority of them second or third generation, say just as fiercely that they are here, have the right to vote and should be able to cast their ballots against rule by Islamic leaders. They all talk in their original regional languages, socialize with one another and frankly look down on Muslims as social and economic inferiors who, they believe, are out to cheat them, extort "donations" and "protection" money or, in worst-case scenarios, as shown by the headlines every day, kidnap and kill.

In the MILF base camp, MILF officers indoctrinate "cadets" through year-round 45-day training courses. MILF soldiers vow "no compromise," no veering from Tripoli, finally approved after Imelda Marcos, at the height of her husband's power under martial law, met Khadafy. Philippine officials, claiming that the agreement to hand over most of Mindanao was a Marcos-era mistake, held out for a deal whereby Misuari would accept some form of autonomy over, say, half the provinces—something the MILF viewed as anathema.

MILF soldiers, when I saw them, made no secret of their suspicion that Misuari might sell out the holy cause. They were committed to holding on to the territory they had, against both the government and the MNLF too, for a complex web of reasons that showed the fragility of any peace, no matter how closely it conformed with Tripoli.

The most obvious reason for the split between the two major Islamic movements is that Salamat takes a strict view of Islamic teachings, in keeping with the worldwide fundamentalist trend. MILF adherents say Misuari, once too leftist, is too secularist for their tastes. They stress the "I" for Islamic, they say, while Misuari prefers the "N" for National—meaning that any government of his would not be all that Islamic. To show their discipline, they have outlawed the use of alcohol and tobacco at Camp Abubakar—and allow only a chosen few to monitor the news on television, otherwise banned for showing material deemed offensive to Islam.

The division between the MILF and the MNLF overflows from religious issues into linguistic and regional ones, reflecting the historic rule of Mindanao by sultans who fought and competed with each other as much as they battled their Spanish colonizers. In the end, these differences may be what count on a grassroots level. Misuari is a Tausug, a people indigenous to Sulu, whereas Salamat is from Maguindanao, the center of MILF power, the province that surrounds Cotabato—and includes the base camp.

People from Maguindanao speak a local language, Maguindanaon, and sometimes the languages of nearby regions, notably Maranaw. They do not, however, understand Tausug or its cousin Yakan, the language of Basilan, the island province between Sulu and Zamboanga. Basilan is also a Misuari stronghold and a focal point of fundamentalist terrorism against the dominant Christians, many of whom still speak Chavacano, which is closely related to Spanish.

At a shop on the main road from which one turns to walk to the MILF base at Camp Abubakar, about ten miles off the road, a merchant told me why the MILF and MNLF could never get along. "We are all Islam, but we are different. I cannot understand them."[4] Lounging around the shop as we talked were half a dozen men, three or four hefting M16s, one or two carrying Chinese-made RPGs (rocket-propelled grenades) and one cradling an M60 machine gun, which he said came from "our factory" but admitted was American-made when I asked to see the serial number.

Outside, banging away with heavy equipment on the road, were several men in civilian clothes whom the MILF soldiers told me belonged to the Philippine army. They were not only out of uniform but also unarmed and unprotected—as part of the ceasefire deal. "They can work on the road through our territory, but they can't send soldiers," said one of my MILF guides. "We are protecting them." There were no glances, greetings, communication between the Philippine army soldiers, from an engineering unit several miles down the road toward Cotabato, and the MILF soldiers.

Talks with both MILF and MNLF leaders on all levels contradict the image that the Philippine government and assorted foreign-aid givers try to give of Mindanao as a great place for investment and development. How could any would-be investor think of plunging seriously into a countryside that might turn into a killing field similar to Bosnia or Afghanistan if the "peace" went awry? What if the MILF refused to support the compromise reached by Misuari and the government? The answer, say optimists, lies in EAGA (East ASEAN Growth Area), an acronym that includes the countries on ASEAN's eastern flank. (They're grouped under yet another acronym, BIMP—Brunei, Indonesia, Malaysia and the Philippines.)

"Investment is up throughout Mindanao," said Noel Kintanar, in the office of President Ramos' special assistant for Mindanao. He attributed the growth to EAGA's role in encouraging trade and investment among member nations. Kintanar came up with figures for foreign investment approaching $2 billion in 1995, some of it for agro-forestry and food-processing around Cotabato.[5] American aid officials funded a program called GEM, Growth with Equity in Mindanao, dedicated to spurring business relationships. Antonio Peralta, a GEM official, saw peace taking hold as economic lures become obvious. "Now the struggle has come to a stalemate with both sides wanting to refine their positions."[6]

The potential for a breakdown in the truce—"stalemate" might be a better word—was so enormous that the MILF was actually trying to improve its image. Walk a mile or two in from the road, accompanied by MILF guides, and one is introduced to El Haji Murad, the MILF vice chairman, in charge of "military affairs." He tosses off enormous figures for the size of the MILF, which he puts at well over 100,000, a figure that is probably best to divide by ten, but what he really is anxious to do is to counter the image of his troops as wanton kidnappers and killers.

"Sometimes we feel we are victims of black propagandists," Murad told me. "They say we are Islamic 'fundamentalists,' but there are two versions of fundamentalism. Something like terrorism is black propaganda, but if it means sticking to the teaching of Islam, we are fundamentalists."[7] Walk another ten miles, along a muddy track impassable to the sturdiest of motor vehicles, on through a village where many of the MILF soldiers live with their families, and one comes upon the training center presided over by Benjie Midtimbang, who trained, along with Haji Murad, with a rebel group in Afghanistan.

"We call these men Mujahadeen," said Midtimbang, invoking the word for Islamic freedom fighters from Afghanistan to the Middle East. He referred to members of the Philippine armed forces as "the enemy." No, "we do not believe in making war," he said, but there was no doubt he was ready. "If we are forced, we will fight to the last drop of blood."[8] Considering the absence of any trace of Philippine authority, that's a vow no one would dismiss as rhetoric. Periodically, MILF guerrillas skirmish with Philippine troops who they say are intruding into their zone. Government and MILF forces both claim to have inflicted losses on each other.

The sense of danger worsened when I got to Jolo, the capital of Sulu, a short flight from Zamboanga and the stronghold of Misuari and his MNLF, several months before Misuari returned to Jakarta for the last round of talks in 1996. The commander of the Philippine National Police on the island knocked on the door of the dingy rooming house where I had checked in and wanted to know what I was doing. "I've been here seven months," Colonel Charlemagne "Charlie" Alejandrino told me. "I have never seen a foreign journalist."[9]

Charlie was not dropping by to kick me out, to send me back to Zamboanga, whence I had flown several hours before, but to acquaint me with realities. "There have been killings in the past month. If you look at the culture, it is only here where the people were not subdued. There was only an agreement with the American government early in this century. The people did not surrender."

To ensure there would be "no incident," the police commander assigned a squad of marines to guard my hotel for the duration of my two-night visit and provided a car with two M16-hefting policemen for excursions around town. Across the central plaza from the hotel, the entrance to Our Lady of Mount Carmel Cathedral testified to the terror that stalks an island province where well-armed guerrillas hold much of the territory against a reinforced brigade of Philippine marines as well as more than 1,000 national policemen.

"On 29 February at 3:30 A.M. they poured gasoline on the front door and started a fire," said the Reverend Robert Layson, parish priest. "People outside smelled the gasoline and started shouting. They did not do extensive damage to the church except for the front door and the ceiling. We used to ask for security only during the masses," but now marines guarded the cathedral round the clock. The priest still conducted services every day at 5 P.M., but he did a shortened version to make sure worshippers were out of there, on their way home, by 5:30 P.M.

"Extortion is rampant, killing is every day," said the priest. "Who's behind it, we really don't know. Our people are very sad and angry and scared." Minutes later, in a homily, he reminded his flock of what everyone already knew: "Killings have been going on almost every day, and most of the victims are Christians."[10]

By 6 P.M., the square and surrounding market areas, where terrorists were known to lurk and occasionally fire on shoppers, were empty. Jolo, an historic port, hub of inter-island trade, once bustling through the night, was now a ghost town. Theoretically a ceasefire prevailed, but Misuari threatened to break it any time the marines moved against his troops, who controlled most of the countryside beyond Jolo. "Many of those who say they want peace have a guilty conscience," said Misuari as he received me at a meeting of his top aides. "They have guilty consciences because they have committed crimes here."[11]

Driven in the police commander's car, I had caught up with Misuari in an MNLF meeting hall near the main mosque in the center of Jolo after the police guards had established liaison with the MNLF under the terms of the truce. Misuari had just returned to Sulu after "preliminary" talks with government negotiators in Zamboanga. He was spending several days psyching up his followers, planning for the next round of talks—and wondering how soon his troops would go to war again. He gave the impression that he would not return to Jakarta as long as the MILF demanded nothing short of Islamic autonomy over the region, as promised in the Tripoli talks 20 years earlier. He was talking as tough as the MILF.

"We get arms from the Armed Forces of the Philippines," Misuari told me, explaining why the MNLF types surrounding the building were sporting American-made weaponry along with some Chinese-made AK-47 rifles. "If I have money, I can buy weapons any time of day." He claimed he got the money from "donations" and denied he was financed mainly by the Organization of Islamic Conference, assumed to be the major source of MNLF funding.[12]

"OIC support is just symbolic," said Misuari, who had spent most of his time since concluding the deal at Tripoli in the Red Sea port of Jeddah in a residential/headquarters complex set up for him by his Saudi hosts conveniently near OIC headquarters. "The OIC will rebuild this mosque," he said, pointing out the window toward Jolo's leading place of worship, several hundred yards from the cathedral. "Look at the dome. You can see where the mosque was hit by shells."

The sight of the mosque inspired Misuari to conjure the memory of the greatest battle in recent memory between MNLF and government forces: the fighting in 1974 in which the MNLF overran the town. "We controlled this city for two days," said Misuari. "Their tanks, their reinforcements came from the sea. We would have conquered them completely, but all the people were fleeing. They were afraid our shells would hit them. They begged us to stop." As it was, Misuari's warriors burned down much of the town before fading into the surrounding jungle. His troops now held the city under a kind of siege, but he blamed the government for ratcheting up tensions. "The purpose is to create a siege mentality in order to create the atmosphere for an anti-terrorism act."

Misuari charged that the marines deliberately staged attacks and incidents, including a recent battle around a mosque outside of the town in which 11 people were killed. He angrily denied that the victims were members of Abu Sayyaf, an extremist MNLF breakaway group blamed for most of the troubles. "They have been portrayed as people associated with terrorist activities. It was the government which is at fault. People went to the mosque for victory celebrations. They were massacred inside. The armed forces were claiming they were Abu Sayyaf. We think they were innocent."

Misuari recounted how he formed the MNLF in 1968 after an especially macabre plot in which more than 30 Islamic trainees, Tausugs recruited from Sulu, were killed after refusing to join in a scheme concocted by then-President Ferdinand Marcos for infiltrating Sabah, the Malaysian state on the northeast corner of Borneo. Marcos' campaign reflected the view, not forgotten by Philippine expansionists, that Sabah belonged to the Philippines, since the sultan of Sulu had ruled the whole region, albeit tenuously, before the Spanish arrived in the sixteenth century. "All of them had relatives in Sabah," said Misuari. "They did not know what they were being trained for. When they learned, they naturally refused. They could not kill their own people."

Most of the victims were shot on Corregidor, the island at the mouth of Manila Bay where they were being trained, and were dumped into the sea. The killings were revealed in March 1968 when one of the trainees, bruised, battered and barely alive, buoyed by a log, was rescued by a Christian fisherman. Marcos' arch-foe, Benigno Aquino, then a senator, made a huge issue of the massacre, selling himself as a defender of all Filipinos, Muslim as well as Christian. Misuari, from his aerie at the University of the Philippines, pounced on the cause. "For nine days afterward we demonstrated in front of Malacañang," said Misuari. "I was still teaching. I was sitting in the park outside Malacañang correcting papers."[13]

Four years later, two weeks before Marcos had declared martial law on September 21, 1972, Misuari resigned his university post and "went underground," mobilizing for war. He saw the struggle against the Armed Forces of the Philippines as part of a sequence of battles that have raged periodically from Spanish colonial times, intensifying after the Americans drove out the Spanish in 1898. "We started war with the Americans in 1902," he reminded me. "Your forces killed more than 600 people in Sulu in 1906." In the United States, the Colt 45 was developed and manufactured in response to the need for a revolver to combat the Moros. General John Pershing—"Black Jack Pershing," the future American commander in World War I—led a force in which he was the lone survivor. "Black Jack Pershing said, 'How can you fight a people who loves death more than life,'" said Misuari. "We fought against the Americans for more than 40 years."[14]

At City Hall, the mayor of Jolo, Soud Tan, did not think the MNLF was that much of a threat. "They can fight for two or three months, no more," he said. "They do not have the resources. They are very poor." Tan, of mixed Chinese and Sulu heritage, admitted, however, that much of what Misuari said was true. He looked from his desk toward a photograph of the governor of the Autonomous Region of Muslim Mindanao (ARMM), formed during Corazon Aquino's presidency with a grand headquarters complex in Cotabato after a plebiscite in which only four provinces, including Sulu, agreed to accept its authority as an entity under the Philippine government.

ARMM represents an attempt at compromise on the principles of Tripoli—a step on the way, perhaps, to creation of an "autonomous" Muslim region that still must bow to Manila. Muslim rebels despise it as a cesspool of corruption, much of it from foreign aid programs that support the ARMM as a device to please the central government while showing goodwill toward Muslims. "The governor of ARMM never comes here," said Tan. "He does not care about us. He is no good. Everybody is corrupt. Everybody has a story. They say we have the longest road in the world. Here they are always building it. The money for the road goes into the hands of officials."[15]

A Muslim descendant of a Chinese trader and a Moro woman, Tan had no doubt the guerrillas got their guns from the armed forces. "Here you can buy weapons. Where can you get guns except from the Philippine government? They cannot account for firearms." Even without arms, he assured me, the Moros would not surrender. Moro warriors, he knew, have fought on empty stomachs, with virtually no fresh ammunition. "People here in Sulu are fond of fighting," he said. "They are not afraid to kill. Perhaps it's part of their survival. There were lots of Americans who were kidnapped and killed here in colonial times." Farmers no longer planted rice, fearing war would engulf the fields. "Nobody is farming here any more. People here prefer to bear arms than ploughs."

The mayor's estimate, however, was not quite correct. Misuari's defiance was a bargaining ploy, a front that gave him the upper hand when it came to negotiating for perquisites and power in Jakarta. Misuari was soon ready to yield to "realities"—and other inducements. Under the "peace agreement" that ended the fourth round of talks in Jakarta in August 1996, the government would form a Southern Philippines Council for Peace and Development (SPCPD) within a special zone covering the 14-province area and nine cities agreed on in Tripoli. The failure of the MNLF to achieve a real independent state was papered over by unofficial admissions that the formula was "a compromise, a transition toward genuine autonomy under the Tripoli agreement."[16]

The fate of ARMM was reserved in the agreement for a second phase, when "the people of the concerned areas" would decide by plebiscite two years later if they wanted to join an autonomous government. The agreement sought, with understandable vagueness, to mollify Muslim fears of loss of the region at the polls to Christian "invaders" by stipulating that congress "may" (not "will") enact a law stipulating "that clusters of contiguous-Muslim-dominated municipalities voting in favor of autonomy" form a new province or provinces within the autonomous region.[17]

Misuari, meanwhile, would more than recognize the current ARMM; he would run for ARMM governor in the election already set for September 9, 1996, a week after the signing of the agreement in Manila. Since the four ARMM provinces, notably Sulu, were largely MNLF territory, Misuari coasted to victory with 86 percent of the votes. Next, Ramos appointed him SPCPD chairman, a post that gave him tremendous leverage over government funds throughout the region. As the first payoff for Misuari's cooperation, the government pledged $200 million for projects within ARMM. Part of the money would go for new jet airports in Sulu and Tawi Tawi, ARMM provinces and the centers of Misuari's strength. The new ARMM governor also was given a commuter jet that ferried him and his aides to planning sessions in Manila and meetings around the country.

"Of course, it's not a perfect arrangement for us," Misuari conceded when I found him in the lobby of the Manila Midtown Hotel, his favorite hangout now that he had emerged from rebellion. "That's all the situation would allow." Busy kowtowing to members of the Ramos government as well as potential investors, Misuari was anxious to get across a sense of security and tranquility in a region where killings and kidnappings were still daily fare in the papers. "These incidents are old grudges," he reasoned. "They are right now the last spasm of a dying era."[18]

Misuari did not think that there would be much trouble about living up to the most important element of the peace—merging the MNLF's 10,000 or so arms-carrying soldiers into the Armed Forces of the Philippines. The terms, though, were vague. After absorbing 5,750 MNLF members as regulars, the government would work to "ensure the eventual integration of the maximum number of the remaining MNLF forces into the Regional Security Forces and other agencies and instrumentalities of the government."[19]

When or how the MNLF would integrate was problematic, whatever was written on paper. Misuari gave the impression that some of his followers were not about to surrender their weapons. "During the initial integration, they require us to keep our firearms," he said. "We are to use our own firearms when necessary. We have our own separate units"—within the Armed Forces of the Philippines.[20]

There were other problems, too. Although "everybody would like to see integration as soon as possible," Misuari had to see when or if the government would make good on its pledges. It was one thing for Ramos to promise this or that and another for the bureaucrats to act. Soon Misuari was complaining that he had almost no funds, and investment was slow, too. He faced a stern deadline. The first phase of the agreement was to last only three years. If he failed to bring about real change in that period, his prestige among Moros, his power, his titles, the agreement itself, would be in jeopardy.

Some influential political figures doubted if Misuari would do much. "We are worried about his willingness to talk to people," said Governor Zacharia Candao, a scion of Maguindanao province. "Misuari in the past was always abroad. Unless he develops a working relationship with the four governors of ARMM, his administration will not be effective."[21]

Members of the rival MILF were less likely to come to terms. "The MILF is going to have a separate peace," said Misuari. "They have given us their assurances they will cooperate," but the instinct of the MILF was to charge them with sellout and betrayal, to resolve never to surrender and keep up the revolt. After weeks of hit-and-run attacks in which more than 150 people were killed and thousands forced to flee from areas that the MILF regarded as its territory, the government and the MILF signed a new ceasefire on July 18, 1997. Two months later, on September 16, after still more skirmishes, they agreed on "guidelines" for the ceasefire, including a ban on deployment of forces by either side into disputed areas. The next day, two MILF guerrillas were killed in a fight with government troops north of Zamboanga.[22]

The pressure was on both sides to talk seriously. "If there is any way we can strike agreement with the MILF to bring peace to the area, we will try," said Candao, as busy promoting new investment in his province as he was in persuading his numerous contacts on both sides to get along for the common good.[23]

How long any agreement would hold was open to question. At the time I was talking to Misuari and Candao, fighting between the MILF on the island province of Basilan illustrated the difficulties. "The MNLF wants to keep the peace," said a top MNLF commander, Jann Jakilan, as MNLF units fought alongside government forces against MILF guerrillas. The harder the MNLF fought on behalf of the government, however, the more determined was the MILF to keep up the revolt around a remote village named Tipo Tipo, up a dirt road in Basilan Island, across an 8-mile-wide strait from the southwestern Mindanao port of Zamboanga.[24]

"The MILF are putting forces into Basilan," a Philippine Army colonel, Edmund Pocado, told me in November 1996 as his troops scoured the area. "The people don't want Basilan to become a battleground, but the MILF seems to have chosen it." Commander Jakilan, a 23-year veteran of revolt, walked unarmed with Philippine Army officers and civilian officials to the village, but his troops, uniformed and heavily armed, remained in a separate camp a mile or so away, supposedly ready to integrate with the army. "Our forces will still exist until such time as the transition is completed," said Jakilan, who had studied engineering in Manila before dedicating his life to the Moro struggle.[25]

Jakilan did not view the signing of the peace—or the election of Misuari as governor of the ARMM—as a sellout brought about by promises of aid and investment. "This negotiated agreement is the fruit of our revolution," he maintained. "Our goal now is the regular autonomous government"—an entity that he made clear should extend over the entire area agreed on at Tripoli.

There was, however, another threat: Christians in Mindanao—several million of whom have migrated to the region over the past century—view any deal with the Muslims as a concession to terrorism. Christian vigilantes have vowed to attack Muslim forces in retaliation not only for the peace deal but for any number of kidnappings and killings by the MILF, the MNLF or breakaway units.

Misuari, in his headquarters in Cotabato, was not perturbed. "I don't see any room for any other group getting more power and influence," he said, dismissing the MILF as serious competition and challenging Christian vigilante propaganda as isolated. "It's the MNLF that is going to have the biggest say over Mindanao and the islands."[26] By early 1997, however, he was less confident. His own accord with the government had "not yet produced anything substantial," he said when asked to help in talks with the MILF. "I could not show them any example."[27]

On the ground in Tipo Tipo, the optimism was not catching on either. A few miles away lay the burned-out shells of two Philippine Army "mestizo" tanks—armored cars with tank-like turrets and cannon mounted on top. Two days earlier, government soldiers had fired at guerrillas, killing one. A few days before that, several government soldiers were killed, this time by MNLF soldiers who claimed to have mistaken them for guerrillas.

The Basilan governor, Jerry Salapudden, leading medical workers to the village to tend to more than 12,000 refugees from the fighting, saw peace with the MNLF as the only way to begin solving the problem. "They are not coming down to surrender," said the governor, who had fought on the MNLF side for 12 years before defecting to the government in 1984. "The only way is to integrate our forces." How, then, do you get them to turn in their weapons? "We will give them new weapons," he replied. "They will turn in their old ones. That is the way." As for the MILF, "Together we will defeat them"—the same promise officials had been making in Mindanao since colonial times.[28]

The parallel between Misuari and Sison, if it failed to endure in ideological principles, lives on in the suspicion that Joma, like Nur, may also have mellowed. The mellowing of Sison, like that of Misuari, appears to have begun when Joma accepted political asylum, and a new base for the Communist Party of the Philippines (CPP), in the Netherlands several months after the 1986 People Power revolution. The self-exile of Joma was significant as a sign that Aquino's idea of "people power" was to mobilize the masses for her benefit and that of her allies, not that of the people at large, as venerated by Joma.

The great irony is that Aquino, a few weeks after coming to power, freed Joma from prison at Fort Bonifacio, where Marcos had jailed him during martial law for violation of the antisubversion law that Aquino later repealed. Joma was on a speaking tour in Europe, garnering support for his revolution, when Aquino's government filed new charges of inciting revolution and rebellion and canceled his passport. Joma and his wife Julieta moved to the Dutch university city of Utrecht, courtesy of the government of the Netherlands, which provided them a living allowance as political refugees. They set up a new headquarters there from which Joma still purported to run the revolt. In exile, Joma dreamed of returning to central Luzon, where he would remold his Mao-style revolution, topple the moneyed elite, drive out their American sponsors and elevate himself to national power.

Jose Maria Sison, chairman not of a ragtag band of jungle guerrillas and urban ideologues but of a politburo and central committee with power over an entire country—might his dream some day come to pass? Might Sison and Misuari clasp hands again—Joma as chairman of the People's Republic of the Philippines, Nur as chairman of an Autonomous (Islamic) Republic of Mindanao? Certainly stranger turns of events have happened in Asia over the generation in which both have been fighting. Certainly, too, Joma, since his youth as a student and faculty member at the University of the Philippines, has shown the driving force, the cruelty along with the idealism, that exemplifies the lives of all successful leaders of popular revolts, *real* revolts, that is, not ersatz exercises in people power.

It was Joma, more than anyone else, who saw the need for a no-nonsense, Maoist-style leadership of the Communist Party of the Philippines. It was Joma who paid tribute to Mao in 1968, nearly eight years before Mao's death, by founding a new CPP on Mao's seventy-fifth birthday, December 26. Like Pol Pot, the leader of the Khmer Rouge scourge that swept Cambodia in the 1970s, Joma spurned the hackneyed cant of members of the old Communist Party, of which he was a restive member. Instead, he derived his inspiration from China's rampaging Red Guards, the foot soldiers of Mao's Great Cultural Revolution of the 1960s.

Was it entirely by coincidence that Sison and Misuari founded their organizations in the same year? Was Joma influenced by the example of

Misuari, who had set up the MNLF eight months earlier? Perhaps also inspired by the spectacle of Muslim rebels in the jungle, Joma moved quickly to establish the New People's Army, led by the romanticized Commander Dante, Bernabe Buscayno, that would seize control, Mao-style, of the countryside.

Joma was determined to do it right. He wanted to make up for the mistakes of the old, now discredited Huks—the Hukbong Mapagpalaya Ng Bayan or People's Liberation Army, successor to the World War II Hukbalahap, the People's Anti-Japanese Army. Huk leader Luis Taruc had betrayed the cause by surrendering in 1954—in an interview with, of all people, Benigno Aquino, then a sensational young journalist. Taruc's guerrillas had persisted since then in Luzon, feeding off protection money from GI bars in Angeles City, assassinating recalcitrant mayors and other foes, but were not getting very far, despite exaggerated claims.[29]

All the while Joma was awaiting the chance to take charge of a movement divided then, as it was years later, between those who wanted to attack the cities, those who wanted to build up in the countryside, and those who simply wanted to kill and extort funds in the name of the cause. Joma was in an excellent position. Since graduating from the University of the Philippines in 1960 he had emerged not only as national chairman of the Kabataang Makabayan, the "below-ground" Patriotic Youth under the aegis of the anti-American Labor Party, but also was secretary-general of the equally militant Movement for the Advancement of Nationalism.

Joma was full of revolutionary fire when he met in one of those typical "back room" interviews with a Time-Life correspondent in 1967. "We will develop the people's democratic power," he promised earnestly. The goal: "to spread nationalism across the masses—from the cities to the countryside, on all levels of society, from the wealthy here in Manila to the poorest peasant in the tiniest barrio." The correspondent described Sison as having "leveled at me his horn-rimmed gaze" before telling him, "We have been caught in the grip of American imperialism too long."[30]

For all the coffeehouse clichés, Joma no doubt believed in serious killing for the cause. Although Joma was no Pol Pot, by the time he and Commander Dante were arrested in 1976, they had not only built on the base of the old Huk movement in Luzon but had managed what the Huks had never accomplished—to spread their movement to the Visayas and to Mindanao. The armed strength of the New People's Army by then was well above 10,000 men, and it was growing at an alarming rate, so much so that Marcos staunchly blamed the NPA for the Plaza Miranda bombing of August 21, 1971. (Years later, NPA defectors revealed that Marcos was right. Joma himself had ordered the attack in which nine people were killed by twin blasts intended for opposition political candidates, all of whom survived, albeit critically wounded.)[31]

The specter of rising communist revolt provided the pretext for martial law a month after Plaza Miranda. The revolt also attracted hundreds of millions of dollars in American advice and other aid, strengthening the armed forces while enriching its leaders as they pursued guerrillas through the countryside. The communists, however, were on the verge of splits that had as much to do with weakening them as did the efforts of Marcos' army and his American ally. The struggle, in gestation when Joma was suffering in an escape-proof, bribe-proof cell at Fort Bonifacio, was whether the NPA should settle for armed struggle in the countryside or take on central power in the cities, notably Metro Manila.

The divisions openly erupted around 1990, while Joma was in exile, increasingly remote, suspected of living a comfortable life befitting his background as a member of yet another property-owning family. Commander Dante, after the People Power revolution and his own release, defected to the government side and was soon running an agricultural cooperative in Tarlac Province, source of the wealth of the Cojuangco family, which assiduously counseled Cory Aquino against land reform. Contradictions in the movement, "underground" in the Communist Party of the Philippines (CPP) and the New People's Army, "above ground" in the National Democratic Front, including Kabataang Makabayan, were too glaring for a cover-up.

In typical Filipino style, the debate erupted into a great semantic exercise whose charges and countercharges, dialectics and dialogue, mingled the verbiage of the international communist movement with that of the armchair intellectuals who had provided so much inspiration for the radicals. (Like Joma, many were the offspring of rich, landowning families in Ramos' native province of Pangasinan in northern Luzon.) The two sides gave themselves names. "Reaffirmists" reaffirmed the strategy and tactics of Joma, advocating limited people's war in the countryside; "rejectionists" rejected the strategy of the reaffirmists, calling for all-out war in the cities.

The furor within the party, typical of power struggles masked by lofty manifestoes, bore little relevance to the crying needs of peasant farmers and workers. "One-Man Monopoly in Party Policy Matters," was the accusatory subtitle of a revealing statement by rejectionists on "party unity and leadership processes." The document attacked a paper on "our urgent tasks" drafted by "Amado Guerrero," Joma's code name, and approved by the Central Committee: "The whole Party upheld its correctness, rectified our errors. But then, this malady of one-man monopoly in Party affairs is precisely what afflicts our Party today."[32]

The new chairman, code-named "Armando Liwanag" (Beloved Light), had upset the rejectionists with an attack entitled "Reaffirm Our Basic Principles and Rectify the Errors." Liwanag was assumed to be another *nom de guerre* for Guerrero (warrior) Sison, said to have reemerged as chairman in 1992.

The writers of this rejectionist diatribe accused the "husband-and-wife tandem," Joma and Julieta, of trying "to make the whole Party swallow all their papers and suppress even the slightest opposition." It seemed significant that this passage was signed by "The Standing Group–Visayas Commission"—an indication of the split in the party in the sugarland of Negros, an island in the Visayas dominated by enormous sugar plantations whose owners treated their workers as serfs. Sugarland was fertile field for an NPA revolt—and for squabbles, sometimes bloody, among factions.

The so-called Visayas Commission, after going through the personal complaints that dominated the mentality of its members, unleashed criticism that applied to Negros but had nationwide application. Liwanag—or Sison—advanced "dangerous proposals in our present conduct of People's War," charged a "critique." The critique made much of his call for "immediate dissolution of large formations such as the battalions and companies of the NPA in the regions and fronts." That concept was blasted as "nowhere to be found in MTT's Strategy and Tactics of People's War."[33] (MTT was Mao Tse-tung, idolized by reaffirmists, less so by rejectionists, unaware that Beijing prefers the spelling "Mao Zedong.")

In the rejectionist view, the flaw was "the danger of feeding small forces to the large concentrations of enemy troops" and limiting "our flexibility and initiative in employing guerrilla warfare to annihilate the enemy one by one. Liwanag's "theory" of spreading the NPA's 25,000 armed members evenly against 250,000 members of the armed forces of the Philippines was seen as "military equalitarianism [*sic*]" that Mao himself had blamed for "setbacks and losses in the experience of the Chinese Red Army." The result, the rejectionists predicted, would be "great losses in our army, organized masses and front territories."[34]

The rejectionist strategy, however, precipitated the losses; the armed forces, equipped by the United States, advised by men such as Colonel Rowe and spurred on during Aquino's rule by Fidel Ramos, now secretary of defense, wiped out the guerrillas whenever they exposed themselves in large formations. The rejectionist campaign was especially disastrous in Negros. "Rejectionists attacked the towns," said Edgar Cadagat, a journalist close to the CPP in Bacolod, the leading city of Negros. "They embarked on an adventurist policy. They were not ready to fend off counter-attacks. The government got back, carried out widespread operations and defeated them."[35]

counter-attacks. The government got back, carried out widespread operations and defeated them."[35]

The military response came after a decade of turmoil in Negros, much of it triggered by Marcos' decision to entrust the sugar monopoly to the island's richest hacienda owner, Roberto S. Benedicto ("RSB"), who shared the wealth with the first family in Manila. RSB manipulated the price of sugar, driving lesser hacienda owners out of business, playing the sugar markets while stockpiling reserves. Profits dwindled and production ceased in many areas in the early 1980s as prices plummeted.

Thus the NPA had no problem recruiting followers for a rampage of killing and burning. Numerous clergymen, including the bishop, Antonio Fortich, an esteemed figure from a landowning family, firmly sympathized with their cause. "There was a time when they really controlled the whole mountainside," said Fortich. "The NPA was sending special communications to the planters of the sugar industry. They said, 'You are not paying minimum wage. You rectify. If not, we will resort to drastic measures.'"[36] One priest, the Reverend Francisco Fernandez, left the clergy in 1980 and took to the hills. He led the guerrillas through much of the mayhem and is now general secretary of the National Democratic Front (NDF), the umbrella group for the entire mainstream left.

The guerrilla struggle for Negros in the 1980s captured worldwide attention. The arrest in May 1983 of nine churchmen, three of them foreigners, including the Reverend Niall O'Brien, all charged in the killing of a local mayor, fueled a crusade that led to the publication of six books, including O'Brien's prison diary.[37] Let loose while their Filipino brethren remained behind bars, the foreigners insisted on going back to jail. Reincarcerated in a military prison, the three escaped after an officer said they were having an easy time. As a condition of surrender, they demanded to go to the same hideous jail as the six Filipinos.

"It was a bit of a hellhole," said O'Brien, freed with the others in July 1984. "I picked up amoeba [dysentery]." The priests also garnered tremendous publicity—not only for themselves but also for the issue of exploitation and suffering on Negros. "The Filipinos allowed the whole world to see us," said O'Brien. "TV crews were there." A Columban colleague of Olongapo's crusading Father Shay Cullen, O'Brien concerns himself with the issues as editor of a Columban magazine in Bacolod, his home for 30 years. "The poverty is a poverty of lost culture and history," said O'Brien, who graduated from Dalgan Park in Dublin just as Shay Cullen was entering. "People are living on the edge of life."[38]

The exploitation had begun under the Spanish, who inflicted all manner of torture, including forced marches bearing crosses unto death, on those who defied the Catholic faith or otherwise showed the slightest sign of resistance. A ruthless Spanish governor in 1856 ordered the massacre of hundreds of villagers in the mountains about 50 miles south of Bacolod—a style of suppression perpetuated under Marcos-era martial law and afterward, under Aquino, who may not have known what was really going on while Fidel Ramos, as defense secretary, ordered the dirty work.

The agent of the worst slaughter, Operation Thunderbolt, was Brigadier General Raymundo Jarque, who climaxed his campaign against the NPA in 1991 with helicopter attacks on NPA hideouts and strongholds in the mountains and valleys, forcing the flight of 35,000 refugees. "He said he was fulfilling the orders of Aquino to wipe them out," said Bishop Fortich, now retired and living in a church home near O'Brien's residence in Bacolod. "I was receiving them here. He said he wants to clear the whole place." O'Brien doubts if martial law under Marcos was so cruel. "About 800 died, many from disease and malnutrition. People have to move. They sell the animals. Marcos wouldn't have gotten away with that. The NPA had to recede back into the inner mountains. This was a way to get Ramos elected"—as happened with Ramos' victory next year.[39]

By the mid-1990s, the CPP was dormant in Bacolod, a city of 400,000 that grew on sugar, fell into depression as sugar prices plunged worldwide, then revived—for the benefit of the owners, not the workers who fled to the city in an often futile search for jobs. Espousing the cause of thousands of underemployed or seasonally employed laborers, the reaffirmists under Francisco Fernandez got an amazing break when General Jarque, no less, defected to the NPA in late 1995.

As is so often the case in squabbles in the Philippines, the root cause was a bloody family quarrel among local landlords—relatives and neighbors living behind high-walled estates in a pleasant seaside town named Pulupandan, a 30-minute drive south of Bacolod. One of them, an attorney, accused his brother-in-law, the mayor, of plotting with Jarque, now retired, to rob tons of prawns from a fishpond claimed by both the attorney and the mayor. The attorney charged that Jarque had threatened to kill him—and had his men murder someone else. The armed forces had delayed Jarque's pension while the case made its way through the courts.

"Jarque lost any shade of hope the case could be won so he turned for justice elsewhere," said a radical priest, the Reverend Ireneo "Bebe" Gordoncillo.[40] The general who once killed civilians was welcomed into the CPP fold. He swore he was only acting on orders previously and now wanted to make up with his former foe. The episode reflected the wildness of a country where salvagings and kidnappings, corruption and thievery are the stuff of daily headlines. Ramos, as president, did nothing; he issued no orders to capture Jarque. Rather, he pleaded for his former subordinate to "come to his senses" and change his mind.

The ultimate twist was the suspicion among reaffirmists that the rejectionists were making a deal with the government. After defecting to the NPA, Jarque spread the word that the rejectionist leader Arturo Tabara was "an asset of the military." Tabara had his own Revolutionary Workers Party, backed up by a 500-member Revolutionary Proletarian Army in Negros. In April 1997, Tabara's force allied with the Alex Boncayao Brigade, named for a slain worker-fighter. The brigade had broken off from the NDF in May 1993 when its leaders in Manila advocated urban warfare. For all the noble words, the reality is the divisions within the CPP mean it is not likely to move beyond statements and demonstrations for years.

"What happened has been a very apparent reduction in military activities attributed to the party," said Satur Ocampo, one of the most knowledgeable veterans of the movement. "As part of the rectification of political-military errors, it was resolved that regular formations were dissolved. The operative principle was there should be only platoon-sized regular formations and all other units must return to squad size to carry out political work. This is mainstream."[41]

Ocampo received me in an ironic setting—a pleasant home in Quezon City's Heroes' Hill district once favored by American counterinsurgency experts. His comfortable residence, owned by the family of his wife, Carolena "Bobbie" Malay, also an activist and lecturer at the University of the Philippines, had been the compound of the CIA land reform operative, Edward Lansdale, who had propped up dubious Philippine leaders in the 1950s before turning his questionable talents to Vietnam. Ocampo, arrested in 1976, served nine years and three months before escaping in May 1985 to the National Press Club overlooking the Pasig River. He and his wife were arrested again in July 1989; they shared a cell for 22 months until her release nearly a year before his.

"From the middle '80s there were large-scale attacks," said Ocampo, now an attraction at radical rallies. "The assessment was the gain of the attacks was less than the cost from '86 to '87"—before the armed forces under Ramos counterattacked. Now he believed "the rejectionists are in a dilemma." He estimated their numbers at 2,000 armed guerrillas nationwide, less than half the regular NPA. "The government recognizes the growing strength of the NPA. They are increasing deployment of troops in anticipation of armed struggle by next year."[42]

The buildup formed the backdrop to yet another startling similarity between the CPP/NPA Muslim revolts—that is, a "peace process." The peace process between Manila and the CPP, however, has staggered even more crazily than the one between the government and the Moros. After the Edsa revolution in 1986, Ocampo surfaced as chief negotiator for the NDF, representing the "above-ground" and "below-ground" apparatus of the CPP and the NPA. Since the CPP was now technically legal, the talks had a fighting chance but broke down as real fighting intensified.

Talks were on track again in 1994, however, when Luis Jalandoni, chief negotiator for the NDF; Joma, as "consultant"; and Howard Dee, ex-ambassador to the Vatican and chairman of the government panel, signed the Joint Agreement on Security and Immunity Guarantees in the Dutch city of Neuwegein. The agreement was to take effect one month before the start of formal talks in Brussels on June 2, 1995, after the May national elections.

There was a neat parallel between the peace process with the NDF and the one with the MNLF. At first, rejectionists said the government had to negotiate with all the opposition groups, including rejectionists. Like the MILF, the rejectionists dropped their insistence on a role at the talks, saying they would judge the results on their merits. There was, however, a difference: the MILF had spurned pleas to send an observer to the talks in Jakarta whereas the rejectionists were never invited to sit at the table.

Still, there was hope. The negotiators were to hammer away at four major areas set as an "agenda" in "the first preliminary agreement" of September 1992. These included (1) international humanitarian law and human rights; (2) social and economic reform, including agrarian, labor and environmental issues; (3) political and constitutional reforms; and (4) cessation of hostilities—with NDF members permitted to carry arms for "self-defence."[43]

The last was the real sticking point, the one that prevented the talks from getting off the ground, just as the issue of plebiscite in Mindanao and the Sulu archipelago frustrated lasting peace between Manila and the Moros. What would count as hostilities? How would each side respond if the other appeared to be taking advantage of such a "cessation," as would certainly happen? Such questions were temporarily set aside after Sotero Llamas, the NDF commander in Bicol, was arrested on May 17, two weeks before the talks were to begin.

The "process" quickly derailed. Both sides turned the arrest of Llamas into a pretext for avoiding each other. The NDF demanded his release, claiming he was listed as an NDF "consultant" for the talks under his code name, Tabo Reyes, and had immunity. A debate ensued on whether Llamas and Reyes were one and the same and whether the appointment was effective, or whether the agreement was effective when the name was submitted. Still, the stage was set; the show was about to go on in Brussels. The NDF, however, refused to attend as long as Llamas was in prison. Ramos said he had no authority to free a man charged with nine crimes, including murder and kidnapping. The curtain rang down before the first number.

While the lines of communications were open, the NDF hoped to broaden its struggle. There were, in early 1996, three main issues: first, the proposal advanced by Senator Enrile, the former defense minister, for an anti-terrorism bill; second, an expanded value-added tax (EVAT), under which the value-added tax in effect for eight years was expanded to 10 percent; and third, an oil-price increase. Such targets were easy. Antiterrorism smacked of an effort at returning to martial law, which Ramos had enforced under Marcos. EVAT and the oil-price increase hit the poor far harder than the rich, who didn't mind paying a few extra pesos here and there while flagrantly avoiding income taxes.

Those issues provided a rallying cry for marches through downtown Manila toward Malacañang Palace. A resuscitated Bayan marshaled a few thousand enthusiasts for a parade in February 1996 to Ayala Bridge, where the marchers halted in orderly fashion for a round of speeches. At the helm was Nathaniel Santiago, Bayan secretary-general and successor to the likes of Joma and Ocampo, who was full of new hope for a revived movement. I met him by the square opposite the downtown post office, a neoclassical structure of the American era, a few hundred yards from Intramuros and across the Pasig River from Escolta, the old Chinese business district. He talked eagerly about the "above-ground" role of Bayan as the CPP's partner in a revolution that was waiting to happen.

"The Philippine left has gone through a process of self-examination, ideological struggles and revitalization," said Santiago as followers straggled into the park before the march. "The left is not divided. In the national democratic process, there are splinter groups. The CPP is holding a rectification movement whose purpose is to repudiate the errors of military adventurism and insurrectionism"—code words for the rejectionist policy. "A few leaders follow the erroneous line. Eventually they were expelled"— the language of a purge. "The splinter group is not more than ten percent." Now everyone, above ground or below, was involved in the "reaffirmation and analysis of Philippine society." Santiago spoke in such an engaging, smiling manner that it was difficult to associate the message with the man.[44]

At 29, however, Santiago was well qualified to inherit the mantle of leader of the Bayan and a future molder of the nation. As a student at nearby Philippine Christian University, he had led 10,000 protesters to the Mendiola Bridge, a flashpoint a few hundred yards from Malacañang Palace, at the height of the People Power revolution. A member of the United Church of Christ, the faith of President Ramos, a small but significant grouping with a reputation for activism, he was expelled from the university two years later for barricading the campus in protest against an increase in matriculation fees. He worked full-time for Bayan and in early 1996 organized a wave of mass protests against the terrorism bill, EVAT and the oil-price hike.

Santiago exaggerated, however, on Bayan's impact. He claimed, with a brash grin, to have created "total paralysis" on February 8 from Mindanao to northern Luzon in a "successful nationwide protest," but the biggest impact was the publicity that night on TV and in the next day's papers. As we strolled through Manila's Chinatown, bystanders, shopkeepers, shoppers, businessmen and workers accepted leaflets and appeared sympathetic but not moved enough to hoist banners or cheer, much less join the parade. Santiago and Crispin Beltran, chairman of the Kilusang Mayo Uno (May First Movement), the "above-ground" union with roots "below ground" in the CPP, were cheered only when they mounted a truck and talked to several hundred of the faithful at Ayala Bridge, over the Pasig River, downstream from the palace.

In an age when Maoism has lost much of its appeal around the world, including China, demonstrators wore Mao buttons with the great helmsman's profile in gold on a red field and olive-drab Mao-style workers' caps—a phenomenon not much seen anywhere else of late. Nobody seemed to espouse the violence that Maoism fed among the zealots of the Great Cultural Revolution in China in the 1960s or among the Khmer Rouge in Cambodia in the 1970s. Those wearing the caps and buttons chatted and smiled as if they were at a festival or indulging in a slightly outrageous fad. Hawkers sold still more of them, the hats clean and folded neat, the pins unscratched, pristine from the shop. When the shouted speeches and grating music ground to a halt, the crowd quickly faded away.

After orating, Beltran offered me his views about the split in the ranks—one that had fostered the rival Bukluran ng Manggagawa sa Pagbabago (Union of Workers for Change) of Filemon "Popoy" Lagman, a rejectionist, brother of a member of congress and former head of the Metro Manila Communist Party. It was a topic that the veteran labor leader, at 63 more than twice the age of most of the people in the crowd, often addressed. He reverted, almost by habit, to the clichés of the great debate, one in which ideologues spend countless hours mulling the question of whether the Philippines is semifeudal or capitalist. Esoteric though such talk might seem, it has a lot to do with whether to wage revolution Mao-style, battling semifeudalism or, as advocated by Lagman and others, on the streets of the cities, taking on the titans of industry and their military protectors head on.

"I am still with the semi-feudal opinion," said Beltran, a one-time taxi driver who joined the movement in 1967 and helped to found the Kilusang Mayo Uno 13 years later. "The solution is the national democratic struggle must be pursued in sort of a national democratic coalition of society. The main target is the bourgeois comprador class. When we fight this class of people, we are fighting the government. The organization of the people is under intensive organizing and political struggle. The CPP is underground in the countryside. They have been weakened because of the internal problems of the left; the downward trend has been arrested."[45]

Why, then, did Joma not come back—in secret, landing dramatically at night from a fishing boat somewhere on the long, ill-defended coastline, joining his cohorts in the jungle, rallying the movement in the field, at the grassroots where it counted? Had he found ideological and other solace in émigré women from Eastern Europe, some of whom he supplied to CPP guests? Did he, truth to tell, prefer the relative luxury of Utrecht, on a Dutch allowance, rounding up funds for the movement, depositing them nobody knew where? Or did he fear that he was at risk for reprisal or salvaging whenever he stepped on Philippine soil for his role in the slaughter at Plaza Miranda all those years ago?

"Joma faces the question of security," said Santiago. "There are leaders historically who work overseas"—Marx in London; Ho in New York, Paris, Moscow and southern China; Kim Il Sung in Khabarovsk; Pol Pot in Paris.[46] The precedents are well known. In the end, though, they went back, as they had to do to lead their revolutions, as Sison also would have to resign himself to doing if his words were to mean anything.

In the meantime, "Joma is not leading day-to-day affairs, he is working with the International Network for Philippine Studies in Utrecht," said Santiago. As if to close the case, Santiago remarked portentously, "Joma has already revealed he was the one who founded the Communist Party of the Philippines"—a "revelation" that was hardly news but may have been good for Joma's fading image. In exile, Joma had the chance to carry on with aid-givers, ideologues, politicos and seminar raconteurs—a spectrum of visitors whom he might never see in the boondocks of his native land.

In looking at the great ideological debate among CPP members and sympathizers, however, one wonders if these people are mesmerized largely by the rhythm of their rhetoric. One might ask the same, to be sure, of the warriors of Bangsamoro, whose oratorical gestures are vastly disproportionate to their actual power. The difference is that the Muslims control large swaths of territory while the NPA exists furtively, in small bands capable of killing, kidnapping and extortion but not much more. Their total strength by the late 1990s was about 5,000 men—down from 26,000 a decade before.

Both movements, however, share a common flaw: they are divided and, all claims to the contrary, likely to remain so. Neither is going to win a war as long as government forces play factions against each other, the extremes against the middle. Perhaps that was why the two best-known leaders of each movement, Misuari and Sison—brothers, "brods," in their halcyon college days—preferred the ease of foreign exile to the hardships of jungle living and jungle fighting at home. The difference was that Misuari had a far larger, richer base.

Like Misuari, however, Joma may have managed the NDF's shows of rhetorical defiance as a ploy. In any event, the months of secret talks between government and NDF negotiators paid off with moves toward yet another deal between government and rebel forces—this time not the Moros but the communists. On March 17, 1997, the two sides sat down again, this time at The Hague, and began yet another lengthy round of talks.

The issues were the same, but some of the characters were a little different. Llamas, granted a reprieve, attended as an NDF representative. The renegade General Jarque, having posted bail of 100,000 pesos in Negros, was a "consultant" to the NDF team. Joma's Julieta led the NDF panel on social and economic reform. This time, to speed up the process, negotiators had two weeks to come up with solutions before moving on to the next item.

Six months later, however, the talks were stalled again. The two sides were still at odds on the first area of discussion, that of human rights. The NDF demanded, among other things, that the government abide by the rules on conduct of war between sovereign states as stipulated by Geneva conventions—a provision that would grant the movement a legitimacy that was totally abhorrent to the government. Some of the negotiators were back in the Philippines, talking secretly but not getting far. General Jarque, still a consultant, appeared to have won a permanent reprieve from prosecution for his defection, advising NDF negotiators in Davao.[47]

Not all the returning NDF negotiators were emissaries of peace. One member of the NDF panel, Fidel Agacoili, was said to have come back with a letter from Sison charging that a "powerful group" in the government had deliberately sabotaged the talks. Soon after his return in September, the NDF stepped up small-scale attacks in southern Luzon and Negros. PNP officials reportedly said the rebels, despite setbacks, had "gained considerable strength and have regained lost arms and territories" in Luzon. In Negros, Tabara's Revolutionary Proletarian Army attacked a patrol, killing two men in a 45-minute battle.[48]

In stage-managing his team, Joma had shown that he knew when to negotiate for personal and political gain rather than wait for change that was not about to happen. Unlike Misuari, however, Sison faced difficulties in finding a place to stay, either home or abroad. The Dutch Alien's Court, in September 1997, refused to grant him permanent asylum after Philippine officials convinced the ministry of justice of the Netherlands of his "terrorist" activities. The decision meant that he would have to appeal to the Dutch supreme court while hunting for another host.[49]

Perhaps the best solution would be for Sison, safeguarded by a truce, to come home—like Misuari, a legitimately anointed leader, a rebel no more. Such acceptance, however, would outrage not only those who had been fighting the NPA but also more radical rebels. Joma's revolutionary foes were even less likely than the MILF to go along with an agreement. Like the Moro extremists, members of the Alex Boncayao brigade and the Revolutionary Workers Party would take up the cause against any compromise construed as surrender to "abusive state agents and diehard capitalists."[50]

EIGHT

"Ten Years On"

The moment you step out of the doors of Ninoy Aquino International Airport, into a swarm of drivers waiting to charge several times the rate of the normal Manila taxis, you feel as though you are walking into cartoonland. You are entering a strip of caricatures, a new face surrounded by comic-book stereotypes. There are the filthy rich. There are the gangsters, the kidnappers, the killers. There are the bargirls and, not always distinguishable from them, the lowly maids. There are the military officers, the police and soldiers, but be careful. They may be one and the same as the filthy rich, or paid killers, or both. Sketch in yourself as the puzzled foreigner, representative of an alien country and a culture that people here have come both to emulate and to hate.

The history of emulation and hatred goes back nearly five centuries, to the killing of Magellan on the beach at Mactan in 1521 after his priests had planted the cross and baptized the natives at nearby Cebu. The difference now is that the foreigners have gone and the targets are shifting. The headlines of Manila's 30 or so daily newspapers may be the world's craziest.

One day you read about a "ghost surgeon"—a distinguished heart doctor who gets his assistants to do the cutting for which he is incompetent without telling the patient beforehand. Or it's a bizarre salvaging, the slaying of a family in a fight for land, or a rush-hour robbery in which the bandits, guns blazing, kill a bank guard and a pedestrian or two. Or it's Imelda, fighting tooth and nail against giving a cent or a peso or a Swiss franc of her purloined, hidden billions. (She refused at one point in 1996 to pay 5.6 million pesos, or about $225,000, owed for refrigerating her late husband's body in his hometown of Batac, holding out, unsuccessfully, for burial in Manila's Heroes' Cemetery.)

The stories go on relentlessly, but there is a common theme beyond that of greed and violence. Through them all runs a current of anti-foreignism—a lot of it anti-Chinese. Suspicion and hatred of the Chinese provides the rationale for waves of kidnapping for ransom—more than 50 cases reported by police in the first three months of 1996. Most of the victims are Filipinos of Chinese descent or Chinese *mestizos,* targeted as Chinese names show up more and more in reports of new wealth and new ventures. A few are foreign passport-holders, as in the case of a Taiwan military attaché's son, a student at the International School, seized in March 1996. The kidnappers demanded more than half a million dollars but settled for a million pesos, not quite $40,000.

Many more members of Filipino-Chinese families are presumed to have been kidnapped and held while their relatives negotiated payoffs in secret. They prefer not to tell police what's happening for fear the kidnappers will murder their quarry or the police will kill someone in a botched rescue attempt. The police say that the families impede rescue efforts by their reluctance, if not downright refusal, to cooperate.

Wealthy families are reported to have stashed payoff money at home in case they need to hand it over in a hurry. They know they will get little sympathy on a mass level. "They are Chinese," a Filipino maid told me. "They have enough. It is not our problem." The kidnappers, however, are not always terribly discriminating. Kidnappings range from big time to penny ante. Just looking well-to-do in a secluded, vulnerable place can be a liability. There are cases of kidnappers holding small children in corners of shopping centers, at pay telephones, settling for payoffs of a few thousand pesos before taking their money and running. (Admittedly, the line between kidnapping and banditry is sometimes blurred.)

The payoffs range all the way up to the national record for ransom—12 million pesos, nearly half a million dollars, for freeing the heir to the fortune of a Filipino-Chinese family in February 1996. The statistics show the risks of trying to foil a kidnapping after the fact. Among 241 kidnapped in 1996, according to the non-governmental Citizens Action Against Crime (CAAC), 23 were killed. The pattern was much the same for 1997—172 kidnapped in the first eight months of the year, said the CAAC, listing nine killed in the first five months.[1]

The big difference was that the kidnappers were greedier than ever. In the first eight months of 1997, 243.6 million pesos, nearly $10 million, was reported to have been collected in ransom. That figure was considerably more than double the 109.9 million pesos' ransom reported paid for all the year before. The CAAC, in its report, noted that ransom totals were "those that are known" and that, "in many cases, ransom payment is unknown."[2]

One of the 1996 victims on the CAAC list was Manuel Ongpin, an architecture student, 19 years old, bearing one of the Manila's best-known names, the son of a wealthy businessman and nephew of two former cabinet members. The kidnappers might have eluded arrest had it not been for the high profile of the victim's family. Sadly, the episode also proved that money and influence do not always talk. The leader of the kidnap gang, high on drugs, may have suspected that the police were after them very soon after seizing Manuel from his car in front of his mother's home in a walled compound at 3 A.M. and stuffing him into their taxi.

Manuel's body, stripped of identification, was discovered beside a secluded road hours later. For days his death was recorded as that of an anonymous salvaging victim, and his body was held in a funeral home south of Manila. Not until the kidnappers asked the boy's father, Luis Ongpin, for his son's ATM banking number did Luis call the Presidential Anti-Crime Commission, an aggregation of doubtful repute run by Vice President Joseph "Erap" Estrada, a former film star and presidential aspirant whom Ramos cannot stand. Luis by then feared Manuel was dead; otherwise the criminals would have tortured the boy into revealing the number.

The "break" came too late—after a friend spotted Manuel's car in a shopping mall near Edsa. Anti-Crime Commission agents staked out the car and arrested two suspects, who led them to six others, one of them an ex-soldier. The agents found nearly $20,000 in pesos handed over by a desperate father, hoping against hope, in response to demands relayed by the kidnappers *after* the boy was dead. Their game over, the kidnappers told agents where to find the body. Luis picked up his son's corpse one day in April two weeks after his family had awakened to find Manuel had not come home.[3]

You know the kidnapping problem is serious when officials worry about its impact on the national image. "The rise in kidnapping cases this year could discourage foreign investment," fretted outgoing Interior Secretary Rafael Alunan. Businessmen warned against flight of capital.[4] Authorities were dismayed when a Hong Kong firm, Political and Economic Risk Consultancy, ranked the Philippines last among Asian countries for safety and security—7.24 on a risk score of one to ten. "I totally disagree with that," said Malacanang Press Secretary Hector "Chito" Villanueva, in the lounge of the Shangri-La Hotel in the Makati financial district after seeing the report. Rather than flaunt such news, he said, the media should "assume a little bit of patriotism . . . since we're trying to promote tourism, investments."[5]

Not for a moment did Villanueva concede that the rating might be well deserved. Nor did he talk about solutions. In the plush surroundings of the Shangri-La, no one suggested that one cure for incompetent policing might be to pay the cops more than the pittance they receive—the equivalent of about $100 a month.

A majority of the police, it is said, live in squatter areas, flimsy piles built on private or government property. There is pressure to drive out the squatters, to obliterate their huts, to toss them all, people and contents, across the countryside, into someone else's backyard or rice paddy. What about the police and other low-paid civil servants forced to live in rows of shanties along rivers that are now sewers, if they are lucky, or just beside open sewers, if they are unlucky? Do they get tossed out too?

Ramos in mid-1995 got the worldwide publicity he loves when he ordered the destruction of Smokey Mountain, an infamous garbage heap near Manila Bay off which scavengers for years had made a living scratching for junk within view of the Manila Hotel—an easy story for journalists doing their Philippine "poverty" feature. The demise of Smokey Mountain, however, did nothing to alleviate the suffering of the 3,500 squatters thrown out of their shanties on the dump, who complained that the flimsy apartment buildings to which they were forced to move were worse.[6] Nor did it do much about the thousands of shantytowns elsewhere. They are eyesores in every city and town, notably in Metro Manila, a crazyquilt of ten cities and seven municipalities. The population, as of September 1995, was officially 9,454,000 but was assumed to have soared well above 10 million, half of whom fell below a vague poverty line with family incomes of less than $2,000 a year.[7]

At the other end of the scale live the wealthy local businessmen, most of whom are ethnically Chinese or Chinese *mestizo,* mixed blood. Newly rich, heirs to great fortunes, foreign executives on fat allowances, diplomats with stylish, rent-free residences—they form the aristocracy. Friends or mortal enemies, they exist in residential districts surrounded by high walls topped by barbed wire and shards of glass, secured by armed and uniformed guards at every portal.

Many of these beautiful neighborhoods have suitably pretty names—Greenhills, Corinthian Gardens, Dasmarinas, Belair. Others are named after people, like Forbes Park, the classiest, for an American colonial governor. Forbes Park derives an extra-special cachet from the residences of the American and British ambassadors, set half a mile apart amid private lawns and gardens suitable for lovely parties, shielded by their own high walls and shrubbery.

They're all called "villages," a word redolent of a quaint, simple place where life is sweet and genteel, children are well scrubbed and schooled, and playgrounds are safe and manicured. Shaggy-haired teens in jeans and T-shirts may amble along the sidewalks, but they're the best protected, the most privileged kids in the Philippines. Their parents tool about in chauffeured limousines or vans with bulletproof tinted-glass windows. Many of the kids go to International School, where Amelita "Ming" Ramos has been admissions director for years, or to any number of other institutions for the privileged. Armed guards are on duty at the gates, as they are at the banks and offices, the nightclubs, the discos and restaurants where the rich, young and old, hang out when they're not in the cooler clime of Baguio, the American-designed retreat in the mountains to the north, or surfing off the white sands of Boracay or still more exclusive retreats.

Fashionable restaurants appealing to every taste and palette fill the heart of Makati and Quezon City, within walking distance of the villages. The elite go by car, fearful of a kidnapping or holdup in the few hundred yards from residence to restaurant, double-parking on narrow streets with no fear of tickets, paying more for food and drink than most clubs charge in the States or Europe. Often, families bring along maids, unobtrusive and ignored in their white uniforms as they feed and mind the pampered tots. Not infrequently, a family's personal security guard or guards wait by the entrance or in the lobby or at a nearby table, dining out with other guards, poised to fire when necessary.

That's how life goes on, shielded by those walls, defended by the best private cops money can buy. For the residents of the villages, wealth guarantees security. They don't need a "better" Philippine National Police (PNP). They don't want any police at all once they're secure behind their walls. They don't trust the PNP inside their villages. They're too afraid the cops are casing their homes, stealing whatever is loose, planning a kidnapping, maybe a killing. For generations, the system has bred contempt for the cops, who everyone knows are among the world's poorest, neediest—and most corrupt. The wealthiest members of society control most of Congress—even if they are not members themselves. They can pay from their own pockets for their own law enforcement.

Intuitively, they do not see why they should have to pay real policemen, members of the PNP, more than their maids. After endless debates and studies, the bureaucrats and politicians can never agree on a serious pay increase for the cops, who go on living in poverty, taking bribes, stealing and killing for money. The higher ranking the cop, the more likely he's on the take—personally accepting the biggest payoffs, controlling those who do the taking for him, running gambling rackets, sharing riches with relatives, cronies, aids and benefactors up and down the structure of governance. Vice President Estrada loved the publicity of chasing after crime with his Anti-Crime Commission, but he was as suspect as some of the people he was after—the more so when his bodyguards attacked a member of Congress at a cockfight for having insulted a gambling lord friend of his. Another day, another story.

The sanctuaries of the rich are not hidden far away. Thousands upon thousands pass these homes every day on their way to and from work. The high walls of the villages border on Edsa, looming gray and ugly above the crowded sidewalks and the 12 lanes of roaring traffic—high enough to discourage the most intrepid thieves and block out the sordid view along with the noise. It was there, in the shadows of those villages, in the third week of February 1986, that a million people poured onto Edsa, cheering on their heroes, never threatening or questioning the basic power structure that endures a decade later, stronger than ever, on either side of the avenue.

"Ten years on," as reports on the state of the Philippines referred to the time that had passed, those who had shared the benefits celebrated the revolution as an almost mystical event. "The tenth anniversary celebration of Edsa's People Power shall serve as the launching pad of 'the spirit of Edsa,'" said Jose Concepcion, the tycoon whose vote-counting National Citizens Movement for Free Elections (NAMFREL) had revealed the cheating by Marcos' people in the ballot-counting for the "snap" election called by Marcos before the revolution. "The Edsa spirit is forever. It will persist as an enduring national legacy. Edsa is for all, capturing the best in the Filipinos. For one glorious moment in 1986, the Filipinos rose above their own weakness."[8]

The day of the tenth anniversary of the triumph of People Power, when Marcos got himself inaugurated at Malacañang, when Aquino was inaugurated in Greenhills, when Marcos, Imelda, their family and some cronies, including Eduardo Cojuangco, had fled Malacañang aboard American helicopters, dawned bright and shining as it had ten years earlier. Ramos, in blue jeans and blue shirt, climbed up to the base of the People Power Monument in front of Camp Aguinaldo, the armed forces headquarters, fronting on Edsa. He received the freedom torch, carried by athletes the length of the Philippines, then held it aloft for the several hundred half-cheering, half-grinning onlookers—and the TV cameras. Helicopters swooped down, scattering tons of confetti and bits of shredded newspapers, sparkling in the sun as they fell like snow.[9]

The president was anxious to counter the negative publicity—polls showed his popularity sinking. His rambling speech was in English, the lingua franca needed to appeal to the powerful and the educated, often divided but still unified by their ability to speak and understand American English. Among the middle class—and on a wider level, among those workers and farmers who speak little English beyond odd phrases—American-Filipino-English also remains the only way to begin to get through to everybody at once. The country is split among 8 major regional languages and 80 other languages and dialects, each reflecting local interests, from the Ilocano region of Marcos to the Tagalog provinces around Metro Manila, down to the Visayas, dominated by Cebuano and Ilongo. Newcomers to Mindanao speak the language of their region, disdaining the languages of the Muslims who preceded them.

Ramos, who is from Pangasinan, where people speak their own lingua franca, senses as acutely as anyone an undercurrent of resentment of Tagalog. It's suspected these Tagalogs think they are "better"—if only because they inhabit Metro Manila and have spread a language and a literature on a more sophisticated level than have the peoples far to the north and south.

Like the analysts who write reports for the International Monetary Fund (IMF), the World Bank or foreign aid programs, Ramos understands on a theoretical level the dangers of income and societal gaps as well as those of region and linguistics. He is sensitive to the explosive divisions that go deep into history. He has a message of reform, for which he desperately needs support against his critics, from the radicals looking for socialist panaceas to the conservatives protecting their holdings. "We may undergo revolution again and again if we do not improve ourselves economically," he reminded the crowd. "Even if we are economically strong, we face the threat of upheaval if we do not manage growth so that it brings social justice and better lives to the poor. We must regain that sense of unity. The worst tyranny is the tyranny of poverty. It still oppresses our people."

Ramos wound up his remarks in bursts of Pilipino, to polite applause, showing himself as not just a man of English but of the people, even though his real message was in English, the same English he used in annual state-of-the-nation speeches and weekly press conferences. How else could he communicate? His speech concluded, the festivities on the big day were just beginning. All day long, Ramos invoked the memory of "Edsa"—an anniversary elevated to the level of a national holiday and crusade. Just as "soldiers and ordinary people united in a desperate battle against a corrupt regime" in 1986, he vowed to "do my best to see fit to be a president of all Filipinos, poor and rich, Muslim and non-Muslim." The hype faced serious opposition, but thousands of police made sure there were no signs of protest.

Ten miles away, in front of the cultural center on which she had squandered untold millions as first lady *and* governor of Metro Manila, where the bodies of workmen killed in construction were still buried in concrete, Imelda was carrying on. Brushing back tears, she led hundreds of Marcos "loyalists," as they were known in 1986 and were still known in 1996, in fervent prayer for the "traitors" who had driven her and her husband from power—then prayed for the Swiss bankers who held most of the $5-$10 billion she was said to have stashed abroad. "May God enlighten them," she said, beseeching the Lord to grant the gnomes of Zurich the "wisdom" not to yield her ill-got funds to the thousands of victims of Marcos-era imprisonment and torture who were suing her.

Across Edsa from Camp Aguinaldo, at Camp Crame, where he had masterminded the final stage of the revolution, Ramos watched a reenactment of the landing of a helicopter bearing a general defecting from Marcos. In the building where he had made his headquarters he breakfasted on tuna, hard rolls and coffee, as I had seen him doing then and there, 10 years earlier, on the last day of the "revolution."

On his way to another round of speeches at the People Power monument, as he walked beside Ming, surrounded by security guards, I asked him to assess his revolution. "It is not quite finished, but we are laying the foundation." Would he get it done by the end of his term in 1998? "Most of it," he said, climbing up on the platform. The celebration devolved into a love-in. Ramos hugged Cory Aquino as she climbed up on the platform beside him wearing a People Power T-shirt—the same trademark yellow that she had worn in her bid for power, for revenge for Ninoy.

Cory, brother-in-law Agapito "Butz" Aquino and Ramos made quite a lineup as they faced another crowd, this time perhaps a few thousand. Ramos suggested that everyone "shake the hands of your neighbor and, better yet, embrace them." That said and done, he offered a prayer to God "that you will grant us peace and order, that you will bring about the economic recovery of the nation." Cory smiled a lot but didn't speak. Butz, eight years younger than Ninoy, talked to me about the gains. "What we fought for is slowly being realized," he maintained. "Ten years is a short time. Definitely the fear is gone. In the provinces the police and military are very well accepted. It's only in Metro Manila there is skepticism. Nobody hates Ramos."[10]

There was nobody around to disagree, but a poster tacked to a nearby wall summarized some of the problems, otherwise unmentioned. "We saved your life at Edsa so save us from corruption, crime bandits in robes, scalawags, drug pushers, insurgents, poverty, religious syndicates, international slaves, tragedy, disasters, calamity and hunger," begged the poster, signed by the "Command of Responsibility." One had to know the language of the press to recognize all the themes. "Bandits in robes" were the judges who take bribes before handing down verdicts; "scalawags" are government workers, also in the news for bribery and graft.

Ramos, however, did not want to hear about the real ills of the system he was trying to run. He concluded his day at a mass on Edsa before a statue of Christ—another monument to People Power between one of the wealthiest "villages," Corinthian Gardens, and two of the largest, most opulent shopping centers, Megamall and Shangri-La Plaza. This time, Ramos got the crowd he wanted—about 80,000 people, members of the charismatic El Shaddai sect led by a Catholic priest who gathered them together for weekly shouting, chanting prayer sessions. What better than for both president and priest than to join forces on Edsa—Ramos glad to have a crowd, the priest basking in star-quality publicity?

Nonetheless, an edge of doubt, of discontent, crept into the observances. As the sun set behind the statue, the specter of a return to the dark days of martial law hung over the scene. The country's top religious leader, Jaime Cardinal Sin, in a homily at the shrine before which mobs had stopped army tanks at the height of the People Power revolution, attacked "spine-tingling proposals against terrorism" put forward by, who else, Ramos. With all the prestige he could muster as his country's best known, most powerful religious figure, Sin, one of Marcos' toughest foes, blasted the proposals as "reminiscent of Marcos' martial law powers," a means to bring about "a virtual return to martial law."

Having sat behind Sin through the mass, Ramos vowed in a speech right afterward, "There is no way a dictatorship can come back because, as your president, I will fight it." Never would he "allow martial law, or any semblance of it." The exchange, near the end of the day, dramatized the problems of a country mired in poverty despite a gross national product rising by nearly six per cent a year. "Has the Edsa spirit really disappeared," asked one paper. One of the most oft-repeated questions was whether the revolt was really a revolution—or "a transference of power from one group to another within the ruling class."[11]

The presence on the platform of Cory Aquino illustrated the point. No one, except perhaps the charismatic Christians packing the intersection below, waving arms on cue, forgot that she was a member of one of the nation's wealthiest families. Aquino, however, was oblivious to all that when besieged by reporters after the mass. "We Filipinos showed the world what kind of people we are," she said as she resurrected the memory of the heady days of her rise to power. "We are a brave people, we are a prayerful people, and we know how to work with the peaceful process." It was the message she had spread as president—one of hope so unfulfilled as to leave people disillusioned with her.[12]

The country was deeply divided, as reflected in the absence of Enrile, Ramos' ally in the coup. Now a senator, Enrile, having fallen out with Aquino soon after she became president, was threatening to sue her for profiting from the sale of dozens of Marcos properties seized by the government. Also absent was another senator, Gregorio "Gringo" Honasan, the ex-officer who had seized Camp Aguinaldo as a prelude to the coup. Gringo's presence would have been too embarrassing. He had been rehabilitated despite his record of five coup attempts against Aquino—some of them staged after he had been captured and then escaped from a navy vessel in Manila Bay by bribing his guards. Cory might not have wanted to see her worst military foe, forgiven by Ramos but never by her.

Amid all the rhetoric, one would hardly expect Ramos or Aquino to admit that their People Power revolution was a celebration, not a revolution. The reality, however, was that life would go on, then as now, under much the same network of leaders who had been running the country since the Philippines became a commonwealth in 1935—four years before the Japanese drove out the Americans after Pearl Harbor. In a struggle between old and new oligarchs, the old had harnessed the people into the power needed to drive out the new. The expulsion of the incipient Marcos dynasty of Ilocos Norte by adherents of a wealthy group of landlords from Tarlac Province represented a change in names but hardly of system.

Revolution, real revolution, remains a distant storm over the political and social landscape of the Philippines. One wonders if there can ever be a revolution in a country and a society united and shaped by Spanish conquistadors and friars, then by American soldiers and bureaucrats. The colonial powers instinctively if not deliberately cultivated a powerful indigenous upper class, offering for a pittance the holdings on which they built their estates, tolerating their corruption and, in the case of the Americans, their abuse of aid funds for the sake of the bases that Washington saw as a bulwark against communism and the Soviet ships and planes then traversing the region.

Leaders of the People Power revolution have trouble comprehending how nonrevolutionary was the movement. Teodoro "Teddy Boy" Locsin Jr., founder of *Today,* one of the better newspapers to have sprung up in the free-enterprising atmosphere, cannot grasp why the world fails to venerate his revolution. After having served the cause as a protester and then as press secretary to Aquino, he wallows in memories of acts of political courage. When I saw him in his office at *Today,* on Edsa, he berated the New York Public Library for failing in 1995 to include the events of 1986 in an exhibit on revolutions around the world. "Is it sufficient for a country to revolt for the sake of freedom," he asked. "Does it always have to be for social causes? It's sufficient to gather in the streets and overthrow a tyranny."[13]

Teddy Boy, as he honestly likes to be called, reminded me of Edsa's role as precursor to the revolt then about to sweep Eastern Europe. "Warsaw, Prague, I would like to think Edsa inspired that possibility. I really think that fighting for your liberty, not having a tyrant, is enough. The people on Edsa were not rich. They didn't want a tyrant over them." For those who might doubt the state of democracy today, Teddy Boy, son of a well-known editor whose family grew rich on sugar in Negros, recalled the terror of martial law. "We're free. You cannot even compare this to a dictatorship. There's no knock on the door at midnight." He was less sure, however, about corruption. True, the siphoning of billions of dollars that characterized the Marcos era "has gone down enormously, but the stealing is worse under Ramos."

For all such doubts, the World Bank in July 1995 gave the economy a blessing of sorts when several visiting officials convened a press conference at the Asian Institute of Management in Makati to say that the government was doing the proper things in opening up the economy. Filipino officials delight in such roseate views, quoting them again and again in luncheons for foreign and local journalists, in propaganda blitzes from Malacañang and in speeches and press conferences. One of President Ramos' prouder moments was his appearance on the cover of *Time* of May 15, 1995. The cover only ran in the magazine's Asian edition, but few Filipinos knew the difference. Ramos distributed hundreds of framed copies of the cover—some autographed by him personally, others with his signature stamped on—for governors and mayors to hang conspicuously in their offices.

Philippine officials respond with aggrieved disbelief when the international organizations turn on them with less than positive notes on the economy's performance. The secretary of finance, Roberto de Ocampo, a smooth-talking product of the London School of Economics, denounced as "unwarranted" an IMF report in mid-1995 that warned of the impact of the government's failure to collect income taxes and carry out basic fiscal reform "even as reforms in the external, financial and other sectors have proceeded apace."[14] Officials, like their radical critics, charged "economic imperialism" when international organizations noted the dangers of "exceptions" under which business people and companies avoid taxes.

The IMF recommended what may actually prove impossible—streamlining the bureaucracy, spending more on infrastructure in order to bring about real improvements in the economy and increasing savings as well as investment. De Ocampo's office produced an array of statistics to argue against the IMF report, claiming, among other things, that gross domestic investment was rising from 21.6 percent of the GNP in 1995 to 27 percent for 1998, whereas the savings ratio went from 16 percent to 23 percent over the same period.[15] Somehow, though, the statistics seemed less than credible against the IMF's criticism. Were the reports of the Philippines' recovery real or hype? Could the country, amid a regional economic tailspin, wind up 35 years under IMF supervision by the end of 1997—or would the IMF withhold approval for a final $334 million in loans while demanding tighter government budgetary controls?

For that matter, was there a correlation between an improving business climate and the departure of American forces? There was an irony in the expulsion of the Americans from the bases. The GNP had begun to rise at about the time of the American withdrawal. No one seriously claimed cause and effect. There was no saying that the GNP would *not* have increased had the Americans been allowed to hang on. Then again, no one says that the GNP would have gone up even more if the Americans had stayed where they were. With or without the bases, however, there was an incipient confidence at the top—a feeling the economy would no longer drift downward under one or another corruptible or incompetent set of leaders.

Ramos fueled the new confidence among the international set, the aid backers and aid-givers, the investors and exporters, with bills designed to attune the economy to an increasingly deregulated, competitive and profitable world. In March 1996, he signed a measure deregulating oil prices so competitors might join the fray unfettered by rules and regulations promulgated by the energy regulatory board. The idea was "to gradually lift government controls over oil prices and profit margins," reported Bloomberg financial news.[16] Within a year, according to plan, the market, not the bureaucrats, was to determine how much customers paid for gasoline and other petroleum products—that is, if it survived all challenges in a ponderous, unpredictable court system.

Around the same time, Ramos signed a measure lowering tariffs and wiping out import quotas on agricultural imports. The law excluded rice from the list, but Ramos hoped it was enough to give an impression of fulfilling a pledge to avoid losing most-favored-nation privileges under the General Agreement on Tariffs and Trade. While living up to the edicts of the World Trade Organization, Ramos tried to placate agricultural interests, some of them supported by the nation's richest families behind the cover of poor, small farmers, by setting up an "agricultural protection tariffication fund" for farmers suffering excessively from the competition. It was an effort at fending off the outcries of foreigners against both leftist and conservative criticism of foreign monetary interests—and foreign domination.

It was all a difficult balancing act. The president's boldest step, however, may have been his effort at making it far easier for foreigners to trade, invest—and make money—in the Philippines. A new law cut the equity that foreign companies had to put up from $500,000 to $200,000 while eliminating the notorious "C" list, under which Filipino companies routinely asked the government every two years to protect them from foreign competition. The measure opened up competition not only in trading but in insurance and also in the distribution of business licenses—all lucrative fields.[17]

Another new law cut prices on imports by basing duties on the price the importer paid for them in the Philippines rather than on an often arbitrary calculation of the much higher price at which the same products were sold in the country of origin. Privatization became a watchword for the era—with de Ocampo claiming nearly $7 billion in profits from sales of overweight, inefficient national companies in the first five years of Ramos' presidency.

As a result of such measures, Ramos faced shrill criticism from all sides, from all levels of society. Poor people said he was forcing oil to skyrocket in price; the rich said they would suffer under intense competition. "Nationalists" railed against Ramos for betraying the national trust, for selling out to the International Monetary Fund, the World Bank, American imperialists and every other foreign interest. Ramos fought back. Competition at the gasoline pump, he argued, would smash "de facto monopoly of big established oil companies by enabling market forces to prevail." He also cited the realities of a changing world and a shifting scene around the Philippines and in Southeast Asia. "The signals are clear. The Philippines is determined, ready and eager to compete in a liberalized multi-trade order. We foresee a number of benefits to the total economic recovery of the country."[18]

Was the Philippines, however, really changing? A national furor—almost a crisis—erupted when the Supreme Court, the same aggregation that had given Imelda her seat in the congress, ruled in March 1997 against the sale of the storied Manila Hotel to a Malaysian company. The court accepted, lock, stock and barrel, the argument of *Manila Bulletin* publisher Emilio Yap that the hotel was a national treasure and should remain in "Philippine" hands.[19]

The hands that wanted it, of course, were those of Yap, whose paper had led a shameful, unabashed crusade to keep the hotel under Philippine ownership, even though Yap's bid did not match that of the dreaded "foreigner." Malaysian leaders, whose Chinese businessmen were major investors in the Philippines, protested they no longer had "confidence" in the country. The foreign chambers of commerce in a joint statement declared, "Challenges should take place prior to the bidding process." In a harsh rebuke of a court whose members were surely influenced by more than just the good publicity always accorded them in Yap's dreadful paper, the statement warned: "Do not change the rules after the game is played and expect to attract players for future biddings."[20] In vain did Ramos criticize the ruling as undermining all he was trying to do.

The flap, however, would blow over. At major centers everywhere, there was a sense of mad expansion amid poverty. Although the lower 40 percent of the people in most key cities lived in shanties, as squatters on other people's land, the top 1 percent were building or managing or investing in apartment blocks, factories, stores or shopping centers. Often they attempted to drive the squatters from their makeshift homes in the search for more land on which to build. Or, corrupt bureaucrats would rent cheap apartments to non-squatters in new buildings intended for squatters. At the same time, tycoons and politicians and bureaucrats battled each other, sometimes in ways that slowed down or stifled projects.

The sense of competitive dynamism, of internecine rivalry, was nowhere so apparent as in the nation's "second city," Cebu, the historic Visayan port where Magellan landed nearly five centuries ago. "We are far ahead of Clark and Subic," were the first words Benson Dakay, chairman of Shemberg, specialists in processing seaweed for food, drink, toothpaste too, as well as a variety of industrial purposes, uttered when I asked how Cebu rated against the two much-publicized new zones.[21]

Comparison between Cebu and Subic seems relevant considering that Subic aspires to become a major port servicing all of central Luzon, whereas for years Cebu has been the major port of the Visayas—and the second-largest port in the Philippines after Manila. Comparisons, though, may not be fair. A glimpse at the port from the bridge connecting Cebu with Mactan reveals a busy, expanding harbor. Freighters pass each other beneath the spans while gantry cranes soar on the horizon. With 2 million people living in the city and surrounding commercial towns, Cebu is an established regional center while Subic remains uncertain how much of a port it's going to become.

In the next breath, though, Dakay, as chairman of Cebu Province exporters, spoke critically, almost despairingly, of delays in the dream for Cebu's emergence—not as an unrivaled number two but, as Metro Manila deteriorates in its own problems, perhaps as number one. "We're behind in implementation, not in planning," he said, over a Saturday lunch that included family members and top managers. "The infrastructure is slow. Everything is too slow. There are billions of pesos to be released. Now the politicians want to have part of the money diverted to their area. We need infrastructure in terms of roads. We need one more bridge. The infrastructure will be delayed."[22]

The importance of the island of Cebu to the country and the region cannot be underestimated. The port in 1995 exported about $1.6 billion worth of goods, more than 10 percent of the nation's total, much of it from an industrial zone dominated by Japanese, American and Taiwan companies on Mactan. "This is a small island, compact," Dakay observed. "Investors like to come here. We have enough skilled manpower." The port and the work force together are ideal for export-processing. "It does not encourage heavy industry," said Dakay, whose seaweed group had total sales in 1995 of about $150 million, equal to the sales of the Timex watch plant on Mactan. Dakay got back, however, to the political intrigue that "slows down our growth," frustrating the dreams of local business interests just as they approach a new stage of development.

The rivalry in Cebu is like no other. Much of it revolves around the titans of the city and the region's leading family. Money politics is the game and Osmeña is the name. The Osmeñas, once hated by Marcos and now, possibly, more powerful than ever, suffer from a problem that differentiates them from members of other clans: they are their own worst enemies. They fight each other. The contest focuses on brothers Sergio III (Serge) and Tomas (Tommy) and their cousins, brothers John (Sonny) and Emilio (Lito). The battle, however, is not between sets of brothers. Rather, the brother of one is allied with his cousin, the brother of the other—and vice versa.

What makes the story more extraordinary than most other family sagas in this society of rich but often divided clans is the history of the Osmeñas over a relatively short period. All the four main power players are grandsons of Sergio Osmeña, a patriarchal figure who sat out World War II in the United States, serving as vice president, then president, of a government-in-exile after the death of Manuel Quezon. Osmeña landed in Leyte with MacArthur in October 1944 but lost his chance to become the first president of an independent Philippines when Manuel Roxas, a MacArthur favorite, albeit a Japanese collaborator, defeated him at the polls in April 1946, two and a half months before Independence Day on July 4. The loss to a member of the pro-Japanese elite, which also included such luminaries as Jose Laurel and Benigno Aquino Sr., was all the more bitter since one of Osmeña's sons, Emilio, a doctor, was executed by the Japanese in 1942.

The old man, however, had a younger son, Sergio Jr. (Serging), who had gladly worked with the Japanese as a businessman in Manila during the war—and ran for president in 1969 against Marcos. Serging might have challenged Marcos again but for the Plaza Miranda bombing. So badly injured as to need medical treatment in the United States, he died in Los Angeles in 1984.[23] Now, the intrafamily battle pits Sonny, the elder son of Emilio, and Serge, the elder son of Serging, against Lito, Emilio's younger son, and Tommy, the younger son of Serging. Sonny and Serge have served in Congress while Lito and Tommy ran successfully for governor of Cebu Province and mayor of Cebu city, respectively, in 1988. As Dakay put it, "The godfather of Cebu is Lito, and the boss is Tommy."[24]

An editor recalled how Sonny dealt the death blow to Lito's aspirations for high office as vice-presidential candidate in 1992. "Sonny killed his brother," said the editor. "He just comes on the air, says, 'What's going on here, my brother is a crook.'" In the Senate, Serge has been as tough as his cousin Sonny when it comes to making trouble for both cousin Lito and brother Tommy. He focused on the "anomaly" of a contract in which property owned by the international airport at Mactan, an American air base turned over to the Philippines years before the senate refused to renew the bases agreement, was leased to a Malaysian-Chinese company for a hotel and casino. Why was there no public bidding on the 75-year deal with which Lito was associated, Serge asked. The "scam," he charged, smelled of more than the usual payoff.[25]

Both Tommy and Lito elaborately spurn suggestions of a comeback in electoral politics. "I think I've put in my share," said Tommy, who stayed on as chairman of the Cebu Investment Promotion Center after Sonny prevented him from taking over the Metro Cebu Development Project. Lito feels the same way. "I don't think I'll run again," he said. "I'm a businessman." Lito also served Ramos as economic consultant with cabinet rank—a position of such influence as to inspire Sonny and Serge to accuse him of conflict of interest in promoting his own projects in Cebu.[26]

In the battle for the wealth, there is little chance that much of it will spread around—or trickle down. All that is clear is that the Osmeñas, if they ever start pulling together, pose a strong regional challenge to those from other regions in power in Manila. Ten years on, all the big names were back. Those "suppressed" under Marcos law vied for the new riches of a relatively liberalized, open economy with those "suppressed" by the anti-Marcos reaction, including the Presidential Commission on Good Government's marvelously unsuccessful efforts at recovering the purloined billions, much less bringing anyone to trial.

One of the most notorious survivors, Eduardo Cojuangco Jr., lives in baronial splendor on a hacienda south of Bacolod in Negros. Danding is a newcomer to Negros, the sugarland that is home to Marcos sugar king Roberto S. Benedicto and a deeply entrenched gentry of other landowners. He bought property there in the early 1970s but did not move from his native Tarlac Province until 1991, after returning from self-exile in the United States. He wanted to improve his image, damaged by association with Marcos and the celebrated enmity between him and cousin Cory Aquino— not improved much by his losing campaign for president in 1992.[27]

That may be one reason Danding, worth more than a billion dollars, clad in shorts and sandals, no socks, drove his jeep to pick me up at the town hall of Pontevedra when I dropped by with no notice, advance call, appointment or introduction, said I was doing research and asked a secretary if I might see him or his son, Charlie, the mayor of the town. Charlie was not in, but Danding gladly drove me to his nearby hacienda, in between new mango groves. Right off, after we sat down in the spacious open-air living room of the home that he had designed in stony Spanish style, Danding offered a disarming analysis— one that is tough to refute. "Ramos is probably going to be better than Cory. People will feel in the end he has not done much. As we go on and on like this, it's going to be harder and harder for the next guy. The so-called miracle economy hasn't trickled down to the masses."[28]

More than ten years on, such words appear like a bizarre satire on an American journalistic analysis of the Philippine scene. One has to wonder how committed is Danding to ensuring that the wealth "trickles down." He leaves no doubt, however, where he stands on one key topic—that of land reform. "I don't think it will work," said Danding, whose 4,500 hectares in Negros were all "sequestered" under the Presidential Commission on Good Government. "A program where you take from those that have to those that don't have isn't going to work." Danding has reason to feel strongly. Officials at the PCGG say they are determined to take over his land and have the authority to do so—a threat that may never materialize in a welter of appeals and other legal maneuvers.[29]

Cojuangco's feelings on land reform make him a philosophical soulmate with cousin Jose "Peping" Cojuangco, Cory's younger brother and campaign manager against Marcos. Danding, however, does not discuss such issues with them. In fact, they don't communicate at all: "I don't see what for. We can't choose our relatives. I feel I haven't wronged them. She apparently doesn't have any love for us." He would, however, like to get on their good side. He said he "turned over all my leaders to Peping in the last election"— the one in May 1995 in which Peping was elected to Congress from Tarlac, while his wife, "Tingting," carried on as governor of the province.

Danding's generosity was part of a deal in which he agreed to pull out of Tarlac Province and settle down in Negros. Vaguely, Danding said that he and a couple of brothers and three sisters shared "community property" in Tarlac, but "I thought it would be nice if I could establish a Visayan branch of the family," especially since his wife, Gretchen, is an heiress of the long-established Offen family up the main coastal road in Pulupandan, on the way to Bacolod. Danding adopts a genial above-it-all attitude as if, in Negros, the politics of Manila were a far-off storm. Rarely does he call on co-crony Roberto S. Benedicto, whose hacienda is just a few miles down the road in La Carlota. "We see each other about four times a year."

Like Lito Osmeña, Danding disavowed any intention of ever running again—also part of the implicit deal with his Tarlac relatives. He professed he was far more interested in cockfighting than politicking. In the walled garden behind his house, 60 fighting cocks were tethered to stakes in between scientifically bred trees and plants, crowing and preening as they awaited their next turn in the pit. "Cockfighting is my livelihood," said Danding, grinning again, showing me around the garden. "It's the breeding side I love the most."[30]

Lately, Danding's noble birds had been disappointing. "I haven't been winning. We haven't been fighting the right competition." The metaphor seemed apt for one who knows what it is to win and lose in the cockpit of a chaotic society. "I enjoyed the reputation of 'number one crony,'" he said, mouthing the "c" word with a grimace. "I stuck with the guy"—Marcos—"and I have no regrets." He hesitated. "Probably he was our best president so far."

Danding got around to the murder of Ninoy Aquino at the airport that day in August 1983—the supreme salvaging in which his name was often mentioned along with those of Imelda and Marcos' military chief, General Ver, as one of the culprits. "I didn't have any participating in his doing it," he said. The circumlocution left one to assume the "his" refers to Marcos, or to Marcos and Ver, the one who had to have plotted the finer details of the meticulously engineered job. Danding went on to the widow, his cousin, the former president. "The Cory administration borrowed more money than he

[Marcos] did in 20 years. Her problem was everybody expected her to perform a miracle." Ten years on, it was still a miracle that everybody talked about—the miracle to come.

The up and downsides of the miracle are clear in Davao, population 800,000. It is the country's third-largest city and port—the most important center on Mindanao and a regional hub too. One of the biggest beneficiaries is another Marcos crony, banana king Antonio Floriendo, whose interests range from a fast-growing food-processing operation to a motor-vehicle franchise. New wealth, local and foreign, is coming in. "Compare 1991 with 1994," advised Warlito Vicente Jr., with the Davao Integrated Development Program, funded by U.S. aid and the city government. "There was 3,400 percent growth. We have been seeing a transformation of Davao from a supplier of raw materials to value-added components."[31]

There was no doubt that the mood of the city had changed from the last time I was there—in February 1986, with reporters awaiting the arrival of Aquino, who was to have flown to Davao for an anti-Marcos rally. In Cebu, Aquino reversed her schedule, returning to Manila as leader of the People Power revolution. I jumped on a plane the same day, driving to the airport by way of Agdao, a wretched shantytown where the initials and slogans of the New People's Army were scrawled on the walls. "Down with Marcos," "NPA Forever," read the signs painted in red by communist guerrillas waging sporadic urban warfare in the slums and terrorizing surrounding farms from bases on Mount Apo, clearly visible from anywhere in town.

Davao had another name in those days too. It was "murder city"—a tribute, as it were, to the city's reputation as murder capital of the world. Almost nightly, a body or two was found on the streets, victims of another salvaging by gangsters, killers-for-hire, communist guerrillas, love rivals, anyone with a grudge. Ten years later, travelling south down the coast toward Digos on the way to General Santos, you heard stories about the NPA building up again. There were reports of sightings and attacks in the hills—and concerns that the standoff was only a hiatus, a break in the action, not a permanent solution.

In a session with faculty members at Ateneo de Davao, the area's leading educational institution, the problems emerged in terms that contradicted the view from the American-aided programs. "The agricultural sector is the lowest contributor to the nation's production," said a politics professor. "In 'Philippines 2000'"—Ramos' pet catchall slogan for a range of programs and policies—"we help the president's strategy of growth areas, but small entrepreneurs are bought out by the big ones."[32]

Land reform was one of the casualties. "Under land reform farmers are supposed to pay back the money," one faculty member remarked. "But farmers cannot borrow from banks. They get loans through cooperatives.

The Department of Agrarian Reform claims success nationally, but farmers end up selling their land. Most of the legislators are landlords themselves. The law says the government has to acquire the land above five hectares. In the end the government is the biggest landlord of all." Ten years on, "We are widening the gap between the upper 10 percent and the lower 40 percent. In the minds of the average Filipino, the greatest source of insecurity is the fear of loss of food on the table."[33]

The indictment applies to an entire country. People Power, everybody knows, was a misnomer. Ten years on, there was a suspicion that nobody could change anything except the appearances of skylines, shopping centers, hotels and malls—none of which had much to do with the well-being of the people in whose name the warriors of People Power marched down Edsa in February 1986.

The Supreme Court, in November 1997, fueled the fears by capriciously striking down the new law deregulating the oil business. The rationale ostensibly was to protect small companies, which had to import all their products against the "big three," Petron, Pilipinas Shell, and Caltex (Philippines), which had refineries and held down prices. The justices couldn't accept a free market "when our economy is in a dangerous downspin," but the ruling jeopardized small companies that had joined the fray to exploit tariff cuts and more competition provided by the law. "Unprecedented," said de Ocampo, professing that he was "stunned" by the ruling.

Apparently the finance secretary had forgotten the precedent of the old days. The new precedent, more than ten years on, evoked the ghost of laws and regulations all supposedly adopted to "protect" a people who had suffered the most at the expense of the Marcoses and their cronies.

NINE

Their Own Worst Enemies

International operators, discouraged by Marcos-era corruption and cronyism, were coming back. By the mid-1990s, the United States rivaled Japan as the Philippines' largest foreign source of investment. "We are the flavor of the month," said Harvard-trained lawyer Ricardo "Dick" Romulo, elder son of Carlos Romulo, a major figure in Philippine foreign policy for 40 years. "They all come for consultations. There were many lean years when no one would pass by Manila for fear of getting shot." Romulo, whose posh Makati law firm is a few blocks from brother Bobby's office at the Philippine Long Distance Telephone Company, did have a complaint. "For me, the influence-peddling is worse than the corruption."[1]

Overall, however, Dick Romulo was irrepressibly positive about the transition from before to after the bases—that is, from before to after the withdrawal of American forces: "The main benefit of the base closing is political. It's robbed the leftists and even extreme rightists of the only issue they had—continued dominance, neo-colonialism of the Philippines." Could such a gain, however, compensate for the economic vacuum around the major bases? "That was 50,000 jobs out the window; that's 50,000 families," Romulo replied. "The entire fallout is a lot of uncertainty. The businessman doesn't know what's going to happen, but at least that issue is gone, that so-called thorn is gone, so we can treat the United States on the basis of mutual business."

The question is what is happening to the infusion of new wealth. Romulo's reply was the obvious one: "Who's getting the money is really due to the structure of this society, which lodges the money in the elite. The classic solution of building the middle class and trickle-down takes a while. What is the shortcut? What is the fashionable way?" Romulo mused but had no answers. "Those who live outside income tax payments" form an upper class; the rest are dunned for real estate and municipal taxes plus EVAT (expanded value-added taxes). "There's an increase in the presence of squatters, which has never happened before." Why, he saw them every day through the tinted glass of his chauffeured limo, "by the railroad tracks, all the way to the underpasses."

If President Ramos had done little about corruption, "commissions" on government contracts and influence-peddling, at least he had given foreigners an impression of pervasive change. "He has succeeded in raising the foreign perception of the Philippines," said Romulo, who represents foreign companies in negotiations. "The main foreign investment is build, operate and transfer"—in which a foreign company builds, for example, an electric power plant, gets it up and running and then turns it over to a local company. "We have a specific law that allows foreigners to build infrastructure. We have started to get transfers of manufacturing facilities from Japan, Taiwan, China, in cars, parts, electronics. We have enough high-skilled people to do the job. That's the bulk of productive investment"—that and investors from the Chinese enclaves of Hong Kong, Taiwan, Malaysia and Singapore, funding hotels, resorts, offices and condos.

Like many other observers, some of them with political and financial axes to grind and knives sharpened, Romulo wondered if Ramos were moving a bit precipitously, just to please his foreign visitors, to impress colleagues at international gatherings such as ASEAN and APEC meetings: "Liberalization has been tremendously accelerated under Ramos. It's too fast. We have to export to live internationally, but most of our exports have high import contents. A true domestic economy must have linkage between local manufacturers and importers." Local tycoons, though, "have to accept the fact that they have to modernize, they have to compete."

Open markets and foreign aid go together. The Japanese, the cruel conquerors of World War II, are the biggest donors—a role that gives them enormous clout in trade and investment as well. The acronym JICA (Japan International Cooperation Agency) is as well known as USAID (U.S. Agency for International Development). While American aid was falling precipitously well before the withdrawal of U.S. forces, that of Japan was rising quickly. Between the People Power revolution in 1986 and the rejection of the bases treaty in 1991, American aid totaled $750.19 million—as opposed to Japanese aid of $4.19 billion. From 1992 to June 1995, Japanese aid came to $2.26 billion, compared to $365.45 million in American funds.[2] Annually, Japanese aid by 1996 amounted to more than $1 billion—compared to $50 million from the United States.

Japan's emergence as "the Philippines' largest aid-giver" is "just one of the many aspects of growing Japanese intrusion in the Philippine economy, in some respects eclipsing the predominance of American business interests in the country," reported *Ibon,* a Bayan-backed journal that debunks government claims and exposes economic and social problems. Japan funnels three-fourths of its investment in the Philippines through the Asian Development Bank, in which Japan holds a third of the shares, or twice as many as the second-ranking shareholder, the United States. A temple of institutional giving, soaring in glass, stone and steel splendor off Edsa, near shopping malls, hotels and other monuments to modernization, ADB channeled 25 percent of $4.65 billion in loans from 1990 through 1994 to Japanese firms.[3]

On the rice-paddy level, such largesse is often less than welcome—and potentially destructive. In the town of Calumpit, up the Pampanga River delta, about 12 miles north of Manila Bay on the way to San Fernando and Angeles, those most affected were up in arms about a Japan-funded project to open the area to shipping while diking it against flooding. "They say they are putting up the project to protect the people," said Roy Padilla, an activist Methodist minister with the Philippine National Council of Churches. "People have to find their own shelter. The government is not doing anything but giving them some food only. There is no comprehensive program. Government officials earn money from these dubious projects. Some of them protect their own residences, putting up fortresses for their houses."[4]

A member of the Calumpit municipal council, Rufino Tolentino, leader of an organization of "anti-delta development" groups, viewed the ADB as a front for Japanese interests: "We will be sacrificed for owners of big hotels, factories, residents of Metro Manila. The Japanese hide their money through the ADB. The Philippines is the third biggest borrower from the ADB. From 1986 to 1992, the Philippines borrowed around $2.4 billion. When this project is finished around 2000, the Japanese will use it as a port and reservoir for import of raw materials and export of finished products. Otherwise, it's too hard for them to transport here."[5]

Tolentino saw the common people as the victims: "The project will not serve any purpose as flood control and irrigation. Farmers and residents will suffer. They don't have any plan for relocating the people." No one, he fears, listens to such pleas—typical of responses to money-making schemes nationwide.[6]

Ibon cited at least three other regions where Japanese aid was compromising local agriculture: "The province of Cavite, south of Manila, is a traditional source of seafood, including oysters and the famous salinas smoked fish. The mining towns in the Cordillera region provide a rich lode of various mineral ores. Mindanao's mountains, valleys and plateaus yield an abundant harvest of agricultural produce and forest products. All these places have one thing in common. They play hosts to various 'development' projects courtesy of Japanese 'aid' money"—all resulting in "rather drastic changes caused by Japanese-funded power plants, industrial estates, roads and other infrastructure projects."[7]

Plundering by privateering entrepreneurs can also wreak havoc on an un-suspecting populace. Disasters are regular news. One evening in September 1995, about 50 miles north of General Santos City, the lake in the crater of a long-dormant volcano named Mount Parker burst open, sending torrents of water cascading down a canyon, sweeping away huts built on a strip of flatland by the stream, inundating farms and shooting hidden boulders through the current. Hardest hit was T'boli, a town named for the T'boli tribal people who inhabit the area. In the heart of the town, in farmland a mile or two from the stream, all was tranquil, but a mad scramble down steep, muddied banks and a walk through fast-moving currents running by flimsy sticks that once were homes revealed a village swarming with grieving relatives and neighbors, now refugees.

Up another muddy bank, at a refugee center in front of a school, T'boli Mayor Dad Tuan (Dad is his real name) said, "My men at the lake say there was an explosion at 5:30 P.M. on September 6 and the water broke out at 6 P.M." An hour later, the currents roared down on the villagers, who were back home for supper, killing more than 40 of them by Dad Tuan's body count and leaving another 70 missing. About 4,000 refugees were massed in the schoolyard and in some nearby fields and homes. "Our problem is lack of food and medicine," said Dad. Some of it got to centers on the other side, but "volunteers" weren't eager to slip and slide down the river bank, then carry it across the stream, risking loss of life, limb and cargo.[8]

The real problem, though, revolved around the question of who did it: "It was not an eruption but an explosion," said Tuan, a T'boli tribesman and former pilot. There was speculation that illegal logging had weakened the earth on the sides of the crater. There was talk of a search for gold in hopes of a strike like those in other veins on Mindanao. Tuan, whose photograph in the municipal hall shows him wearing an 18-carat, diamond-encrusted gold ring, swore to me, "no logging, no mining here."[9]

Government volcanic experts saw no man-made reason for the crater wall to have weakened—no signs of anyone logging or searching for gold. There must have been too much rain, they said. Then it turned out the experts had jumped to that conclusion without visiting the area. As the public outcry mounted, illicit logging *and* a secret gold hunt were exposed. It was also dis-covered that T'boli officials were involved.

What else could one expect from a system in which payoffs are the norm at every level of society? As regularly as people are salvaged and kidnapped, ships are wrecked, drowning hundreds; mines collapse, trapping miners; hillsides are stripped of forests and topsoil, starving crops; and industries spew contaminants.

Such was the case on the island of Marinduque, where giant Marcopper Mining wiped out virtually all life in two rivers by dumping mine tailings, lahar-like sludge, over a four-year period, killing or sickening thousands of people and their livestock. A UN report painted the scene in Pinatubo-like terms. The river system was "so significantly degraded as to be considered an environmental disaster," it concluded, citing "the total loss of aquatic life and biological productivity from the affected areas." Among "additional impacts" were "total loss of the beneficial use of the rivers for domestic and agricultural purposes, e.g., livestock, fishing, laundry, bathing and crops" along with "reduced access" and "increased health risk due to immersion."[10]

The UN report warned of worse to come as the waters rose in the rainy season to "threaten the health and well-being of local communities." The company, it seemed, had been discharging the mine tailings from a highly productive source of copper ore into the open-cut site of an abandoned mine pit, which had finally burst through "a disused drainage tunnel near its bottom." Nor had the company managed to close the tunnel after the disaster. "The failure by Marcopper to completely stem the flow of tailings from the tunnel to date," said the report, "reflects the lack of risk assessment, contingency planning and monitoring. . . ."[11]

Through it all, the system goes on unchecked except when a disaster involving mass loss of life momentarily exposes its flaws. Ensuing investigations make headlines, then are forgotten amid more payoffs—until the next disaster. Ten years after the People Power revolution, people realized, not a single member of the old Marcos entourage—no crony, no official who benefited from the system—had done a day in jail. "Has anyone of these crony owners been prosecuted and jailed," asked commentator Randy David. "Has anybody been sent to jail for dissipating the assets of sequestered companies, or for squandering scarce resources of government in a futile effort to run or to safeguard these companies?"[12]

David doubted the integrity of those who came after Marcos almost as much as those who had once served the deposed, deceased dictator. He believed that "the public officials who took power after Marcos failed to pursue the cases against the regime because they were overwhelmed by the enormity of the task of prosecuting the Marcoses and their cronies." They were not only "intimidated by their complexity and the danger of opening an entire Pandora's box that could incriminate nearly everybody in the business community" but were also "quite content to seize some crony properties through sequestration and use these for their own purposes while the status of these assets awaited resolution."[13]

The cases against Imelda Marcos represent the most visible disgrace of the system—the justice system and the society that supports it. Her lawyers had no trouble delaying review of a conviction in 1993 by filing a "motion for reconsideration"—a procedure that enables the rich to escape almost anything. No one believed that she would ever serve the term of 18 to 24 years meted out by the judge after a trial for graft and corruption that had dragged on for 20 months. The Supreme Court in September 1997 ruled that she still had to stand trial on charges of transferring funds from government accounts to her own, but in the end she counted on the high court. Had not that august body revealed its loyalty to her by letting her take a seat in Congress—even though she had long since left her childhood home of Leyte, from which she had run for office?

The effort to retrieve a portion of the fortune she and her husband had banked in Switzerland showed the power of unlimited funds and influence on a global scale. The government and "10,000 human rights victims" were suing separately, but a decade after Marcos' flight the case was still in pretrial stage amid conflicts among agencies. One of them was the PCGG, which Salonga had chaired until he decided to run for the Senate and lead the attack on the American bases.[14]

A U.S. federal court ruling in Hawaii in 1995, holding the Marcos estate liable for $2.1 billion for the human rights victims, had no immediate impact. The Swiss Supreme Court ruled that it could release none of $500 million acknowledged as held by two Swiss banks until a high court in the Philippines found Mrs. Marcos guilty of at least *something*. The PCGG chairman, Magtanggol Gunigundo, hotly denied as "a tale out of Arabian knights" a claim by lawyers for the victims that government officials had sold gold acquired in a deal with the Marcos family—and had colluded with Swiss banks to salt the $2 billion in proceeds in secret accounts. "There is no negotiation for the sale of this alleged golden hoard," Gunigundo told me.[15]

The story got even better when the American lawyer for the human rights victims in Los Angeles said Ramos himself held Marcos assets in Swiss accounts. The source was said to be a memo by the retired Swiss judge in charge of a trust for some of the Marcos wealth. The judge, however, labeled the memo a forgery, and Ramos called the tale "a conspiracy of falsehood and fabrication." For once he had Imelda on his side. She gladly denied that she or Ramos or anyone else had withdrawn Marcos assets from Swiss banks. "The Marcos wealth is not ill-gotten," she gloated.[16]

When I saw Salonga in semi-retirement at his home in a gated, guarded village in Pasig, a short drive off Edsa on the eastern fringe of Metro Manila, he was defensive about why he had quit the PCGG after only a year and a half. "I think I recovered as much as could be recovered," he said. "I was drafted by Cory Aquino to run for the Senate." He linked his position on the bases to his brief effort to recover the Marcos billions: "Because of the bases, the Americans were willing to see Marcos accumulate hidden wealth." He accused the business community of betraying him in the end: "I should have had a lot of money for the 1992 election. I lost because all the businessmen who had pledged to help me got out after my stand on the bases."[17]

Salonga belatedly suggested that Ramos name "a special team of able, untainted prosecutors, headed by a competent person of integrity and dedication, and with the advice of an eminent three-man body of distinguished citizens" to work on the cases against Imelda and her brother, Benjamin "Kokoy" Romualdez, who had once tended both their interests by serving concurrently as ambassador to the United States and as governor of Leyte Province.[18] The idea seemed fine—until one recalled that Salonga had abandoned the same cause to pursue his quest for political glory.

Did there now exist an "untainted prosecutor" or "competent person of integrity" willing to work full time on the issue of hidden wealth? The answer was almost certainly no. "These cases which cry for justice one way or another have not been moving for a long, long time," noted an article in *Kilosbayan Magazine,* the journal of Salonga's own Kilosbayan, People Action, an organization he established to promote his causes after his poor showing in 1992. Unless Ramos "does something about it and soon," said the magazine, "there may be no cases of plundered wealth to talk about *after* the 1998 elections."[19]

But how, the article asked, could the opposition in Congress "be expected to demand speedy justice when some of their leaders are deeply involved in the ill-gotten wealth cases against the Marcoses or were waltzing with the dictator during those fateful years."[20] The web of inner connections, of blood relationships, of obligations, was endless. As Salonga lectured me, "Debt from within, cronyism, is part of our culture."[21] Cronyism, however, goes far beyond "debt from within." It extends to the exchange of numbers of overseas bank accounts, the handout of expensive gifts, the dispensation of positions, directorships, stocks, bank loans, free hotel rooms and airplane tickets, donations and allowances—and 10 percent off the top.

"Not all Filipinos are corrupt," said Salonga, in a show of national sensitivity, as I pressed for details that he was not about to give. More than ever, the cronies, Imelda included, were in a position to pay off old friends and colleagues, even old enemies. Whatever wealth some of them may have lost, if any, they were presumed to have recovered—with interest. "And the blame goes to the Presidential Commission on Good Government," said one writer, charging that it "has miserably failed to recover the 'ill-gotten wealth' of these people." Since its creation, in fact, the PCGG had recovered the peso equivalent of about $400 million, compared to its original goal of $8.5 billion—the minimal estimate of the Marcos loot, including $3.5 billion in Swiss banks.[22]

The renaissance of the cronies made a mockery not only of the People Power revolution but of the validity of President Ramos' drive toward

"Philippines 2000," whose aims did not include a solution to the puzzle of the hidden wealth. "The PCGG had awesome powers and plenty of opportunities to seize the assets of the Marcoses—and their cronies," according to a summary of the debacle. "But it squandered them."[23]

Prosecutors acknowledged that the cases would not be solved for 10 or 20 years—that is, never: "The Marcos heirs have succeeded in blocking the PCGG's attempt to turn over their Swiss accounts to the government. They have eluded conviction in U.S.-filed cases by winning these cases outright or entering into one-sided compromise agreements with the PCGG." At the same time, "the Marcoses' cronies took advantage of the sloppy handling of the cases by PCGG lawyers to regain control over their sequestered firms."[24]

The list of the cronies is a rogue's gallery of tycoons and confidence men, killers and bullies. Among the wealthiest, after the widow Imelda, is Eduardo "Danding" Cojuangco Jr., who escaped some of the heat in Negros while fighting for a fortune of nearly a billion dollars that he pumped into a number of companies, including San Miguel, the brewery. In deals reached in 1990 and 1991, Danding's Negros neighbor, Roberto S. Benedicto, retrieved directorships in about 20 of his companies while paying a pittance of $16 million in cash and agreeing to surrender stock certificates worth much more in two Manila television stations—a small price for rehabilitation. Six years later, Gunigundo complained, "We still don't have the shares in our hands."[25]

Lucio Tan, who once "owed" nearly a quarter of a billion dollars, remains the nation's richest man, flying high as chairman of Philippine Airlines after winning his three-year fight for control of the money-losing national flag carrier. That done, he won a series of court decisions rejecting the government's efforts to get his flagship company, Fortune Tobacco, to pay millions more in taxes—and then sued the bureaucrat who went after him.

The worst of the cronies find life overseas to their liking. "Kokoy" Romualdez and former military chief Fabian Ver, the likely mastermind of Benigno Aquino's assassination, live unobtrusively in North America, their assets largely untouchable and increasingly forgotten. Herminio Disini, who made $100 million in commissions on an aborted deal with Westinghouse to build a nuclear power plant in Bataan, hangs out in a castle in Austria.

The PCGG sees out-of-court settlements as an easy way to get quick judgements and dispose of cases. Lawyers for the cronies charge that profiteers with close connections to the leaders of the People Power revolt, including Aquino, are buying up sequestered companies for bargain-basement prices. Some companies, once taken over by the PCGG, are reported stripped bare of their assets. Imelda charged that the PCGG seized a mansion of hers for a friend of Cory but neglected to mention that she had owned the property secretly through a front. That omission did not stop

Imelda from filing charges of theft, graft and corrupt practices after the property was auctioned off for what she said was less than half its real value. The case is one of about 50 involving the Marcos family in its prolonged campaign to cling to its fortune.[26]

The scramble for the stolen billions conjures the image of television documentaries in which wild animals maul one another in greedy quarrels over freshly killed meat. There is not a chance that justice will be done. Even if someone eventually goes to jail as a symbol, a scapegoat, hundreds of others who profited from the looting of the Philippines, both before and after Edsa, in the old order, the new order or both, will remain not only free but also richer than ever.

A PCGG official once estimated that recovery of all the ill-gotten wealth of the Marcoses would suffice to repay the entire national debt of $26 billion owed at the time of the People Power revolution. Imelda embellished on the estimate, twitting PCGG investigators by saying that gold certificates willed by her late husband to the Filipino people were worth much more— possibly the whole debt as of a decade later, more than $40 billion. There was one problem. The gold certificates were "missing." Moreover, said the PCGG, the only Marcos will filed in court in the Philippines showed that he had left his entire estate to Imelda and their two daughters and son.[27]

Is corruption in the Philippines worse, however, than that in its ASEAN neighbors? Yes, according to a poll conducted by Dow-Jones' Asian subsidiaries, the *Far Eastern Economic Review* and its television sibling, Asia Business News, asking executives to judge the civil service of their countries. The poll showed 44.5 percent rating the Philippine civil service as "very corrupt," at the top of the list ahead of Indonesia, whereas 22.2 percent called the Philippines "corrupt" and 33.3 percent pronounced it "somewhat corrupt." (No one checked the box for "not corrupt.") Business leaders, their self-interest piqued by the need for bribing immigration, customs and tax officials, rated the Philippine civil service *last* in efficiency— 62.5 percent called it "inefficient," whereas *none* found it either "highly efficient" or "efficient."[28]

The money flows in ways too numerous to count. Members of Congress with power over public works have been known to name the contractors for projects. "It is an open secret that the kickback given for this consideration amounts to 10–20 percent of the projects costs," said one study. Another case in point cited by the study: appropriations "in the national budget for non-existent hospitals and health personnel." One member of Congress was caught "appropriating funds for a private foundation that he himself heads," but "front-line revenue-collecting agencies" were by and large the biggest losers.[29]

Filipinos often rationalize corruption by claiming that the same—and more—goes on in Indonesia, Thailand, Malaysia and even communist Vietnam. "That survey does great injustice to our civil servants," said Press Secretary Villanueva, on the defense again. "I don't think there is any country, even the western countries, that is immune to graft and corruption."[30]

No doubt, but the government "ombudsman," Aniano Desierto, amid calls for his own resignation for accepting gifts, estimated "the government suffers an annual loss of 40–50 billion pesos in undeclared taxes and 10–20 billion pesos out of the current appropriation due to funds diversion or misappropriation. . . ." Those figures, in dollars, came to $1.6-$2 billion per year lost in taxes and another $400-$500 million from corruption. Or, as Desierto put it, the amount "would either be capable of creating 830,000 jobs or 3,300 kilometers of concrete road or 50,000 kilometers of barangay-to-market roads or 50,000 school buildings." Indeed, he added, "Such staggering losses can pay our foreign debt at $40 billion in 20 years."[31]

One crucial difference between the Philippines and other ASEAN countries is that the wealth acquired by graft and bribery elsewhere tends to go back into local economies—for more investment, more profits, more payoffs. The billions looted in the Philippines tend to go overseas, to Swiss accounts, investments in real estate, homes in America, as they did before Marcos' demise. The Swiss accounts of the Marcoses are the tips of a huge iceberg. Filipino entrepreneurs see the deposit of their booty abroad as an end in itself—safer and more desirable than exposure to shaky investments and fraud at home.

There is, however, a mirror image of the flight of capital from the Philippines, where it was earned or stolen, into foreign bank accounts. That is the billions of dollars sent back by the masses of Filipinos who flee overseas in search of jobs. While the Imeldas and Dandings and RSBs fleece the economy, untold millions, mostly from poor families far from the centers of money and power, toil abroad in often debasing, degrading jobs for pittances—and remittances that go back home. From a handful of Ilocanos shipped to the pineapple plantations of Hawaii in the early twentieth century, the number of Filipinos overseas has soared to well over 7 million, 2 million in the United States alone.

The amount of money remitted through normal banking channels by Filipinos in all categories overseas came to $7.56 billion in 1996. OFWs (overseas Filipino workers), those who sign contracts with employment agencies or companies, remitted $4.3 billion. Migrants—workers and students on expired visas—remitted much of the rest. Total income sent home through all channels by all Filipinos abroad was assumed to have been much higher, well over $10 billion, including cash hand-carried into the country. Considering that the Philippines' trade deficit was $11.84 billion in 1996, one had to view remittances as essential to the country's economic survival.[32]

The Philippines' greatest export, in other words, is people, most of them in menial jobs, but many employed in fields ranging from health care to engineering to journalism. Many more are in the nebulous category of "entertainer," including the thousands singing in combos, in discos, in ballrooms, piano bars in luxury hotels and nightclubs around the world plus thousands more masquerading as "cultural dancers," go-going in sailors' bars in Hong Kong's Wanchai district, stripping and inviting customers for sex in Japan's "pink cabarets" and back-alley *nu-doh gekijo* (nude theaters), all *yakuza* domain.

President Ramos in 1996 sought to elevate respect for OFWs by having them officially called just that instead of OCWs (overseas contract workers), as they were previously known. That term had taken on a negative connotation for its association with another demeaning term, DH (domestic helper), the largest single job category for those sent abroad on contract.

The elitists at the apex of governance and society in the Philippines, however, look with disdain on the vast majority of OFWs, whatever they're called. The educated and well-to-do are upset because they are sometimes confused with OFWs—and treated at airports, in restaurants and on streets from Hong Kong to the Persian Gulf as if they too were lower class. Instinctively, they hold the OFWs in contempt as social inferiors—poor, semi-literate, ill-mannered. A typical OFW is fortunate to know enough English to communicate as a maid or a servant, chauffeur or cook—categories whom the rich of the Philippines treat as low life as surely as do the oil-rich Arabs or wealthy overseas Chinese.

While pumping their profits into foreign accounts, Philippine tycoons and taste-makers would like the government to do all it can to discourage Filipinos from working overseas in such large numbers. "The policy of the government is to reduce immigration as we improve our economy," said Felicissimo Joson, chief of the Philippine Overseas Employment Administration, set up to advise and manage the daily exodus of Filipinos bound for work projects abroad. "It is not the policy of the government to use employment as an export industry."[33]

Joson spends much of his time worrying about the unhappiness and tragedy that befalls overseas workers, hundreds of whom drown in shipwrecks, die in industrial accidents, or commit suicide every year. Many more return with stories of having been beaten by their employers, cheated on contracts, or tortured and whipped in Saudi jails for such infractions as drinking alcohol or petty thievery.

Their stories, told matter-of-factly, with smiles of relief that it's all over, come as a shock to a foreigner who can't see why they don't sue, don't file charges and don't make a huge fuss, as they certainly could in the United States.

Yolanda Malicdan, now running a small cooperative, weaving cloth on a loom in a village near Baguio, quit her job as a maid for a wealthy family in the United Arab Emirates after the wife, a woman in her late twenties, hit her on her back with a water pail and on her head with the heel of a shoe, injuring her so badly that she had to go to the hospital. Yolanda's offense: the woman's baby had run out of the bathroom in the middle of a bath and disturbed the family. A scar is visible on Yolanda's forehead. "My employer paid me, and I left. I tried several times to call our embassy, but they can do nothing."[34]

Arab women are the worst, said Yolanda, but Arab men also beat maids—when they are not molesting them. "The Arabs use their headdresses. They pull it off and hit with that. It's hard and heavy. I heard of a co-worker who needed an operation after she was hit." Sometimes the employers pay for medical treatment. Sometimes the maids quit, with or without compensation. Never, however, do they go to the police or the courts, which they know would be dead set against them—and might hold them responsible for the crime.

The plight of Filipino maids has been in the newspapers for years, but two cases captured headlines and imaginations as never before. The first was that of Flor Contemplacion, a maid who was hanged in Singapore in March 1995 for the murder nearly four years earlier of another maid and a five-year-old boy in her care.

The case turned into a sensation in the Philippines, touching the rawest nerves of a people who believed a bully-boy was again doing them wrong. Diplomatic relations with Singapore were almost but not quite broken, top officials were accused of not caring or doing enough to protest Flor's fate, and Secretary of Foreign Affairs Roberto Romulo had to resign, while the ambassador to Singapore was recalled. Flor never denied her guilt, but that did not stop speculation that the dead boy's father had killed the maid after the maid accidentally drowned the baby. ("Flor was framed," Yolanda believes, as does almost any Filipino who has worked as an OFW. "She was forced to make confessions.")

The second sensational case was that of Sarah Balabagan, a Muslim girl from Mindanao for whom an unscrupulous employment agency had lied about her age, saying that she was in her twenties to get her a passport and a job as a maid in the United Arab Emirates. Sarah's crime was to have murdered the elderly man of the house, stabbing him 34 times with a kitchen knife as he tried to rape her. Fragile and frightened in the photographs, Sarah aroused even wider sympathy when it turned out she was really 15. Initially, a local court in June 1995 sentenced her to seven years and a net sum of $13,000 in "blood money" for the victim's relatives. It was all in accordance with Islamic Shariah law—$40,000 owed the family for wrongful death minus $27,000 awarded her for having been raped.

Three months later, however, a Shariah court retried Sarah and sentenced her to death. As the world cringed at the prospect of her execution, UAE President Sheikh Zayed ibn Sultan an Nahayan, anxious about his country's image in the West, especially the United States, the source of billions of dollars worth of arms, passed the word down for the victim's son to settle for blood money. Although the son had a right under Shariah law to insist on the death penalty, he accepted from Sarah's dirt-poor family the sum of $41,000 raised from private donors and relayed through the Philippine embassy. Then, in November 1995, an appeals court gave her a year in jail and 100 lashes—unspeakably brutal but preferable to the image of her frail, blood-spattered body sagging from a post.[35]

Both cases riveted attention in the Philippines on the OFWs. Pictures of bruised and battered women are staples in the tabloids, which are big sellers among Filipino workers overseas. Philippine embassies are besieged by Filipinos asking for help from cruel employers. Sometimes Filipino diplomats are accused of a different form of cruelty—and venality. OFWs in Saudi Arabia in 1996 charged the Philippine ambassador and the embassy's OFW welfare officer with "selling" Filipinas to Arab, Pakistani and Palestinian men to work as maids. They said the pair had displayed "gross negligence and arrogance" toward OFWs—and did nothing for those who had fled from cruel Saudi employers, then were held by the Saudi Social Welfare Administration, where guards raped them.[36]

OFWs rate Arabs as the harshest and overseas Chinese a solid second. All told, an average of 35,000 cases of abuse are reported each year by OFWs for offenses ranging from arbitrary changes in contracts, including reduction of pay, to beatings and rape. The worst offenders, in terms of the numbers of arrests of OFWs, abuses against them and disputes with employers, are newly rich overseas Chinese in the ASEAN neighbors of Singapore and Malaysia. Next on the rogues' list are Gulf Arabs in the United Arab Emirates, Kuwait, Libya—and Saudi Arabia, which attracts the most OFWs.[37]

How much, however, do Filipinos in high places care? Ramos, off to the Gulf in March 1997, yielded to a UAE demand that he ban a sensational Filipino film, *The Sarah Balabagan Story,* which portrayed rich Arabs as venal, cruel, woman-hating cowards.

"The world should learn to realize that we are helping the world," said Isodoro Aligada, a congressman who spent 14 years in Saudi Arabia as an engineer and project director. He believes the lot of the OFWs has improved as a result of the damning publicity. "When they have a Filipino maid or a Filipino driver, they're proud of them," he said. Trouble sometimes breaks out when a wife becomes wary of the attention her husband is lavishing on the maid. "These countries are not used to having a maid. When you get a maid who is looking good, the jealousy comes out."[38]

For solace, Filipino maids flock like birds to downtown parks and squares on days off in cities from the Persian Gulf to Asia. In Hong Kong's central district, opposite the Star ferry, on Statue Square between the ritzy Mandarin Hotel, the colonial Legislative Council and some of the glistening banks that form the colony's skyline, hundreds of them gather on Sundays, picnicking on Filipino-style food, reading Manila newspapers, exchanging gossip.

Worried about their future after Hong Kong's transfer to Chinese rule on July 1, 1997, most of the colony's 140,000 Filipinos preferred to stay on. Thousands had given up jobs at home as teachers, clerks and secretaries to work as domestic helpers, sweeping floors, doing laundry and minding babies for higher pay for the former colony's upper class. "I miss my home," said a DH from Marcos' province of Ilocos Norte in the Ilocano region, spawning ground of millions of OFWs. "There is no work there. It is much better here"—where maids average $150 a week, ten times more than schoolteachers in the Philippines.[39]

"Endless poverty, rampaging unemployment and other social problems force Filipinos to work abroad," said *Ibon,* reporting that nearly 2,000 contract workers leave the Philippines every day, more than a third of them for unskilled service jobs. "Poverty caused by an iniquitous social and political system has practically driven Filipinos abroad." Whereas unemployment in late 1994 was 8.4 percent, *under*employment was more than 20 percent, and upward of three-fourths of the people lived below the poverty line.[40] The truth is, the Philippines cannot do without the billions earned by OFWs. Remittances are legally required of male OFWs with families back home and are sent voluntarily by millions more—female OFWs or men and women who are no longer OFWs but migrant workers, often living and working overseas without proper visas or passports.

Like everything else in the Philippines, deploying hundreds of thousands overseas fosters rackets of all sorts. "Filipino migrant workers are the most exploited and abused among [the] Filipino working class," observed *Ibon.* "They are exploited and abused not only abroad but right in their own country."[41]

Routinely, agencies in Manila and other centers with large numbers of relatively poor people seeking salvation on OFW incomes vastly overcharge, beyond legally set maximums, for placement. Less typically, they collect fees, even land titles, for jobs that do not exist. As in all other agencies and offices of governance, the rackets flourish with bureaucratic connivance—one syndicate operated inside the Philippine Overseas Employment Administration, under Administrator Joson's nose, and in embassies abroad.

Occasionally, President Ramos "ordered" the Department of Labor and Employment and the Department of Justice to go after illegal recruiting. The best incentive for him to act, as in Smokey Mountain and much else that he did, was the embarrassment of negative publicity. In January 1996 he demanded prosecution "without delay" of "members of the syndicate which recently recruited 'tourist workers' for Malaysia" after "the mass arrest by Malaysian authorities" of Filipinos sent to Malaysia for jobs that did not exist—and forced to work illegally.[42] The woman in charge of the syndicate, presumably tipped well in advance, was nowhere to be found. Ramos' people were not serious about stopping illegal recruiting, any more than they hoped to do much about abuses against Filipinos on legitimate jobs overseas.

The question is whether the Philippine governing system, regardless of who nominally controls it, is serious about anything beyond improving the statistics for the next conference or the next review by the IMF or World Bank. The atmosphere in the Philippines might be more attractive for business but remained clouded in Ramos' quest for NIC (Newly Industrialized Country) status by the year 2000. The growing trade deficit—already $9.09 billion for 1995, up from $7.85 billion the year before and double the deficit of $4.02 billion for 1990—conspired with double-digit inflation, declining agricultural production, even a decline in foreign investment to raise doubts about the image of turnaround.[43]

The looting of Clark—an assault that Philippine society would prefer either to forget or to dismiss as a murky happening for which no one is to blame—remains a symbol of the looting of Philippine democracy. The headlines are full of bickering among senators and representatives, but all of them represent the same class that ruled under Marcos and before, with origins dating from their collaboration with Spanish and then American colonialists. Are a few monopolies, such as Philippine Airlines and the Philippine Long Distance Telephone Company, open to competition? On paper, yes. In fact, the lineups shift, there are more teams in the league, but the players remain much the same.

The spirit of looting also pervades land reform—not surprising considering that almost all members of the Congress are either landlords or protégés of landlords. One device of Congress is to force through exemptions under the comprehensive agrarian reform program for money-making cattle farms and fishponds. Another is to request approval for turning farmland into industrial or housing estates. How much long-term income these would generate remains uncertain. Three-fourths of the manufacturing in the Philippines remains at the cottage-industry level—packaging, handicrafts and the like.

The economic downturn that shook the region in 1997 reverberated through the Philippines in the form of a sagging stock market, declining peso, soaring interest rates and rising oil prices. Growth in industry steadily decelerated in 1997 amid fears that the country had lost some of its allure for foreign investors. The governor of the Bangko Sentral ng Pilipinas (the Central Bank of the Philippines) acknowledged that a "too high interest rate to support an unrealistic exchange rate will obviously be detrimental to business and the economy as a whole."[44]

At a meeting with IMF officials in Hong Kong, according to one report, Philippine financial officials "showed a touch of pragmatism by ever so gently" explaining why they might not be able to liberalize financial services as quickly as suggested by the World Trade Organization. Finance Secretary de Ocampo explained to WTO chief Renato Ruggiero that the Philippines preferred a "moderate path of financial liberalization."[45] The ultimate fear if the downturn persisted, as indicated by the Supreme Court nullifying oil deregulations, was that the Philippines and other countries might revert to protective measures of the sort that had been so ruinous under Marcos.

Most alarming was the failure of agricultural production to keep up with rising needs. The looting extends to the food needed for a population growing by about 2 million a year—70 million by the middle of the 1990s, certain to go above 80 million by the turn of the century. Poorly implemented land-reform schemes, Chinese traders and the weather were three of the reasons advanced for the decline in rice production in 1994. (So much for the green revolution of "miracle rice" developed with American aid at the University of the Philippines' institute in Los Baños. Farmers say they don't have enough money for the fertilizer needed to grow it.) Cartels may be to blame for hoarding, but Philippine rice production is only 2.6 metric tons per hectare as compared to 3 tons in Vietnam and 4 tons in Indonesia—countries that definitely should not be more advanced agriculturally.[46]

Democracy in the spirit of many of the idealists who waged the People Power revolution may prove as ephemeral in the Philippines as in so many other Third-World countries, including all the other members of ASEAN. The democratic spirit faded slowly as Ramos, frustrated by the problems inherited from Aquino, from Marcos, from generations before them, tried in various ways to assert authority, to bring about order, to see if the wealth might somehow trickle down. It was difficult to say where or who were his real foes—political forces, once his friends and allies; Marcos "loyalists" paid off by one crony or another, Imelda included; tycoons battling over new opportunities in investment or, conversely, fighting liberalization in order to protect commercial fiefdoms.

Leftists saw Ramos from a different perspective—as a dictator in the mold of Lee Kuan Yew of Singapore or the Indonesian ruler Suharto, who rose to power in 1966 by smashing the communists after their abortive coup of September 30, 1965. Noted Antonio A. Tujan Jr., a top Bayan editor:

"Ironically, the neo-liberal development framework being followed by the Ramos government requires the imposition of fascist rule along the lines of Singapore's constitutional authoritarianism." Ramos-style "liberalism," he said, was "only for the capitalist class, especially the foreign ones, and requires the stifling of dissent."[47]

Such assertions reflected the endemic suspicion of the foreign capitalist forces whom Ramos strove to bring into the Philippines on a scale never imagined by any of his predecessors. The greatest irony was that radical "nationalists" actually shared common cause with political and business interests anxious to stave off foreign competition in favor of their own often inefficient enterprises. In the maelstrom of conflicting forces, the left never mentioned the alternatives to "transnationals:" no new ventures at all in key fields *or* ventures by local tycoons, who paid far less than most of the dreaded foreigners in "the capitalist class."

The radicals were right, however, in perceiving the signs of reversion to authoritarian rule. It did not seem coincidental that Ramos should appoint dozens of retired generals and colonels to key posts. He knew them from his military days, and he felt comfortable with them. Some of them formed the crux of a group called "Friends of Steady Eddie," the president's nickname. They put out glossy-covered books containing his speeches. National Security Adviser Jose Almonte, the former general involved in recruiting ex-officers into the government, handed me a set of four books of Ramos' speeches at the end of an interview in which he heaped scorn on revolutionaries, both rightists and leftists.

"The rebels of RAM have joined the political mainstream," he said of the band of military men who staged the coups against Aquino. "The RAM is centrist, not rightist"—a self-interested judgment considering that Almonte was a prime mover behind RAM in the early days when the initials stood for the Reform Armed Forces movement. (Later, RAM was construed as the acronym for the Tagalog Rebolusyonaryong Alyansang Makabansa.) At the same time, Almonte linked improvement in the lives of the poor to market-opening. "By bringing down the tariff barriers that feathered protectionists, these are among reform measures that contribute to pulling the roots of the rebellion." The inference was that lower tariff barriers would lower prices—and encourage local industry to hire more people too.[48]

Raul Manglapus agreed—almost. "Protectionism should be a thing of the past," he told me. Away on a speaking tour when Marcos imposed martial law, the president of the Philippine National Oil Company and former senator had spent more than thirteen years in the United States during the period of martial law, returning the day after the revolution on Edsa. Five years later, he was negotiating the bases agreement with the Americans, heaping on absurd financial demands before completing the deal the Philippine Senate rejected.

Manglapus did not appear to have changed his philosophy much since then. "There may still have to be some basic industry subject to tariff protection," he said carefully. Take petrochemicals. "All around Southeast Asia you will see the petrochemical industry is highly protective. I am for a reasonable protection of petrochemical because it is a basic industry."[49] That argument might suffice for the people who regulate the industry, but it ignored the impact of high tariffs on petrochemicals on the costs of local industries buying their products—and on consumers.

Manglapus also wanted petrochemical firms to set up operations on the Bataan peninsula, a region still harassed by NPA guerrillas but comfortably near his Philippine National Oil Company facilities. A Taiwan company preferred a safer location in Batangas Province near Manila, close to both the Caltex and Shell refineries. The issue turned into a political football amid customary charges of payoffs after a judge upheld a demand by the congressman from Bataan for the Taiwan company to invest in his district—and the company decided not to invest at all.

Manglapus forgot all that while appearing to favor free markets: "I am for lowering of tariffs in areas with free investment"—a distinction that might get blurred depending on who was making policy to suit whose whims.[50]

There was also a convenient rationale for avoiding pursuit of corruption at every layer of government. Seamlessly, not pausing, Almonte brushed off observations that little of the "hidden wealth" of Marcos et al. had been recovered, that little had changed for most people: "Even if they recover a billion or so, it is nothing, it's a drop in the bucket. You cannot solve the problems in three years. The most we can do is just put the Filipino house in order. My reaction is to resolve the problem through a systemic approach, not on a case-by-case basis. We are creating conditions by which corruption will be minimized. Like in tax reform, we are introducing the principle of growth. Like in the customs, we are bringing down tariffs so there is no more smuggling."[51]

The program, on paper or in an interview, sounded logical. Only after hearing dozens of horror stories, after reading reports of smuggling, cheating, graft and bribery everywhere, does one realize on what a theoretical plane Almonte was talking. Nothing if not ingratiating, Almonte sounded like a bit of a leftist himself as we chatted on in his office complex not far from Edsa. "Our poverty is so deep-seated, we are confused," he said, pressed for what the government might do. He held the Americans in large measure at fault for the feudal system. "The Americans used the local elites as their conduit of control."

One wondered how much Almonte really believed his own words in view of his background in intelligence, especially since he was now charged, among other things, with coordinating all the intelligence gathered by government agencies. Here was a man who had the information needed to extract favors and payback and loyalty from throughout the armed forces and much of the civilian establishment as well. For him and for his boss, the mission was to form an impregnable base to build an edifice capable not only of carrying out programs but also of perpetuating power. All else—the looting, the hidden wealth, people power—was of little relative import.

To that end, the Armed Forces of the Philippines, down to 100,000-plus troops, supplemented by the Philippine National Police, was no more than an internal peacekeeping organization. "Our modernization plan is not enough," said Almonte. "If we can have one small slingshot, maybe we can manage. As far as internal threats, we are confident we can handle them."

Defense Secretary de Villa, in charge of modernizing the armed forces, dealt in similar generalities. "There's always a chance for some upheaval anywhere," he averred, but he wasn't sure where. Like Almonte, he acknowledged neither Moro nor NPA guerrillas as a threat, and failed to mention the vulnerability of a coastline of more than 8,000 miles surrounding as many islands over a distance from north to south of 1,150 miles.[52]

A Ramos clone who yearned to follow him as president in 1998, de Villa displayed a disturbingly cold vagueness. "The Philippines is not expecting an aggression as we have experienced from World War II," he said, when pressed on what the armed forces were for. "We cannot say we are prepared, we cannot say we are not prepared." He professed "we're not worried about anything," but for safety's sake still counted on American expertise, if not the American weaponry that stopped coming after rejection of the bases treaty. "The historic association with the United States is going on. We conduct exercises every year. We're not about to discard that."[53]

One reason for de Villa's reluctance to say more was that Lulu Ilustre, spokeswoman for the armed forces, was there, minding a tape recorder on the coffee table between us. Ilustre had already warned me not to ask questions about the looting of Clark—the topic that sent her into a paroxysm of rage afterward. It was as though the looting of Clark, of the treasury, of government agencies, of the people who earn the most for the country by laboring under often humiliating conditions abroad were matters that the de Villas, the Almontes, preferred to ignore while advancing their own aims and those of their boss. Their world, behind the walls of their compounds off Edsa, appeared as removed from Philippine realities as that of the nearby luxury hotels and malls.

In this unreal setting, it is possible to forget that the days of the American military presence, if not American power, are not quite over. The Joint U.S. Military Assistance and Advisory Group (JUSMAAG) moved to the "Rowe compound" in the U.S. embassy's Seafront facility overlooking Manila Bay after the assassination of Colonel Rowe in 1989. Then, as U.S. military aid plunged sharply after the failure to renew the bases treaty two years later, it retreated up Roxas Boulevard to a suite of rooms in the venerable embassy building by the bay.

Those facilities seemed more than adequate as American military assistance dwindled to materiél already in the pipeline and the number of people in the group plunged from several hundred to six. As a symbol of the shift, the JUSMAAG was renamed MAG, for Military Assistance Group. The adjective "advisory" was deemed unnecessary since the Americans claimed no longer to dispense "advice." They might drop in on Philippine units at brigade level but no longer ventured into the field, surveying the troops in small-unit action, where it really counted, as they had when Colonel Rowe was telling the Filipinos how to beat the NPA.

Strangely, however, a year after the last Americans had left Subic Bay, joint exercises resumed under the rubric, "Balikatan"—shoulder-to-shoulder. The war games were a vestige of imperial glory that was. From late 1993 to mid-1996, small elements of the U.S. Army, Navy and Air Force coordinated with their Filipino counterparts in order, as a joint press release stated, "to enhance their joint capabilities to respond to mutual defense efforts and civil military operations pursuant to the Mutual Defense Treaty of August 30, 1951."[54]

Behind the language of the press release lay a carefully calculated effort by both the Philippines and the United States to get along militarily after the bitterness engendered by the bases debate. Soon after President Ramos visited the United States in November 1993, the two sides staged Balikatan '93, the first joint exercise since the last Americans had pulled out of Subic a year earlier. Ramos showed up at the games—a strong symbolic gesture, since no Philippine president had ever before graced such an exercise with his presence.

There were other signs of life in the old alliance. About $100 million in military assistance approved before 1992 was flowing into the Philippines, mostly for armored vehicles and spare parts. The Mutual Defense Board, set up in 1958 with Philippine and U.S. representatives, was busy at Camp Aguinaldo developing plans for defending the Philippines and stockpiling materiél in case of attack on the Spratly Islands.[55]

The bitterness lingered on, though. Around the time of the second anniversary of the U.S. pullout from Subic, the government in November 1994 said "no" again—this time to something named ACSA (pronounced axe-uh). The acronym stands for Acquisition and Cross-Servicing Agreement—a deal for giving American planes and ships "access" to some of their old haunts for $12 million worth of routine purchases and servicing a year. The question was whether U.S. warships would gain "access" if the United States resumed military aid, including sales, all of which had dried up except for a paltry million dollars a year for training Philippine officers in the States.

"Access" remained a dirty word. The whole issue was just too sensitive politically, especially when one considers the implications of a section of the agreement providing for "storage service." The term, to Filipino nationalists, sounded an awful lot like a euphemism for "base." What could be the meaning of "storage" other than to "base equipment"—and the men to go with it?[56]

Each year, meanwhile, the war games got a little more intense. By 1995, the two countries were ready for by far their biggest show since the American pullout in the form of Balikatan '95. This time, all services from both countries participated, and the games escalated to participation by one Philippine and one U.S. Army brigade. Marine and navy units from both countries operated off Cavite, while the Philippines' few F-5s, relics from a generation ago, flew in tandem with U.S. Air Force A-10s.[57]

The mood was one of self-conscious rapport. Officers on both sides were terribly polite. There was a deliberate effort not to appear arrogant, hostile or overbearing. The Americans did not talk in condescending tones or terms to the Filipinos, historically patronized as "little brown brothers." Nor did the Filipinos show off the superiority of a new nationalism—or, for that matter, pilfer (much) American hardware or duffel bags. The Americans made a show of checking with the Filipinos before talking to me.

The war games were so inconspicuous, so low profile as to attract almost no notice. Both sides clearly preferred it that way. No more than a thousand Americans, many of them reservists, were flown in. Their mission was not a secret, but no one was after publicity. An "incident," everyone knew, would be ruinous.

The only deterrent to future war games, it seemed, was the size of the Pentagon budget. In the new era of goodwill, there was no reminder of the expulsion of American forces, of the looting of Clark, of the theft and graft that undermined the military establishment as surely as any other government agency.

These Americans, here for annual training, showed no more than a hazy awareness of a recent past. Many not only were ready to forgive and forget but also seemed not to care. "For us, it's one of many exercises in the theater," said an American officer. "For them, it's a premier event." Five years after the Senate "said no," the bases seemed irrelevant and unnecessary, not worth the trouble.[58] "WHERE'S THE WAR?" asked the caption on the front page of the *Manila Times* under a layout showing American forces in an exercise in Cavite across Manila Bay in the spring of 1996.[59]

Suddenly, however, the Americans discovered that one war, at least, wasn't over at all. After years of uncertainty, The Philippines' Department of

Justice, in December 1996, said the old Status of Forces Agreement (SOFA), under which the United States had primary jurisdiction over American military people on active duty while the Americans still clung to their bases, was no longer legal. Absent a new agreement, the Philippines wanted jurisdiction over anyone charged with breaking the law—including foreign servicemen.

The response from the Pentagon was almost instantaneous. There would be no more war games, no Balikatan, without a new SOFA similar to agreements the United States had with about 70 other countries with which it conducted war games. The bottom line was that the United States did not want to risk leaving its servicemen behind if they were accused of breaking the law during an exercise. The goal of American diplomacy was "immunity," which the United States could waive in the case of serious crimes similar to the marine rape case on Okinawa.

The debate touched a raw nerve. No top Philippine leader, no matter how ostensibly pro-American, wanted to run the political risk of having sold the national patrimony to the country that had once lorded it over them with its bases. "Status of forces is really a misnomer because there are no forces based here," Ramos said when I asked him about the SOFA talks. "We would like the exercises, the port visits, the exchange."[60]

The American ambassador, Thomas Hubbard, denied the United States wanted "blanket immunity from Philippine law for its forces." The goal, he insisted, was to "clearly define the circumstances" governing jurisdiction. The fear was, "The longer we go without resolving the legal protections issue, the greater the risk that the security relationship will drift."[61] The Philippine Senate would have to ratify the deal—a process sure to provide an excuse for another round of nationalist attacks and further undermine what diplomats still called a "special relationship."

And what about the impact of a fresh influx of American ships and planes on toxic waste—an increasingly contentious issue amid persistent reports of dangerous levels of contamination around former power plants, motor pools and landfills at Clark and Subic? The State Department upset Filipinos by contending there was no requirement on the part of the United States to clear up all toxic waste before giving up the bases—but claimed credit for having done what it could to prevent an imminent risk. That was less than reassuring to CDC President David. In September 1997, as Philippine and U.S. officials were entering a new round of SOFA talks, he closed a dozen areas at Clark identified as dangerous by toxicity tests. Worried about the impact on investors after the *Philippine Star* broke the story, David stated that the areas were "neither accessible nor populated."[62]

The top American military leader in the region, Admiral Joseph Prueher, commander-in-chief of the U.S. Pacific Command, sought to counter sensational reports that the United States was bargaining hard for the right to dock ships and land planes at will in the Philippines in return for goods and services. "There is not an effort going on to get an ACSA agreement at this time," he said, but he pointedly reminded Filipinos that about 400 vessels a day passed through the South China Sea.[63]

Truth to tell, however, there was no immediate threat from any outside power. The Chinese would have had to vastly increase their presence in the Spratlys to provoke the United States into sending troops into combat. American diplomats and military strategists might have done better to have dropped the issue and let the Filipinos debate and decide the matter among themselves. The Filipinos were playing a game—for American aid, for power within their own system. In the end they would have to agree on a face-saving phraseology for immunity that would placate not only the United States but other countries, including ASEAN partners, if they wanted any of them to join in war games for "mutual defense."

More disturbing than the threat to more U.S. exercises was that posed by the system of influence and petty corruption that had grown up around the armed forces, as shown so publicly in the looting of Clark. Many Philippine military officers, with interests in real estate and other lucrative sidelines, seemed suspiciously prosperous. To them, military exercises with the United States were a diversion from more profitable enterprises.

A senior American military officer came close to answering the question of where was the war. "I knew my counterparts," he said in polite under-statement. "I knew they all seemed to be well off, and I knew it would be very difficult to do that on what was being paid to them. Therefore they either had to have acquired some wealth or they had some other means of in-come."[64] The Filipinos, having looted themselves, not the foreigners who exploited them, now floundered in the uncertainty of a new era in which they may find they are their own worst enemies.

TEN

New Frontiers

Sarangani Bay runs ten miles wide and twenty miles long, an indentation into the southeastern corner of Mindanao, a mysterious region of jungle and conflict, commerce and civilization far removed from the rural slums of Luzon or the urban squalor of its cities and towns. Here, on this last frontier, there are no great stone churches built by the Spanish friars, no rusting relics of the remains of an American military base, no bars that once catered to brawling American GIs and contractors, no out-of-work bargirls wishing the American dollars were still pouring in for them and their extended families.

General Santos City, whose namesake had died in Japanese captivity after persuading thousands of people to move from Luzon and the Visayan Islands and settle the area, is a miracle waiting to happen—a potential industrial and commercial hub in the emergence of a once obscure corner of Southeast Asia.

General Santos City—"Gensan" for short—also has emerged as a redoubt of American power and money in a country that is largely unaware of the potential for American resurgence on this last frontier. In Gensan, the signs of a rebirth of American power are everywhere—in the beautifully paved highway through town, in the burgeoning seaport on one of the world's greatest natural harbors and, most of all, in the new airport with its USAID-financed 10,000-foot airstrip.

In a country where it is fashionable to blame "the CIA" for everything, to suspect that any American asking hard questions about current political and economic problems is a CIA agent, General Santos City has a unique distinction. It is hard to believe, gazing on the graceful airport overlooking the bay on the far reaches of town, that someone, somewhere, at or near the center of power in Washington does not have a grand design for conversion of all that infrastructure to military purposes when and if war ever threatens the region and American interests are at stake.

Everyone here is sure that "the CIA" has a scheme for this place, but actually most of the development is a remnant of an almost forgotten mini-Marshall plan initiated for the United States by Elliot Richardson after the demise of Marcos. As a reward for the victory of the forces of good, as Aquino and her allies were then perceived, over evil, which Marcos certainly was, the United States organized a consortium of aid-giving countries in a program for pooling assistance and bailing out the Philippines from the morass of debt piled up during the Marcos era.

The program, patterned after soldier-statesman George Marshall's plan for reviving Europe after World War II, might have extended much more deeply into the Philippine economy had the United States had to provide all the funding promised in return for renewal of the bases agreement. With the forced withdrawal of American forces, Gensan remained a focal point of a reduced U.S. aid program under the aegis of a "multilateral aid initiative," then the "Philippine Assistance Program."

The $205 million American aid program for the city would never have happened had George Shultz, then secretary of state, not endorsed it long before the vote on the bases. "I was involved in the preparation of the concept in 1988," said Danilo Zamudio, project director for SOCSARGEN (South Cotabato Province, Sarangani Province and Gensan), one of five regions marked by Manila for special development. "Our project was selected to construct a fishing port, establish an agriculture processing facility. We had to build a wharf. We envisioned we have to improve our air transport system. We asked for $30 million in aid."[1]

With Shultz's personal approval, in June 1988 the Manila mission of USAID dispatched consultants. The Americans also financed a master plan for another focal point of national development, CIC, the Cagayan de Oro to Iligan "corridor" on Mindanao's northwestern coast. The difference between CIC and SOCSARGEN is that planners envision the former as providing sites for iron and steel and cement plants, joint ventures with foreign companies, and the latter as a center for light industry, notably food processing.

The Americans may have also seen Gensan's strategic position and enormous natural harbor, Sarangani Bay, as large enough for the entire Seventh fleet, as a successor to Subic Bay, or perhaps Subic Bay, Cubi Point and Clark combined. At any rate, Gensan is where the United States chose to plunge its aid rather than in the CIC; or in CALABARZON, stretching from Cavite through Lagunas and Batangas and Rizal and Quezon provinces in Luzon; or in the Panay-Negros Agro-Industrial Development Project; or in the Samar Integrated Areas Development Project (on the island where U.S. troops slaughtered hundreds of rebellious "natives" at the height of the Philippine "insurrection" around 1900).

"If you compare the various areas of Mindanao, you will select General Santos," said Zamudio. "This area has both the agriculture and the fisheries.

We have industries that are agro-related—corn, seed-processing, five tuna canneries." SOCSARGEN is indeed an agricultural Eden, the source of one-fourth of the corn grown in the Philippines, three-fourths of the cotton and the only place where asparagus is harvested on a large scale—suitable for export, fresh-frozen and juicy throughout Australasia.

American agro-interests were already solidly entrenched. Cargil was pouring out coconut oil, Dole Pineapple was canning fruits and vegetables and Dole Seafoods was processing fish products long before the arrival of American aid. With new investment from the Philippines' own Republic Food Corporation, as well as from Taiwan and other Asian countries, Zamudio predicts that Gensan in a few years will match Davao, a four-hour bus ride north through jungle-covered hills overlooking sweeping beaches.

At City Hall, Mayor Rosalita Nuñez reveled in the talk about a renaissance of American influence: "American aid is creating a big impact—under the right kind of local leadership. There's a joke. They say, 'You're a favorite of the Americans. They are going to transfer the bases here. We will improve our stock. We will be taller, with longer noses.'" She readily admitted American interest may be more than economic, much less altruistic. "They say the Americans want to 'guarantee security,' and, 'You can't isolate yourself from the rest of the world.' I have even heard the Seventh Fleet will be outside Sarangani Bay." She smiled, quickly qualifying the remark. "That's hearsay."[2]

Amid high-level planning and politics, one knowledgeable voice has been that of a Catholic Marist brother from New York. Robert McGovern—Brother Bob—investigates and encourages the prospects for the city from his base at the local Notre Dame College, the city's leading educational institution, one of eight Notre Dame colleges and universities in Mindanao. In 1983, while Marcos was still in power, covering up the assassination of Aquino in August in the face of discontent at home and disillusionment in Washington, Brother Bob persuaded USAID to provide the funds for the Notre Dame Business Resource Center—the birthplace, the instigator, for many of the ideas for the city.

"We had set up this center on our own in 1975 before we approached USAID for help," said Brother Bob, who grew up in upstate New York, resolved in his teens to become a Marist—and, in his thirties, volunteered for service at Notre Dame, run by Marists. "USAID was trying to help the Philippine government stimulate economic development. They saw what we were doing here resembled what they were trying to accomplish. They were thinking, 'We help you expand your work so we can see the benefits of your work.' We knew there was lack of information. We built up a data bank and profile studies of industry."[3]

No one had any real idea of the potential for General Santos until Brother Bob pointed the way. The first revelation of his research was the untapped riches of the seas—a resource that one would have thought local fishermen thoroughly understood.

"The fishing industry only grew into a big industry after 1975," said McGovern, who picked up all his economic expertise on the job. "What helped was the building of artificial islands in the Celebes. The tuna started to linger because the artificial islands attracted small fish. At first we'd catch tuna by hook and line. We knew this was a big industry, but the largest group of poor people were also in the fishing sector, and fishing was heavily infiltrated by the New People's Army. When the statistics were gathered, people realized this thing was a gold mine."[4]

His comments reflected the contagious nature of the excitement behind the push for infrastructure development. "People said, 'If we're going to move products, we better improve the roads. With the roads and more produce we'd have to improve the port.'" It was then, as ideas were traded between General Santos City and Manila, that the American AID mission, buoyed by the mini-Marshall plan, came to support a specific, tightly focused project that might make a difference. "USAID decided to pick up the airport, the road and the port. The Philippine government wanted to start new growth centers. In Mindanao, they wanted to take the pressure off Davao and Cebu."

Foreign entrepreneurs have shared in the explosion of Gensan, now bursting with about 400,000 people. "When I came here with Dole Pineapple in 1968 none of the streets was paved," said Donald Partridge, a transplanted Oregonian who retired from Dole—and, with his Filipino wife, owns and operates the plant that prints the labels for the cans in which Dole and other companies package their products. "We continue to expand in our business." Partridge, training his three sons to take over, believes Gensan "will probably outdo all the other cities in Mindanao"—if not the entire region. "We were very fortunate," he said. "There were a lot of people who said it was too much money in one place, but we needed all of it— the port, the airport and the road system."[5]

Some of the enthusiasm fades, though, when conversations turn to the issue of who benefits from all the expansion. "Aquino listened to some bad advice," said McGovern. "She undercut herself all the time." Aquino's ineffectiveness translated into the failure to address the underlying problems of land reform, rice shortages, wages and basic health and welfare services. "The new money is not trickling down fast enough to head off the social problems we have here. Unless it trickles down faster, you are sitting on a social time bomb."

One issue that Aquino never began to comprehend was the refusal of the rich to pay more to middle-class professionals as well as day laborers, fishermen and farm hands. "If a Filipino nurse is only going to get 2,000 pesos a month and she can earn that in one weekend in a hospital in New York, there has to be an improvement in wage scales," said Brother Bob.

Mayor Nuñez despairs over the contrast between the vibrancy of the rush to build—and the failure of all the programs for enriching the community to have any impact on real poverty. "Today I spoke to the street children," she said. "They asked, 'Why are we called street children?' From there I rush to the induction of Jaycees. I told them we are subsidizing an NGO for the education of street children. There are 700 of them in the city, aged 6 to 15. I said to the Lions and Jaycees, 'It's not a sin to be rich, but to be rich without a social conscience is definitely very bad.' The filthy rich don't even consider the plight of the laborers. They say, 'We are giving them just wages,' but justice is not enough. It's a big mess."[6] The reality is, average wages in SOCSARGEN are far below the cost of living.

It is difficult to fathom the gap between the drive to grow and the poverty of a large underclass. A Japanese banker, Haruo Kawai, inspecting the port area, sees the region as hovering on a great divide. "For Japanese, it's the time to invest," he said. "After Ramos, we don't know what will happen. The Philippines will not grow if they lose this chance."[7] Kawai was touring the new projects with other bankers. At the SOCSARGEN development office, the tour began with a slide show, *Gateway to Opportunity*.

Engineers on the sites exude the drive of the new frontier they are building in the midst of poverty. "I have probably 20 engineers," said Roy Ventura, chief of party of the Wadell Engineering Corporation, headquartered in Burlingame near San Francisco, as he looked out on the USAID-funded wharf. "They are all doing a super job. The people here are tremendously easy-going." Almost in the next breath, however, he acknowledged the problems. "It's a very poverty-stricken area. There is a process here where you have to use payola to get things. I refuse to do it and sometimes suffer as a result."[8]

The payola ranges from the 50 pesos, less than $2, that a mechanic on site has to pay to "expedite" registration of a car to the thousands of dollars that companies sometimes cough up to "facilitate" the unloading of containers full of valuable machinery. Such problems reflect not only the corruption of Philippine society but also the preoccupation of an entire class with petty enrichment—and no concern about the suffering of many more to whom profits from payola are far out of reach. "I'm a registered professional engineer," said Ventura, "but I had to get signatures on my drawings." For a thousand pesos, nearly $40, government engineers signed his specs. It's a fee that technically may not be a bribe—but amounts to the same thing.

Beneath the bribery level, there is thievery, as pervasive as the bribery and the poverty. "We have our own guards 24 hours a day," said Ventura, but that's not enough to keep the thieves from sneaking into the facilities at night, sometimes by boat. "They've stolen equipment, siphoned gas out of equipment." Security guards, fearful of getting salvaged, are powerless against organized bands. "They say they have no idea who they are, cannot describe them and otherwise keep their mouths shut."

Ventura linked it all to the desperation to survive. "These people are very poor. They live in nipa huts 8 by 12 feet. They have no water, no light. You can get a piece of plywood and lean it against a fence, and they'll live underneath it." He pointed to a row of shops at the turning toward the new wharf. "It's a typical little village of lean-tos. They scrounge for a living. They live on the dump over there. It's a pattern. It's got to be ended."

Out at the airport, a 45-minute drive from downtown but still within the limits of the city, team leader LaVerne Humphreys was battling to open the runway and terminal on schedule in the face of still more revolt by the poor and dispossessed. The Badjao, a seafaring tribal people living in shacks down the road from the airport, on the way to a dump site, had no chance of threatening the barbed wire and security guards surrounding the giant facility. Humphreys contemplated the contrast between the dreams exemplified by the airport and the nightmare beyond the gleaming concrete.

"You could put the whole Seventh Fleet in here and not even see it," Humphreys observed as he looked down from the runway toward the bay. "If they get the infrastructure in, they could feed Southeast Asia. This is ideally located, and the expansion is unlimited. Everyone's a little gunshy with all the unrest down here. You don't go to the beach." Anyway, the coral was no longer so entrancing. Local fishermen had dynamited away about 80 percent of it—the principal problem with dynamite-fishing. "Then they squirt Clorox into crevices, and the lobster staggers out. They cyanide a lot too"—a method in which the water is poisoned and half-dead fish are hauled onto boats to be sold in Hong Kong, where live if slightly poisoned fish fetch higher prices than totally dead ones.[9]

Although Gensan is safer than other cities on Mindanao, Humphreys saw open revolt around every bend in the new American-paved road, in the hills around the bay, even on the beach. Twice, terrorists have kidnapped his landlady from her ranch near the airport, demanding ransom for her return. "Once we drove up and saw a guy scuba-diving. There were guards on the beach with automatic weapons, Uzi rifles. He said, 'I've been kidnapped two times, I won't let it happen again.' One day my driver started to go faster than hell. He said, 'There's a car following us.' He had window-tinting, so they couldn't see who was in our car. These AID guys from Manila, all they'll ride is a bullet-proof car."

No matter how much Ramos wanted the airport, he could not just order the army or national police to guarantee its security any better than they were able to protect the port. Theft occurs regularly, sometimes spectacularly. "One day all the scaffolding was gone," said Humphreys. "Another time they stole a boat." The presumed culprit were the forlorn Badjao, living in their nipa huts up the road from the main gate leading to the contractors' compound and the airstrip. "They'll kill you at the drop of a hat. We've never had an imminent threat, but a month ago the police said there are rumors, so go home early."

The priority placed on completing the airport, formally opened in mid-1996, hardly exonerated the project from the usual corruption. Humphreys tolerated a lot but got upset when the graft seriously interfered with the job. "There's always grease money for everything," he said. "This is probably the worst place I've worked from the point of view of corruption. It's infinitely worse than Africa and Indonesia. I have spent 35 years overseas. This is the poorest place I've ever been—and the most corrupt. It takes a month to get duty-free stuff through customs."

Humphreys, however, preferred to view the airport from a long-range perspective—one shared by many, Filipinos and Americans alike: "About six months ago a Filipino said the airport is the first part of a large program. Ten years from now this will be the center of all activities in Southeast Asia"—commercial *and* military.

It is possible to envision just that scenario if tensions increase in rivalries among ASEAN nations, or between ASEAN nations and foreign powers, for some of the economic spoils. At stake are not only the profits from light manufacturing and agricultural products but also a windfall from the natural resources of the sea, ranging from fish harvested with reckless impunity to untold reserves of oil, gas and other minerals.

"This is all new," said Brother Bob, stopping his van beside a container ship at the new wharf. "This is the first computerized terminal in the whole country." Across the wharf, pens filled with pigs awaited loading for the two-day voyage to slaughterhouses in Manila. "All this was filled in from the sea. They used to transport them 25 kilometers to get them to the boats."[10] At the airport, cargo planes were taking on fresh vegetables along with "sushi-quality" tuna, caught that day for nonstop flights to Japan and, the other way, to Australia.

Alex Sunderman, a USAID official from El Paso, Texas, was getting ready to leave in January 1997. "In terms of American aid funds for infrastructure in the Philippines, this is it," he said. "I'm the last guy." In the heart of EAGA (East ASEAN Growth Area), the next giant Asian center was up and running.

On the other side of Mindanao, to the northwest, far out in the South China Sea beyond the long island of Palawan, the sparks were already flying in what has been largely a diplomatic and propaganda war for a little-known island chain claimed in whole or in part by half a dozen powers, notably China, Taiwan, the Philippines and Vietnam, also by Brunei and Malaysia. Named for the British navigator who charted the islands in the nineteenth century, the Spratlys are a cluster of atolls, some of which are below water most of the time, none of which is inhabitable year round. They have assumed importance in recent years with the realization that a fortune in oil and gas lingers beneath the shallow waters.

The rumor mill grinds with ever more sinister theories. One of the more intriguing has it that the contest is all a CIA plot, or at least that America is encouraging China in its claim to the islands and all the oil beneath and around them. The reason, according to the story, is that the Philippines would then have to beg for American military aid and the United States would have to set up a new base on the Philippines.

In reality, the contest for the Spratlys suggests a scenario involving a strange new friend—Vietnam. An historical irony is that the Philippines, in the 1960s, sent about 2,000 troops to Vietnam, the Philippines Civic Action Group, as a show of support for the United States. The group, led by one Major Fidel V. Ramos, had pacification-type duties, but its presence gave the United States the right to list the Philippines as a Vietnam War "ally."

The Philippines' worst offense, though, may have been to cooperate with the United States on providing a rear base area. Marcos negotiated Washington out of using Clark, the largest U.S. air base outside the United States, for bombing runs over Vietnam, but the base was vital for training, resupply and medical evacuation—and as a transit point for planes going elsewhere. Subic, as America's largest navy base anywhere, was even more important. Warships ranging from nuclear submarines to aircraft carriers refueled and refitted there for duty off Vietnam.

Since those days, however, the alliance between Hanoi and China has deteriorated sharply. First, China seized the Paracels, north of the Spratlys, in 1974, a year before Hanoi's victory in the South. Then, China backed the Khmer Rouge through nearly four years of bloody rule over Cambodia—and attacked Vietnam's northern frontier at the end of 1978.

Most recently, China's expanding army outraged both the Philippines and Vietnam by seizing some water-covered atolls in the Spratlys during the 1994 monsoon season and building unearthly-looking facilities serviced by Chinese navy vessels, thinly disguised as trawlers. The Chinese, who had quietly occupied nine of the islands in the 1950s, jumped from their destroyer base off Fiery Cross and moved in on Mischief Reef, whose subsurface atolls shelter a horseshoe-shaped lagoon that forms an anchorage four kilometers long and two kilometers wide.

While no one had any idea what was going on, the Chinese mysteriously erected four octagonal structures on steel stilts and pilings rooted in the coral. The cluster, they said, was "a fishing village." Philippine authorities did not discover the mischief on the reef until January 1995, and they want people to believe that the Chinese miraculously threw up the structures in November and December when the monsoon was too severe for patrol boats to ply the turbulent seas and report on troubled waters.

Later, after film of the structures made the television news and was shown around the world, China protested vehemently, warning of "stronger measures." Now Filipinos fret over a more dire possibility—that China will build a small airstrip right on the reef, several feet below water at low tide but inches above the waves at high tide. It would be an engineering "miracle"—but one that could happen. Somehow, the more China protests its desire to avoid conflict and just be friends, the more menacing are its deeds. Even as Ramos was ingratiating himself with China's President Jiang Zemin at the 1996 APEC summit in November 1996, reports filtered out that China was increasing its garrison on Mischief Reef.[11]

The Chinese soon showed how unlikely they were to change policy despite occasional reassurances. More than a year after their presence was first discovered on Mischief Reef, they were reported to have built "administrative structures"—"one or two fishermen's quarters" linked by walkways to the original. They are nipa huts, not made of metal or concrete, but new antennae sprouting up from the structures suggest their importance as a listening post and relay facility for China's own propaganda broadcasts.[12]

As obstreperous as the Chinese from the mainland are the Chinese from Taiwan, home of the anticommunist nationalist Chinese. Nationalist China occupied Itu Aba, an island slightly larger than Pagasa, after World War II and has held on to it unchallenged for all the years since the communists drove nationalist forces from the mainland in 1949. Communist and nationalist China alike cite the discovery of Han dynasty artifacts on some of the islands as proof that all China, whether the "communist" one headquartered in Beijing or the "nationalist" regime on Taiwan, has sovereignty over the Spratlys, if not the entire South China Sea.

Both the Philippines and Vietnam believe passionately that the Chinese, both communist and nationalist, should get out of the atolls and stop making the Philippines, Vietnam, Malaysia and Brunei so uneasy about the ones they occupy. All four are bound by a mutual sense of obligation through ASEAN, a strictly economic grouping but one with inescapable military overtones. No one remembers Philippine support of the Americans in Vietnam while contemplating the struggle for the South China Sea.

To the Philippines, the Spratlys are Kalayaan (Freedomland), a last frontier never occupied by the Spanish or the Americans. The Japanese built air and submarine bases on the islands in World War II, but they were unknown to Manila until Tomas Kloma, owner of a small fishing fleet and chairman of the Philippine Maritime Institute, "discovered" them in 1951, declared the "Free Territory of Freedomland" on July 5, 1956, was scared off by Chinese fishermen—and "sold" them to the Philippines for one peso.

One of the biggest islands out there, the one that makes Kalayaan a legal municipality, the place that the Philippine claims is really settled, is Pagasa, its 32.6 hectares overrun by something more than sand but less than jungle, 200 nautical miles west of Palawan, two hours and 15 minutes away by light plane. Pagasa was basically forgotten, even after Kloma found it again, until the 1970s when the Spratlys inexorably began to surface as an international issue and the Philippines decided it was time to clarify its claim. Among the first things the government, then ruled by Marcos under martial law, did was to build a 2,000-meter airstrip on the island.

As a show of legitimacy, Pagasa now boasts a lighthouse, a municipal hall and multi-purpose building, a post office and clinic, plus a housing project inhabited mainly by 75 to 100 construction workers. There are no really permanent residents, a fact indicated by the absence of women, much less families, but life is not totally austere. There's fishing and swimming off a white sand beach. A recreation hall features karaoke and billiards. There is also an elected "mayor" who claims Pagasa as home although he lives most of the time in Puerto Princesa, Palawan's capital.

Vietnam and Malaysia are also muddying the waters with actions based on claims prompted in large part by the aggressive attitude of the Chinese. The Vietnamese, after the humiliation of the Chinese seizure of the Paracels and their victory over the U.S.-backed Saigon regime in April 1975, did what they could in the Spratlys. They occupy half a dozen atolls mostly outside the area claimed by the Philippines and have dug deep into the largest, Pugad, sending in tanks as artillery pieces, dispatching marines and patrol boats. So close is Pugad to Philippine-held Parola Island that a Vietnamese marine swam there one day and defected.

The brouhaha is about the environment, marine life, resorts and fishing rights, but what really fuels it is what's below the shallow ocean floor around the atolls. "There is black gold underneath," said Arturo Carlos, a dentist and former board member and local coordinator for Alcorn Production Philippines, an oil company that has drilled off Palawan's northwest coast. The results have not been promising "due to water intrusion in the oil," but the sense of hidden wealth adds urgency to the confrontation.[13]

"We got outmaneuvered by the Chinese," said Navy Captain Rex Robles, deputy commander of Westcom, the military's western command, headquartered in Puerto Princesa. "You wake up one day. You see somebody in your backyard. You say, 'Wait a minute, my grandfather used to live here.' He says, 'Let's talk this over,' but he refuses to leave. He is not a gentleman.

He is sitting in your backyard. I would say, 'First get out of my backyard.' Now they are enhancing their presence."[14]

At his headquarters at Westcom, Robles spoke from perhaps a special point of view. As a former leading light of the Reform Armed Forces Movement (RAM), he was among those who spearheaded the anti-Marcos alliance after Ninoy Aquino's assassination in 1983. Closely identified with Juan Ponce Enrile, the former defense minister, Robles joined the fight against Cory Aquino after determining she had little idea what she was doing as president. Held in detention for nine months after the coup attempt of August 28, 1987, he was exiled to Westcom to get him out of the way.

He still tends to be outspoken, as he was in the old days as a member of the RAM steering committee, RAM spokesman and a favorite contact for the foreign press, but few people come down from Manila to visit him at his quiet posting by the sea. He was glad to talk, and he marveled at the ingenuity of the structures the Chinese have built on Mischief Reef. "You look at this, either iron or concrete," he said. "There is a lifting effect that lifts this structure, but they don't fly off. The octagonal shape of the roofs means the winds can only bite at certain portions at a time."

Robles saw encroachment on Mischief Reef as signaling Chinese designs on the entire area, including the seas much closer to Palawan. "It is a prime oil and natural gas area. Portions have been dug up and found to be productive. The Chinese could turn against the Filipinos. The United States comes in and pacifies the area, stabilizes it, and then capitalizes on oil." Robles smiled, then added, "That's my private idea."

The real unanswered question: Who is there now to protect the Philippines if it cannot defend its own frontiers in a looming regional struggle that is still only a cloud on the far horizon of the South China Sea? The Philippines, until its Senate "said no" to the bases, counted on American air and navy patrols so routinely that no one considered the gaping void their absence would create. Not a word was said about the black holes in the Philippine radar system—once so conveniently filled by American radar screens and patrol planes laden with electronic equipment.

Such matters assumed greater import in early 1996 when some vessels flying Chinese flags intruded upon Philippine waters. Shots were exchanged and Filipino patrol boats gave chase—but reportedly turned back when they ran low on fuel. The Chinese vessels were presumably on a smuggling mission, just one the Filipinos happened to have spotted among the many that slip through their porous net. Bureaucrats pointed out that the incident, mysteriously not revealed until four days after it happened, was well north of the Spratlys—off Capones Island, not far from Subic Bay. The defense secretary, Renato de Villa, offered the comforting assurance that they were "pirate" ships in a region noted for low-level piracy.

No one noted the irony of the locale of the battlefield—in waters once traversed by U.S. Navy vessels on sea lanes above Subic. No one wondered about the exposure of the Philippines to a Chinese threat that won't go away. No one asked how the Philippines could respond more than haphazardly with only five frigates and a few dozen patrol boats defending its long coastlines. Spotting the enemy, whether smugglers or poaching fishermen or, some day, divers and drillers defended by warships lurking just over the horizon, was left to chance—and fate.

In reality, the military brass was more interested in profiting from smuggling than in stopping it. The suicide of a young naval ensign aboard the frigate *Bacolod* epitomized the priorities. Only after the officer's well-connected family demanded a full-scale investigation did the truth emerge in early 1997: the officer was murdered after threatening to expose the vessels' role in transporting illicit goods and people in and out of the country. It should have come as no surprise that a top navy admiral, in retirement, figured prominently in the scandal.

Luminaries from the Philippine film and television world gathered on the slopes of Club John Hay for the annual celebrity golf tournament. Fans asked for autographs, posed for pictures with their favorites, and clapped and cheered as the stars teed off for the first round of a day that ended with a banquet and speechfest, all in a mountain setting first exploited by the Americans in the early years of their rule as a cool retreat from the heat of Manila.

The celebrities booked into cottages built in the 1910s and 1920s. The white frame structures, in a row above the golf course, harked back to the days when Club John Hay was Camp John Hay, and the clubhouse down the road was the focal point of the social whirl. Then as now, to get to Baguio, travelers trek up the hairpin curves of the American-built Kennon Road for respite in a community designed by the American architect Daniel H. Burnham as a "garden city" for about 30,000 residents. His vision was more than fulfilled. In an idyllic layout of pleasant streets winding around crowded slopes, life centers on the wide-open green of Burnham Park, where a bust honors his memory.[15]

Today, however, the city is bursting with about 300,000 people, a third of them students at any one of seven colleges and universities and 93 elementary and secondary schools, more than half of them private. Once serene and remote, guarded by a handful of American forces for fellow Americans and their guests on rest and recreation from tough duty elsewhere, John Hay resembles a large public park swarming with people from town along with well-to-do vacationers.

It has been that way since July 6, 1991, when Frank Hilliard, then serving as base closure officer, formally shut the base. The transition, compared to that at Clark, where Hilliard served for the next few turbulent months as assistant base closure officer, was polite. There was a turnover golf tournament, as befit John Hay's best-known tradition, and none of the looting that Hilliard was soon to witness a few hours' drive down the slopes in Pampanga Province. "It was very businesslike," said Hilliard.[16]

The Department of Tourism more or less followed the example of the U.S. Air Force, which had run John Hay after the Americans recaptured it from the Japanese after bombing most of the city to the ground near the end of World War II. The idea for the first few years was to make the place work as it had for so long, maintain the golf course to perfection, open the cottages, restaurants and facilities to the public and somehow make a modest profit.

Gradually, however, the vision of a playground accessible to all Filipinos faded. The Department of Tourism, deciding it could not maintain the cottages quite as the Americans had done, stripped them of the cooking facilities that had once made them homes away from home for foreigners for $10 a day. "I don't know what they did with all those stoves and refrigerators," said Hilliard, "but for sure I know many of the former John Hay employees are well off."

There were other problems, too. "We spent $750,000 putting in a sprinkler system for the golf course which now doesn't work," said Hilliard, who manages the local Attic Inn, a hangout for the foreign community a few miles from John Hay. The Americans introduced a "recapture system" in which water sprinkled over the course drained into short wells, which in turn pumped it back into the reservoir. "All of these pumps were stolen. The sprinkler heads are mostly gone. They don't have a recapture system so they consume tremendous amounts of water"—a bitter issue in the dry season.

Hilliard credited the Department of Tourism with having otherwise done "a tremendous job of maintaining the golf course" but saw deterioration— "potholes, buildings in disrepair"—everywhere else he looked. "The infrastructure is really hurting. Filipinos are not yet attuned to preventative maintenance. That mentality carried over to the management of John Hay." One problem: lack of funds. "We generated $6 million a year in revenue to maintain operations. We got another $6 million tax money for the infrastructure. The Filipinos never understood that. They saw $6 million coming in revenue and thought they could make money. They've been losing steadily."

The Philippine solution was to lease the 244-hectare heart of the special economic zone—except for the historic summer residence of the American ambassador and a Voice of America transmitter. The collegial atmosphere evaporated when John Hay entered a new era in October 1996 with the signing of a 25-year lease by a real estate consortium. The group would invest $110 million in two hotels, a condo and shopping mall but, said the Bases Conversion Development Authority, would "ensure environmental safeguards."

No one, however, believed that a master plan would keep a developer from breaking the rules for a profit when the authorities weren't looking—or were sufficiently well paid not to look. "It's going to become very high price," said Hilliard. "It will be unreachable to the local population. That's what's causing problems. Economically it's viable, but not for the locals."

Activists among Igorots, the mountain people grouped in tribes spread over the Cordillera region, are furious. The locals, most of them members of the Ibaloi tribe, which dominates the immediate area, remember ancient tales of how they were driven off the land when Baguio was a village of a few hundred people. They claim ancestral rights to much of John Hay and the nearby Philippine Military Academy and proselytize through their elected politicians as well as such groups as the Cordillera People's Alliance and Cordillera Resource Center in Baguio.[17]

"They plan to develop John Hay into Disneyland, but the people don't like it," said Paul Fianza, at the Cordillera Resource Center. "John Hay is Baguio's last watershed. You permit development, you're flushing your future."[18]

Fianza, a member of a prominent Ibaloi family, offered what may be a simplistic explanation for why John Hay costs so much. "The reason it's losing is, when the president comes with his friends, he doesn't pay." Throw in all the other high-level free-loaders, politicians and hangers-on, and the point may be valid. That's not so bad as long as everyone else can get in, too. "Before, when the Americans were here, Filipinos needed a gate pass. Also, local taxis were not permitted on the grounds. In terms of access, you can say it's open, but if a private developer comes, it will be the same as when the Americans ran it."

The Cordillera People's Alliance is still more emphatic. "We definitely do not want the kind of development they want," said Minnie Degawan, secretary-general. "That entire area is still ancestral domain. The ownership of John Hay is not yet resolved." She contrasts the luxury of John Hay and the grand summer homes of Baguio with the life of the vast majority of people crowding the city. "It's counted as the summer capital, the tourist center of the Philippines. More than half of the people do not have water. People do not know what these GNP figures are all about. It's the standard of living they're concerned about. People are having a harder time now than before."[19]

The anger rises when one goes out of town, among tribal people fighting to hold on to individual plots and tracts against inroads from the lowlands—some of them led by big-time multinational companies, others by entrepreneurs smelling the opportunities on untouched slopes or under the ground.

"What the people want is John Hay should remain with them," said Raymondo Bolos, a Kankanaey, one of the two major Igorot linguistic groupings, along with Ibaloi, in the province. Bolos, a farmer and part-time gold miner on the slopes southeast of Baguio, a few miles beyond some of the city's most opulent summer homes, believes passionately that "there should be some way the people will not be taken out of the picture."[20]

Bolos, however, is far more concerned about issues close to home. The open pit of the Benguet gold mine cuts an ugly gash into almost a mountainside opposite the main road through his village. "For years they tunneled into the mountain. Open-pit mining is just recent, in 1990. We were the first ones who objected. We picketed. They stopped at the height of the animosity. When we called the people to maintain the picket, the people did not come. They resumed two years later. We presented our demands: 'Since you are getting minerals, please do something for the community.' They promise to build a road. They repair only. They promise more. Now they say, 'no money.'" Nor does Benguet bring that much prosperity. "Before they had 10,000 employees, now 1,000."

Mining in the Cordillera is a matter of raging dispute, not only now but for the entire history of foreign intrusion in the region. In pursuit of gold the Spanish sent the first expeditions of conquistadors and missionaries to the Cordillera in the late sixteenth century; four centuries later, to encourage foreigners in the same pursuit and reap dividends for his own government, Ramos, on March 6, 1995, signed the Philippine Mining Act. Designed to bring in technology needed to cure "an ailing industry," the act offers enticements that denizens of the Cordillera view as disturbing as the Spanish expeditions. For an investment of $50 million, an investor receives 81,000 hectares of land for 50 years plus 100 percent of equity and 100 percent repatriation of profit and capital, along with numerous other benefits.[21]

"Why is it that up to now, there remain so many among us who are poor," editorialized the Cordillera People's Alliance in its official journal. "Where has all the wealth gone which they have taken from our homeland? Look: our mountains and forests have been destroyed because of the logging and the numerous mines which have been a source of money for our nation, the Philippines."[22]

While Bolos farms a hectare or so, two of his brothers run the family's own crude mining operation on a nearby slope. He pointed out the sluices, the little tailpond, the ore waiting to be ground, all on his property. It's a makeshift routine, much of it done by hand or rudimentary machines—for centuries a kind of cottage industry of the Igorots of the Cordillera. In the end, after sifting again with chemicals, the tailings wind up at Benguet, which buys them for a pittance by the truckload, then sifts them yet again with its sophisticated electronic equipment for the tiny specks that evade the homegrown process.

"In an hour you can get your salary for one year if you are lucky," Bolos offered, repeating a line that's an old saying where he comes from, "but in a year you get nothing if you are unlucky."[23]

Lucky or not, there's no avoiding Benguet. Bolos had to admit that his brother-in-law works there as a supervisor, and many of his neighbors toil there too. "We make just enough to survive," said Bolos, whose wife, two daughters and a sister in Hong Kong sent back the remittances needed to build their cement home and that of his mother, an ancient widow living in the house in back. Bolos worries about not having proper title to his land—not a problem among Igorots but a pretext for lowlanders to nibble away. "We claim ancestral land. Our great-grandfather was born here. So long as we deal with them correctly, nobody is difficult with us. It is more or less a question of being vigilant."

Otherwise, the people—not just the highland Igorots but impoverished lowlanders too—will be looted out of existence. There is no way to avoid the theft of their common Philippine heritage, whether it's the hardware of Clark going out the front gate on trucks or the ore from the mountains sluicing into the machinery of the multinationals. The question is whether they can hold their own against the forces of both old and new regimes, relentlessly grinding at the foundations of their lives as the country rushes toward Philippines 2000.

The specter of the most serious looters—the old Marcos cronies and their equally dangerous rivals, the new breed of Filipino-Chinese investors—poses a threat to a people as far removed from the region's "new" prosperity today as they were under martial law. One of the most terrible figures from the Marcos era, "never-say-die" Imelda, made a disturbing appearance in Baguio in 1996 to deny another old charge against her—this time that her husband Ferdinand, as president, had ordered soldiers to confiscate the solid gold, diamond-encrusted Buddha from a treasure hunter who had found it buried by Japanese soldiers in World War II.

Imelda, showing off, scratched the golden-painted surface of the statuette, seized by Baguio police in 1971 and held in a vault in a Baguio courthouse, all to prove that it was a cheap, brass imitation. "How could this be gold," she asked the reporters gathered in the courthouse. "Just rub it, and you can scrape it off. It is all paint." She offered to ship the imitation to Marcos human rights victims suing for $2 billion in America. "I will pay for the freight and give it to them with love."[24]

Imelda shrilly denied any substitution of golden Buddhas. She said she would gladly open her bank vault in Switzerland to show the real Golden Buddha to anyone who wanted to see it if it were there. Nobody challenged her and asked her to open the Swiss vault, which she had been fighting mightily to keep shut to investigators and human rights victims for a decade. It was her way of dramatically displaying her innocence—though few believed her convoluted story. "We know the truth," said Bolos after Imelda's publicity stunt was splashed on the front pages. "She cannot fool people here."

Imelda, irrepressibly Imeldific to the last, had brazened her way past her record of thievery and made a remarkable comeback. From her base in Congress, she was constantly doing political favors. Might she run again in 1998—not for president, as in 1992, but for vice president, perhaps on a ticket with Erap Estrada, the incumbent actor/vice president?

Such a ticket almost made sense. Estrada had played the nationalist hero in an anti-American film, *Aguila* (Eagle). The film, financed by leftists and produced at the height of the debate over the bases, was full of scenes of American soldiers abusing Filipinos. Having been driven out of Malacañang with the help of the Americans, Imelda considered herself one of the abused. To columnist Art Borjal, Erap and Imelda make "the ideal team of the genuine opposition, that segment of the political spectrum that has refused to recognize the legitimacy of both the Aquino and the Ramos governments."[25]

Could it be, more than a decade after Edsa, there was still a widespread view that Aquino and Ramos did not rule legitimately? As long as two years before the 1998 election, presidential politics were dominating the headlines. The wars between elitist factions, molding the masses to support them in their personal feuds, raged in the Congress and in the walled "villages" of the rich. The wars also raged in a countryside dominated by the three Gs of "goods, gold and graft"—separate but related to the other three Gs of "gambling, golf and girls," on which Clark hopes to enrich itself. As always, local politicians guaranteed the votes for whatever faction they had promised to deliver them in return for more goods and gold.

Amid the politicking, word spread anew: Ramos wanted to run for reelection after all. Casting himself as above the fray, Ramos denied it again, but Alberto and Carmen Pedrosa, he a former ambassador, she a columnist, the proud parents of a CNN International news anchor, Veronica Pedrosa, gathered signatures for a vote for the amendment. They campaigned under the aegis of PIRMA (People's Initiative for Reforms, Modernization and Action). Security adviser Almonte was perceived as the movement's mastermind along with two other members of the cabinet, but they could hardly have spearheaded the movement without the approval of Ramos.

There was a catch. Aquino, ineffective though she was as president, saw the 1987 constitution as her crowning achievement and the one-term presidency as one its vital points. With Cardinal Sin as her ally, she battled against change in the constitution with a passion that she had never displayed for land reform, hidden wealth or anything else other than vengeance for Ninoy. The Supreme Court, whose powers Ramos would have dearly liked to curb, ruled—by a 9–5 vote on March 19—the petition invalid.

The campaign devolved into a personality contest with Estrada counting on box office appeal to defeat any Ramos favorite. So did all the other contestants, including the powers behind the powers. The greatest of these was Cardinal Sin, who rallied the entire Catholic Church of the Philippines behind him to squelch a never-say-die effort on the part of the "Friends of Steady Eddie" to get around the Supreme Court decision. Filipinos at once came up with a term that showed their sardonic view of it all. "Cha-cha," for charter change, was in the headlines every day.

If a nationwide referendum was a non-starter, what about a constituent assembly in which both houses of Congress might approve an amendment? Sin and Aquino would have none of it. To them, the apparition of Ramos in Malacañang for another six years beyond June 1, 1998, conjured the worst memories of Marcos.

On a rainy Sunday afternoon, 25 years after Marcos had declared martial law and had Ninoy Aquino arrested on September 21, 1972, Cardinal Sin was assured of a huge crowd. All he had to do was order his priests to cancel their masses and bus their flocks to downtown Manila. He would celebrate the mass himself. He had hoped the crowd would approach a million but was thankful when as many as half a million, by generous police estimate, gathered under umbrellas in the Luneta park by Manila Bay in front of the Manila Hotel, where a number of the well-to-do among them had reserved rooms. Behind him in the grandstand was a panoply of politicians, including some leading "presidentiables," Fil-English for anyone running for president. Among them: Estrada and Senator Macapagal-Arroyo.

"We have gathered today disturbed by national crisis," the cardinal intoned in his homily. "It has been the crisis of a nation lost. A crisis of truth. A crisis of national life."[26] Cory was at her fiery best. "Today there is a dark wind blowing across our country again—the wind of ambition, a gathering storm of tyranny," she shouted to the cheering multitude. "We are here to shield that flame so that the light of democracy will not go out in our country again." The rhetoric level increased as she read from her prepared text. "Do your worst, we will do our best to stop you," she screeched, to more cheers, "and we, the people, will prevail."[27]

There was only one problem. Ramos, returning the day before from a 10-day overseas trip that had included a meeting with Boris Yeltsin in Moscow, had upstaged the ralliers. First, he told a cheering crowd in Davao, "I will not run for president, period, period, period." Then he called for a constitutional convention after the election in which delegates from across the country could vote on sweeping changes. "The 1987 constitution is not adequate to take care of the Philippines' future," he told reporters after arriving at Metro Manila's Villamor Air Base three hours before the rally.[28] Manila headline writers had a new catchphrase, "con-con," for the unwieldy "constitutional convention."

Estrada joked to me that he hoped Ramos' "period, period, period" pledge was not "period, period, period, comma," but Ramos made clear that he meant it.[29] "The Sept. 21 Luneta rally was only the tip of the iceberg of widespread public opposition to extending the presidential term," wrote editor and columnist Amando Doronila, blaming Almonte and other cabinet members promoting cha-cha for "shocking miscalculations" made by Ramos.[30]

When the Supreme Court, two days after Sin's mass mass, unanimously rejected a PIRMA motion asking the court to give Comelec permission to verify the nearly 6 million signatures on the referendum petition, Ramos said the decision was "a clear verdict that citizens cannot avail themselves of the people's initiative . . . at this time." Thus he hoped to "lay to rest any unfounded speculations about my own position."[31] Cha-cha, this time, had failed, but the battle was far from over.

While Ramos aspired for elder statesman status, Aquino would battle on to save her proudest achievement—a constitution drafted by a commission of 50 or so handpicked members who had been answerable to no one. Neither she nor Sin was likely to give up easily—even though Ramos was not in power. Their concern was the perpetuation of their own power and influence in a struggle that had little if anything to do with the welfare of the people who had launched Aquino to People Power. "We are here again as we were in Edsa in 1986," said Cory. "People-Prayer-Power 1986 and People-Prayer-Power 1987. We want to impress upon the leaders of today and tomorrow that we will come here as often as needed."[32]

There was no doubt that she meant what she said. It was all a grotesque satire on a democracy looted by an insufferable class system and a legacy of corruption—the basis of power in a nation adrift after a revolution that had done more to confirm than to change the structure of Philippine society.

Notes

Chapter One

1. *Today,* August 29, 1995.
2. *Philippine Daily Inquirer,* September 2, 1995.
3. *Business World,* September 12–13, 1997.
4. *Today,* December 1, 1996, contrasted the figure for the 1996 GNP increase of 7.1 percent with that of the 5.4 percent increase in GDP, gross domestic product. Remittances from abroad may have reached $10 billion in 1996, accounting for at least two-thirds of the difference between the GNP and GDP figures.
5. Herminio Aquino, chairman of the congressional committee on Mount Pinatubo, interviewed by the author, Manila, September 1997.
6. Mrs. Ramos made these remarks at a luncheon of the Foreign Correspondents' Association of the Philippines, Westin Philippine Plaza, Pasay, Metro Manila, August 31, 1995.
7. Noel David, interviewed by the author, Guagua, September 1995.
8. Max V. Soliven, editorial page column, *The Philippine Star,* September 4, 1995.
9. Paul Hutchcroft, "The Political Foundations of Booty Capitalism in the Philippines," paper presented at the annual meeting of the American Political Science Association, Chicago, 1992, p. 5.
10. The Reverend James Reuter, interviewed by the author, Manila, October 1995.
11. Roberto Romulo, interviewed by the author, Makati, November 1995.
12. Nicholas Platt, interviewed by the author, New York, July 1996.
13. Raul Manglapus, interviewed by the author, Fort Bonifacio, Metro Manila, November 1995.
14. Platt, interviewed by the author, July 1996.
15. Manglapus, interviewed by the author, Fort Bonifacio, November 1995.
16. Cheney and others made this remark on several occasions at the height of the debate in the Philippine Senate, September 1991.
17. Nicholas Platt, foreword to *Background on the Bases: American Military Facilities in the Philippines,* 2nd ed., U.S. Information Service (Manila: 1988), p. 3.
18. Ibid.
19. Jose Almonte, interviewed by the author, Quezon City, Metro Manila, September 1995.
20. Ibid.

21. Ibid.

22. Ben Serrano, column, *Gold*Star Daily* (Cagayan De Oro), September 4, 1995.

23. Ibid.

24. Max Soliven, editorial page column, *The Philippine Star,* September 13, 1995.

25. Reuters wire, September 12, 1995.

26. President Ramos, in a press conference at Malacañang Palace on July 26, 1995, attended by the author, acknowledged the exercise, which he said was routine training under planning for a year.

27. Renato De Castro, "Philippine-United States Security Relations in the Post–Cold War Era: From Bilateralism to Cooperative Security?" unpublished paper, Manila 1996, p. 9.

28. Ramos' remarks, on October 18, 1995, were reported in the Manila newspapers on the same day. He was on his way to New York to address the United Nations' fiftieth anniversary observances. Text of his remarks was provided by Malacañang press office.

29. General Renato de Villa, interviewed by the author, Camp Aguinaldo, September 1995.

Chapter Two

1. Pete Soledad, interviewed by the author, Clark, September 1995.

2. Kelvin S. Rodolfo, *Pinatubo and the Politics of Lahar: Eruption and Aftermath, 1991,* (Quezon City: University of the Philippines Press and Pinatubo Studies Program, Center for Integrative and Development Studies, 1995), p. 79. Rodolfo, a geologist at the University of Illinois Chicago, arrived in the Philippines on June 13, 1991. He quotes here from the *Manila Times,* April 6, 1991.

3. *Nova,* "In the Path of a Killer Volcano," WGBH-TV, Boston, February 9, 1993; program transcript, Journal Graphics, Denver, p. 5.

4. Ibid.

5. Ibid.

6. Ibid., p. 6. See also Rodolfo, *Pinatubo,* pp. 127–28.

7. *Nova,* "In the Path," p. 7.

8. Colonel Ron Rand, interviewed by the author, Washington, D.C., July 1996.

9. Major General William Studer, interviewed by the author, Washington, D.C., July 1996.

10. *Nova,* "In the Path," p. 8.

11. Ibid., pp. 8–9.

12. Ibid.

13. Major General Studer, interviewed by the author, July 1996.

14. Ibid.

15. Ibid.

16. Steven Campbell, interviewed by the author, Angeles City, May 1996.

17. Ibid.

18. Colonel Rand, interviewed by the author, Washington, D.C., July 1996.

19. Campbell, interviewed by the author, Angeles City, May 1996.

20. *Philippine Flyer,* Special Edition, September 30, 1991.

21. *Nova,* "In the Path," p. 9.

22. Ibid.

23. Ibid., p. 10.

24. Ibid.

25. Rodolfo, *Pinatubo,* pp. 8–9.

26. *Philippine Flyer,* Special Edition, September 30, 1991.

27. Rodolfo, *Pinatubo,* pp. 8–9.

28. *Nova,* p. 11.

29. *Philippine Flyer,* Special Edition, September 30, 1991.

30. Major General Studer, interviewed by the author, Washington, D.C., July 1996; *Nova,* "In the Path," p. 11.

31. *Nova,* "In the Path," p. 12. "Andy" is Andy Lockhart, also of the U.S. Geological Survey. Colonel Rand, interviewed by the author, Washington, D.C., July 1996.

32. *Nova,* "In the Path," p. 12.

33. Katherine Bruce, interviewed by the author, Seoul, Korea, December 1996.

34. *Philippine Flyer,* Special Edition, September 30, 1991.

35. Rudolph Littleton, interviewed by the author, Angeles City, May 1996.

36. Colonel Jules Ferreira, interviewed by the author, Subic, November 1995.

37. Rodolfo, *Pinatubo,* p. 79.

38. Ibid., p. 83. Rodolfo cites the *Philippine Daily Inquirer,* July 14, 1991.

39. Pete Soledad, interviewed by the author, Clark, September 1995.

40. Rodolfo, *Pinatubo,* pp. 111–112.

41. Ibid., p. 81.

42. The Nova/WGBH special provides these statistics.

43. Colonel Arthur J. Corwin, "Memorandum for Convening/Appellate Authority," January 31, 1994. This unpublished memorandum was provided for appeal of court martial of Captain Chen Almacen.

44. Ibid.

45. Major General Studer, interviewed by the author, Washington D.C., July 1996.

46. Ibid.

47. Ibid.

48. Rodolfo, *Pinatubo,* pp. 50–51.

49. Ibid., p. 45.

50. Alfie Lorenzo, "Lito Lapid: Uncrowned Box Office King!" *Star Special,* a Sunday supplement of *Abante,* May 19, 1996, p. 8, provides the descriptive term for Lapid.

51. Dr. Ignacio Valencia, interviewed by the author, Guagua, September 1995.

52. Ibid.

53. *Manila Times,* October 19, 1906, quoted in John A. Larkin, *The Pampangans: Colonial Society in a Philippine Province* (Quezon City: New Day Publishers, 1993), p. 219.

54. Kelvin Rodolfo, "The Question of Pinatubo Dikes Revisited," paper presented at the National Institute of Geological Sciences Journal Club, University of the Philippines, Quezon City, September 4, 1995, pp. 2–5. (Italics are boldface in the original text.)

55. Ibid.

56. Kelvin Rodolfo, memorandum to Chairman Richard J. Gordon, Subic Bay Metropolitan Authority, September 7, 1995.

57. "People Power in Pampanga," editorial, *Manila Standard,* October 11, 1995.

58. Antonio Fernando, interviewed by the author, September 1995.

59. The author accompanied Ramos and his party on the trip to the lahar region, October 12, 1995.

60. Vigilar offered this defense of the plan on numerous occasions, including briefings during the trip of October 12, 1995.

61. "Rosing" was the Filipino name for the typhoon, dubbed "Angela" internationally. The Department of Social Welfare and Development, Manila, provided the statistics the day after the typhoon in a press release. Ramos offered his criticism in remarks broadcast by national and local television and radio stations, monitored by the author, several hours after the storm was over.

62. *Manila Standard,* October 14, 1995.

63. Angeles City reporter, interviewed by the author, Angeles City, November 1995.

64. Ramos and his aides visited the dike on May 9, 1996. The author accompanied them.

65. *Manila Bulletin,* May 21, 1996.

66. Angeles City reporter, interviewed by the author, Angeles City, May 1996.

67. *Philippine Daily Inquirer,* September 6, 1997.

68. Ibid., September 3, 1997.

Chapter Three

1. Clark Development Corporation (CDC) guide, interviewed by the author, Clark, August 1995.

2. Colonel Arthur J. Corwin, "Memorandum for Convening/Appellate Authority," January 31, 1994.

3. Steven Campbell, interviewed by the author, Angeles City, May 1996.

4. John Cummings, interviewed by the author, Angeles City, February 1996.

5. *Philippine Flyer,* Special Edition, September 30, 1991.

6. Cummings, interviewed by the author, Angeles City, February 1996; Colonel Ron Rand, interviewed by the author, Washington, D.C., July 1996.

7. Captain Edelberto Ocampo, interviewed by the author, Angeles City, May 1996.

8. Ibid.

9. Frank Hilliard, interviewed by the author, Baguio, May 1996.

10. Captain Allan Ballesteros, interviewed by the author, Clark, August 1995.

11. Angeles City reporter, interviewed by the author, October 1995.

12. Ramon Tulfo, "On Target: Military pilferers," *Philippine Daily Inquirer,* March 27, 1991.

13. Associated Press wire, February 21, 1991.

14. Tulfo, "On Target."

15. Captain Ballesteros, interviewed by the author, Clark, August 1995.

16. Corwin, "Memorandum."

17. "Assignment of Errors and Brief on Behalf of Appellant," *United States* v. *Captain Chen G. Almacen,* U.S. Air Force Criminal Court of Appeals, Case No. ACM 31268, August 18, 1995.

18. Ceferina Yepez and Captain Allan Ballesteros, interviewed by the author, Clark, August 1995.

19. U.S. Information Service, *Background on the Bases,* 2nd ed. (Manila, 1988), p. 16.

20. Captain Ballesteros, interviewed by the author, Clark, August 1995.

21. Philippine Air Force officer, interviewed by the author, Clark, September 1995.

22. Captain Ballesteros, interviewed by the author, Clark, August 1995.

23. See William Henry Scott, *The Discovery of the Igorots: Spanish Contacts with the Pagans of Northern Luzon* (Quezon City: New Day, 1974), pp. 1–7.

24. Colonel William H. Dassler, director, assessments and training, Defense Nuclear Agency Field Command, Kirtland Air Force Base, letter to "Convening Authority," January 1, 1994, "Subject: Clemency Petition—General Court Martial, United States v. Almacen."

25. Captain Chen Almacen, interviewed by the author, Torrance, California, June 1996; other U.S. military officers, interviewed by the author, Washington, D.C., June-July 1996.

26. U.S. military officer, interviewed by the author, Washington, D.C., July 1996.

27. Colonel Dassler, letter to "Convening Authority," January 1, 1994.

28. Colonel Arthur J. Corwin, sworn statement, Ramstein (Germany) Air Force Base, August 5, 1992.

29. Captain Almacen, interviewed by the author, Torrance, June 1996.

30. Ibid.

31. *Philippine Daily Inquirer,* October 24, 1992.

32. *Philippine Star,* October 25, 1992. Both the *Philippine Daily Inquirer* and the *Philippine Star* misspelled Dassler's name—the former called him "Dasher," the latter "Dashler."

33. Captain Almacen, interviewed by the author, Torrance, June 1996; Frank Spinner, interviewed by the author, Washington, D.C., July 1996.

34. *Philippine Daily Inquirer,* October 24, 1992; *Philippine Star,* October 25, 1992.

35. Catjoe Tayag, "EXCLUSIVE! USAF Agents, Lawyers Arrive; Clark Looting Probe On," *Angeles City Inquirer,* October 7–13, 1993.

36. Ibid.

37. Ibid.

38. Ibid.

39. Captain Ocampo, interviewed by the author, Angeles City, May 1996, described the sequence of events surrounding his role and that of the Aetas in the case.

40. Robledo Sanchez, interviewed by the author, Angeles City, May 1996.

41. *United States* v. *Captain Chen Almacen,* Department of the Air Force, Air Force Legal Services Agency, USAF Judiciary, Pacific Circuit, Jennifer J. Snider, Captain, USAF, detailed defense counsel, Clarence P. Guillory, Captain, USAF, individual military counsel, October 27, 1993.

42. Captain Almacen, interviewed by the author, Torrance, June 1996.

43. Ibid.

44. Captain Ocampo, interviewed by the author, Angeles city, May 1996.

45. Carlito Ganzon, interviewed by the author, Angeles City, April 1996.

46. Chen G. Almacen, Torrance, California, letter to Virgilio Almacen, Sablan, Philippines, January 20, 1996.

47. Virgilio Almacen, Judy Almacen Semon, interviewed by the author, Sablan, May 1996.

48. Corwin, "Memorandum."

49. Major General Studer, interviewed by the author, Washington, D.C., July 1996.

50. U.S. military officer, interviewed by the author, Washington D.C., July 1996.

51. Major General Studer, interviewed by the author, Washington, D.C., July 1996.

Chapter Four

1. Retired American military officer, interviewed by the author, Washington, D.C., June 1996.

2. Philippine Air Force officer, interviewed by the author, Clark, September 1996.

3. Colonel Ron Rand, interviewed by the author, Washington, D.C., July 1996.

4. Philippine military officer, interviewed by the author, Clark, September 1995.

5. John Cummings, interviewed by the author, Angeles City, October 1995.

6. A former American official, interviewed by the author, May 1966, described these and subsequent details on the transition at Clark.

7. Frank Hilliard, interviewed by the author, Baguio, May 1996.

8. Colonel Rand, interviewed by the author, Manila, November 1995.

9. Ener Lumanlan, interviewed by the author, Angeles City, August 1995.

10. CDC guide, interviewed by the author, Clark, August 1995.

11. John Osmeña, in a conversation with the author, October 2, 1997, acknowledged having made this remark as reported at the time but distanced himself from a scandal that was now history—and of no political value. "I have no first hand

[*sic*] information about the matter," he stated in a fax to the author on the same date. "What I have is simply gossip from the grapevine which is worthless to a journalist." For that reason, he said, "talking to me would be a waste of time."

12. Lumanlan, interviewed by the author, Angeles City, August 1995.

13. CDC tour guide, interviewed by the author, Clark, August 1995.

14. A former American contract supervisor, interviewed by the author, Angeles City, May 1996, provided these and subsequent details on the schools.

15. Colonel Rand, interviewed by the author, Washington, D.C., July 1996.

16. Former American contractor, interviewed by the author, Angeles City, May 1996.

17. Colonel Rand, interviewed by the author, Washington, D.C., July 1996.

18. A former American official, interviewed by the author, May 1996.

19. General Romeo David, interviewed by the author, Clark, August 1995.

20. Ibid.

21. William Kwong, interviewed by the author, Angeles City, May 1996.

22. *Sydney Morning Herald,* July 12, 1995; *The Australian,* Canberra, July 12, 1995.

23. Ibid.

24. Max Ross, president of the Angeles City Tourism and Businessperson's Association, interviewed by the author, Angeles City, August 1995.

25. News release, Office of the Press Secretary, Malacañang, Manila, July 5, 1995. Ramos ordered the Department of Foreign Affairs to work with foreign governments to curtail sex tours, the PNP to arrest those involved, and the Department of Social Welfare and Development to assist "victims of sexual trafficking and prostitution."

26. Colonel Rand, interviewed by the author, Washington, D.C., July 1996.

27. Major General Studer, interviewed by the author, Washington, D.C., July 1996.

28. Colonel Arthur J. Corwin, "Memorandum for Convening/Appellate Authority," January 31, 1994.

29. Ibid.

30. Cesar Lacson, interviewed by the author, Clark, November 1995.

31. *Ibon Facts & Figures,* Vol. 18, No. 20 (October 31, 1995), p. 3. "Clark Special Economic Zone: Business as Usual" is the title of the entire issue.

32. Ibid.

33. Bryan Johnson, *Four Days of Courage: The Untold Story of the Fall of Marcos,* (Toronto: McClelland & Stewart, 1987).

34. Johnson, interviewed by the author, Angeles City, August 1995.

35. Quoted in *Childhope Southeast Asia and Oceania Newsletter,* Vol. 2, Nos. 1–2, (January-June 1992), from "Our Man in Manila," Sean O'Malley, *Saturday Night* magazine (Toronto), December 1991, pp. 40–45, 84–88, 90.

36. Johnson, interviewed by the author, Angeles City, August 1995.

37. Dave Carlson, interviewed by the author, Angeles City, August 1995.

38. Ross, interviewed by the author, Angeles City, August 1995.

39. John Cummings, Margaritaville menu, Angeles City, 1995.

Chapter Five

1. "Won't Go Back to Subic Anymore," *Book of Navy Songs,* (Annapolis, U.S. Naval Institute, 1926), rpr. in Gerald R. Anderson, *Subic Bay: From Magellan to Mt. Pinatubo* (Dagupan City, Philippines, privately printed, 1991). (Tubig—changed to "tubic" to rhyme with Subic—means "water" in Tagalog.)

2. Anderson, *Subic Bay,* p. 37.

3. Ibid., pp. 42–44.

4. *Stars and Stripes* [Tokyo], September 27, 1985.

5. Judge Cesar Ventus Bada, *The Genesis of a City (The Olongapo Story),* (Philippines, city of publication not cited, privately printed, 1994), p. 260. The author was a presiding judge in Olongapo's municipal court.

6. Joseph Collins, *The Philippines: Fire on the Rim* (San Francisco: The Institute for Food and Development Policy, 1989), p. 259. Collins quotes Gordon as saying, "And don't write that in your book because they're going to say I'm an ambitious young man."

7. Ibid.

8. Ibid., p. 260.

9. Rodolfo, *Pinatubo,* p. 52.

10. Ibid.

11. Ibid.

12. SBMA aides, interviewed by the author, Subic, August 1995.

13. *Asiaweek,* owned by Time Warner and published in Hong Kong, is well known among the relatively small number of Filipinos who buy foreign publications. Lea Salonga is a household name throughout the Philippines for her success both at home and abroad.

14. *Rising Above the Storm,* video (Subic: Pacific Hollywood Corporation, 1994; updated version, 1996).

15. Michael Sellers, interviewed by the author, Subic, August 1996.

16. *Rising Above the Storm,* 1994.

17. Ibid.

18. Richard Gordon, when encountered by the author outside SBMA headquarters, November 1995.

19. SBMA volunteers, interviewed by the author, August and November 1995.

20. The author attended the function at SBMA, August 1995.

21. Ibid.

22. Doroteo Rocha, interviewed by the author, Olongapo, August 1995.

23. Kate Gordon, interviewed by the author, Olongapo, August 1995.

24. Ibid.

25. The author attended the dialogue, November 8, 1995.

26. The author attended the *asalto* and the events preceding it on the evening of August 5, 1995.

27. The author attended the anniversary ceremony, November 24, 1995.

28. Manila Newsfeatures and Commentaries, *Manila Chronicle,* January 20, 1996.

29. Foreign businessman, interviewed by the author, Subic, November 1995.

30. SBMA aide, interviewed by the author, Washington D.C., May 1995.

31. For a fuller summary, see Gary Silverman and Rigoberto Tiglao, "At Your Peril: Foreign firms find themselves bogged down in Philippine politics," *Far Eastern Economic Review,* Hong Kong, January 23, 1997, pp. 48–49.

32. Introduction to *The Truth About the 1991–1993 Management of the Subic Bay Metropolitan Authority (SBMA) Under the Chairmanship of Richard J. Gordon as Reported in the Findings and Recommendations of the Commission on Audit (COA)* (Olongapo: privately printed, 1996).

33. James Gordon Jr., interviewed by the author, Quezon City, August 1995; Robert Couttie, interviewed by the author, Olongapo, November 1996.

34. Foreign businessman, interviewed by the author, Subic, December 1996.

35. Richard Gordon, interviewed by the author, Subic, November 1996.

36. *Sun-Star Clark,* Mabalacat, Pampanga Province, April 1, 1996.

37. Richard Gordon, interviewed by the author, Subic, November 1996.

Chapter Six

1. The author witnessed all the events described here and interviewed City Hall "volunteers" as well as protesters throughout Olongapo on APEC Day, November 25, 1996.

2. Conrado Tiu, interviewed by the author, Olongapo, November 1996.

3. Foreign restaurateurs, interviewed by the author, Olongapo, May 1996; aides of the Reverend Shay Cullen, interviewed by the author, Olongapo, May and November 1996.

4. Victor Fitzgerald, interviewed by the author, Olongapo, December 1995.

5. ABS-CBN television news, May 7, 1996; *Philippine Daily Inquirer* May 8, 1996.

6. ABS-CBN television news, May 7, 1996.

7. Associated Press wire, May 8, 1996.

8. Michael Clarke, interviewed by the author, Olongapo, November 1995. Clarke had copies of the advertisement and subsequent communications in his possession.

9. The Preda media office showed the author a videotape of the ITN footage, Olongapo, November 1996, broadcast in London on "News at Ten." CNN broadcast the piece on its "Inside Asia" program.

10. Ibid.

11. Joselito Herrera, interviewed by the author, Manila, December 1995.

12. *The Sun* (London), November 15, 1995.

13. *The Star* (London), October 31, 1995.

14. Michael J. Clarke, letter to the editor, *Foreign Post* (Makati), May 9–15, 1996.

15. Clarke, letter to Mayor Katherine Gordon, May 17, 1995.

16. British diplomat, interviewed by the author, Makati, May 1996.

17. Michael Douglas Slade, interviewed by the author, Angeles City, November 1995.

18. *Sunday People,* London, May 25, 1975.

19. Slade, interviewed by the author, Angeles City, September 1997.

20. *The Observer,* London, December 22, 1996; "Knives out for Pork Pie Pae-dophile," ran the clever headline. (One year and five months earlier, on August 22, 1995, the tabloid *Daily Star,* London, had headlined, "Pork Pie Pervert Faces Life." The Preda media office provided copies of the articles.

21. "Defender of Children," Yorkshire (England) Television, produced by Tim Tate, October 1995.

22. J.V. Cruz, "Fr. Shay Cullen's ego trip at Filipinos' expense," *The Sunday Chronicle* (Manila), November 5, 1995.

23. Adrian C. Manalad, "More pedophiles arrested—none convicted yet," *What's On in Manila and Expat Philippines* (Makati), December 10–16, p. 1.

24. Press release, British embassy, Manila, September 26, 1997.

25. NBI lawyer, interviewed by the author, Olongapo, November 1995.

26. Preda Foundation (Olongapo), press release, May 16, 1996. Preda had a bet-ter claim on the arrest of British child-murderer Brett Tyler, seized after a Preda aide, Rolando Vergara, found him from a photograph provided by Scotland Yard. Vergara watched Tyler's home in Olongapo, where he was holding "mass" on Sundays for kids. Deported to England, Tyler was sentenced along with an accomplice to life in prison for killing a nine-year-old boy.

27. United Nations Children's Fund (UNICEF), *The Progress of Nations* (New York: Division of Communications, UN Children's Fund, 1995), p. 34. Children were defined as those below the age of 18.

28. Foreign volunteer worker, interviewed by the author, Cebu, December 1995.

29. The Reverend Shay Cullen, interviewed by the author, Olongapo, August 1995.

30. Les Wagner, interviewed by the author, Olongapo, November 1995.

31. Bar and restaurant owners and workers, interviewed by the author, Olon-gapo, August, November 1995.

32. The Reverend Cullen, interviewed by the author, Olongapo, November 1995.

33. Amelia Juico Gordon, interviewed by the author, Olongapo, December 1995.

34. Ibid.

Chapter Seven

1. Dr. Samuel Tan, interviewed by the author, University of the Philippines, February 1996.

2. Tes Pacaba, "The Bottomline," *Ibon Facts & Figures,* Vol. 18, No. 13, July 15, 1995. The issue is entitled "The Crux of the Moro Plight."

3. "More About the Moros," ibid., p. 3.

4. Shopkeeper, interviewed by the author, Matanog municipality, Maguin-danao Province, February 1996.

5. Noel Kintanar, interviewed by the author, Davao, September 1995.

6. Antonio Peralta, interviewed by the author, Manila, February 1996.

7. El Haji Murad, interviewed by the author, Camp Abubakar, February 1996.

8. Benjie Midtimbang, interviewed by the author, Camp Abubakar, February 1996.

9. Colonel Charlemagne Alejandrino, interviewed by the author, Jolo, March 1996.

10. The Reverend Robert Layson, interviewed by the author, Jolo, March 1996.

11. Nur Misuari, interviewed by the author, Jolo, March 1996.

12. Ibid.

13. Ibid.

14. Ibid.

15. Soud Tan, interviewed by the author, Jolo, March 1996.

16. MNLF spokesman, interviewed by the author, Cotabato, February 1996. The Tripoli agreement stipulates 13 provinces. The number was expanded to 14 when South Cotabato Province was divided, adding a new province, Sarangani. Misuari and Ambassador Manuel T. Yan, chairman of the government "peace panel," signed the agreement "with the participation" of the Organization of Islamic Conference.

17. GRP-MNLF Peace Agreement, Manila, 1996.

18. Misuari, interviewed by the author, Manila, October 1996.

19. GRP-MNLF Peace Agreement.

20. Misuari, interviewed by the author, Manila, October 1996.

21. Zacharia Candao, interviewed by the author, Cotabato, November 1996.

22. *Philippine Daily Inquirer,* September 14, 1997; *Philippine Star,* September 16 and September 17, 1997.

23. Candao, interviewed by the author, Cotabato, November 1996.

24. Jann Jakilan, interviewed by the author, Tipo Tipo, November 1996.

25. Colonel Edmund Pocado and Jakilan, interviewed by the author, Tipo Tipo, November 1996.

26. Misuari, interviewed by the author, Manila, October 1996.

27. Kyodo News International, April 14, 1997.

28. Jerry Salapudden, interviewed by the author, Isabela, November 1996.

29. See Ron de Paolo, "Report of a Week Among Philippine Killer-terrorists, the Huks," *Life,* July 10, 1967, pp. 20–25.

30. Arthur Zich, "The Many Faces of Philippine Communism," ibid., pp. 25–28.

31. See Gregg Jones, *Red Revolution: Inside the Philippine Guerrilla Movement* (Boulder: Westview Press, 1989).

32. *Crisis of Socialism Strategies of Action . . .* Concerned Members of the Communist Party and . . . Other Organs and Units of the Party (Manila 1993), pp. 41–42. The book does not contain a title page and does not cite a publisher or author as such. The cover lists the above topics, giving the impression they are the title, while the "concerned members" citation appears at the end of a brief preface. The cover also lists the topics in Tagalog translation, *Krisis Ng Sosyalismo Istratehiya Ng Pagkilos at Internal Na Demokrasy, Pag-Aaral Debate Diskusyon Paglalagom,*

Malalimang Muling Pagsusuri at Pagpapanibagong-Sigla. The book is divided between English and Tagalog. The material quoted here appears in English. Liwanag is also a code name, meaning light or clarity.

33. Ibid., pp. 63–64.

34. Ibid., p. 63.

35. Edgar Cadagat, interviewed by the author, Bacolod, January 1996.

36. Bishop Antonio Fortich, interviewed by the author, Bacolod, January 1996.

37. Niall O'Brien, *Seats of Injustice* (Dublin: O'Brien Press, 1985). (The coincidence between the name of the author and that of the publisher was just that, a coincidence.) See also Alfred W. McCoy, *Priests on Trial* (Victoria, Australia: Penguin, 1984.) McCoy, author of numerous eye-opening studies on, among other things, the sugar industry in Negros, interviewed the priests in prison.

38. The Reverend Niall O'Brien, interviewed by the author, Bacolod, January 1996.

39. Bishop Fortich and the Reverend O'Brien, interviewed by the author, Bacolod, January 1996.

40. The Reverend Ireneo Gordoncillo, interviewed by the author, Bacolod, January 1996.

41. Satur Ocampo, interviewed by the author, Quezon City, May 1996.

42. Ibid.

43. Ibid.

44. Nathaniel Santiago, interviewed by the author, Manila, February 1996.

45. Crispin Beltran, interviewed by the author, Manila, February, 1996.

46. Santiago, interviewed by the author, Manila, February 1996.

47. Satur Ocampo, interviewed by the author, Manila, September 1997; *Philippine Daily Inquirer,* September 19, 1997.

48. *Philippine Daily Inquirer,* September 3, 1997.

49. *Today,* September 12, 1997.

50. Choong Tet-sieu and Antonio Lopez, "A Question of Strategy; The Rebels Choose: Peace Talks or Killer Squads," *Asiaweek,* April 18, 1997, p. 34.

Chapter Eight

1. "Kidnap Watch Statistics 1993–1997," Citizens Action Against Crime & Movement For Restoration of Peace and Order, Manila, September 1997.

2. Ibid.

3. *Business World,* May 3–4, 1996. "Citizen's anti-crime group describes kidnapping: It's a cottage industry!" was the headline over the article, by Carlo M. Santos.

4. *Philippine Star,* March 31, 1996.

5. Reuters, May 5, 1996. The rating scale, based on interviews with foreign business executives, ranked Singapore at the top with a score of 1.25. Next was Japan, then Hong Kong, Malaysia, Taiwan, South Korea, Thailand, India, Vietnam, China and Indonesia.

6. *Philippine Star,* November 29, 1995; *Manila Bulletin,* November 30, 1995.

7. Media Research and Development Office, Malacañang, provided the statistics.

8. Jose Concepcion, briefing on plans for the tenth anniversary of the People Power Revolution, Manila Hotel, February 16, 1996.

9. The author, who had witnessed the People Power revolution on Edsa, attended the tenth anniversary observances, February 25, 1996.

10. Agapito Aquino, interviewed by the author outside Camp Aguinaldo, February 1996.

11. These comments appeared on February 24 in the *Manila Chronicle* and *Philippine Daily Inquirer* respectively. For days before the anniversary, all papers ran commentaries, editorials and features.

12. The author attended the mass and accompanying speeches.

13. Teodoro Locsin Jr., interviewed by the author, Makati, December 1995.

14. Roberto de Ocampo made this remark at a luncheon of the Foreign Correspondents' Association of the Philippines, Westin Philippine Plaza, Pasay, Metro Manila, July 20, 1995.

15. Department of Finance, Office of Fiscal Policy and Planning, September 1997.

16. Bloomberg financial newswire, March 28, 1996.

17. *Foreign Investments Act of 1991 R.A.* [sic] *7042 As Amended by RA 8179* (Makati: Department of Trade and Industry, 1996). RA stands for Republic Act.

18. President Ramos, speech, Malacañang, March 28, 1996.

19. *Philippine Daily Inquirer,* March 26, 1997.

20. "Statement of Concern," issued jointly by the American, Australian, Canadian, European, Japanese, Korean and New Zealand Chambers of Commerce of the Philippines, February 1997.

21. Benson Dakay, interviewed by the author, Cebu, December 1995.

22. Ibid.

23. Resil B. Mojares, "The Dream Goes On and On," in *An Anarchy of Families: State and Family in the Philippines,* ed. Alfred W. McCoy (Quezon City: Ateneo de Manila University Press, 1994), p. 316.

24. Benson Dakay, interviewed by the author, Cebu, December 1995.

25. Cebu newspaper editor, interviewed by the author, Cebu, December 1995.

26. Tomas Osmeña and Emilio Osmeña, interviewed by the author, Cebu, December 1995.

27. Eduardo Cojuangco Jr., interviewed by the author, Pontevedra, January 1996.

28. Ibid.

29. Cojuangco offered these views during his interview with the author, January 1996.

30. Ibid.

31. Warlito Vicente Jr., interviewed by the author, Davao, September 1995.

32. The author met with faculty members at the Ateneo de Davao after having lectured there, September 1995.

33. Ibid.

34. *Asian Wall Street Journal,* November 6, 1997.

Chapter Nine

1. Ricardo Romulo, interviewed by the author, Makati, November 1995.

2. *Ibon Facts and Figures,* Vol. 19, No. 3 (February 15, 1996), p. 2. The entire issue is entitled "Japanese ODA to the Philippines."

3. Ibid., pp. 3–5,

4. Roy Padilla, interviewed by the author, Calumpit, September 1995.

5. Rufino Tolentino, interviewed by the author, Calumpit, September 1995.

6. Ibid.

7. "Maleficent AID," *Ibon Facts and Figures,* Vol. 19, No. 3 (February 15, 1996), p. 1.

8. Dad Tuan, interviewed by the author, T'boli, September 1995.

9. Ibid.

10. UN Environment Program-Water Branch, *Final Report of the United Nations Expert Assessment Mission to Marinduque Island, Philippines* (Nairobi: UNEP/Department of Humanitarian Affairs Environment Unit, September 30, 1996), p. 69.

11. Ibid., p. 71.

12. Randy David, "Admitting Guilt: Will We Ever See a Filipino Roh Tae-woo?" *Kilosbayan Magazine,* (December 1995), p. 9. The article holds up the trial in Seoul of two former South Korean presidents as an example of a country pursuing corruption.

13. Ibid.

14. The case was often front-page news. Mikael G. Aquino, Manila Newsfeatures and Commentaries, *Sunday Times* (Manila), January 12, 1992, summarized the problems at that stage.

15. Magtanggol Gunigundo, interviewed by the author, Manila, September 1997; *Today* and the *Philippine Daily Inquirer* front-paged stories on the alleged deal, September 26–27, 1997.

16. The story was splashed on the front pages of Manila newspapers on October 1, 1997. Among the headlines: "Swiss account bears Ramos name," *Today;* "President Dragged into Marcos loot mess," *Manila Standard;* "WHAT SWISS ACCOUNT?" *People's Journal.*

17. Jovito Salonga, interviewed by the author, Pasig City, February 1996.

18. Bayani Villaneuva, "Imelda Goes to Congress—What Next? Part II," *Kilosbayan Magazine* (December 1995), p. 16.

19. Ibid.

20. Ibid. The title of Raymond Bonner's *Waltzing with a Dictator* inspired the "waltzing" phrase.

21. Salonga, interviewed by the author, Pasig City, February 1996.

22. Mikael G. Aquino, Manila Newsfeatures and Commentaries, *Sunday Times* (Manila), January 12, 1992.

23. Ibid.

24. Ibid.

25. Gunigundo, interviewed by the author, Manila, September 1997. The *Philippine Star,* August 12, 1996, reported that Benedicto had assured the PCCG that he would return the shares.

26. Gunigundo, interviewed by the author, Manila, September 1997.

27. Ibid.; *Manila Standard,* August 2, 1996; *Philippine Star,* August 10, 1995.

28. "Asian Executives Poll," fax survey conducted by the *Far Eastern Economic Review* and Asia Business News, administered by Asia Studies Ltd., Hong Kong, *Far Eastern Economic Review* (May 30, 1996), p. 27.

29. Eric Gutierrez, "Clouded Vision: Reporting from Manila," *Worldpaper,* April 1997, p. 5.

30. *Today,* Manila, May 30, 1996. Most other newspapers reported Villanueva's remark, and columnists from several followed up with commentaries the next day.

31. Aniano Desierto, speech before Philippine accountants' organization, Davao, July 18, 1996.

32. Philippine Overseas Employment Administration, under the Department of Labor and Employment, and the Department of Trade and Industry provided the statistics.

33. Felicissimo Joson, interviewed by the author, Pasig City, February 1996.

34. Yolanda Malicdan, interviewed by the author, Itogon, May 1996.

35. See *State Department Human Rights Report, United Arab Emirates, 1995* (Washington, D.C.), p. 8; *Amnesty International Report 1996* (London), p. 309.

36. *People's Tonight,* May 15, 1996.

37. *Ibon Facts & Figures,* Vol. 18, No. 9 (May 15, 1995), pp. 6–7. The entire issue is on the topic, "Filipino Migrant Workers: The Price of Labor Export."

38. Isodoro Aligada, interviewed by the author, Pasig City, February 1996.

39. Filipino hotel chambermaid, interviewed by the author, Hong Kong, June 1995.

40. *Ibon Facts & Figures,* Vol. 18, No. 9 (May 15, 1995), pp. 2–3.

41. Ibid., p. 6.

42. Presidential News Desk, Office of the Press Secretary, Malacañang (Manila), January 17, 1996.

43. Economic and Social Statistics Office, National Economic Development Authority.

44. *Today,* September 26, 1997.

45. *Business Daily,* September 26, 1997.

46. *Ibon Facts & Figures,* Vol. 18, No. 21 (November 15, 1995), pp. 7–8. The theme of the issue is "No Food Available," the initials a play on the government's National Food Authority.

47. Antonio A. Tujan Jr., "Bursting the Ramos Bubble: 1995 Yearend Briefing, Sociopolitical Situation and Projections" (Manila), leaflet published in 1995.

48. Almonte, interviewed by the author, Quezon City, September 1995.

49. Manglapus, interviewed by the author, Fort Bonifacio, November 1995.

50. Ibid.

51. Almonte, interviewed by the author, Quezon City, September 1995.

52. de Villa, interviewed by the author, Camp Aguinaldo, September 1995.

53. Ibid.

54. *Media Release for Combined Philippine/U.S. Exercise Balikatan '95,* RP-US Mutual Defense Board, Camp Emilio Aguinaldo, Quezon City, October 22, 1995.

The release concludes, "The statement has been coordinated with the RP-US Mutual Defense Board, the Armed Forces of the Philippines, and USCINCPAC," U.S. Commander-in-Chief Pacific, headquartered in Honolulu.

55. Renato De Castro, "Philippine-United States Security Relations in the Post–Cold War Era: From Bilateralism to Cooperative Security?" unpublished paper (Manila, 1996), pp. 11–16.

56. Ibid., pp. 21–22.

57. Ibid., p. 21.

58. U.S. army public affairs officer, interviewed by the author, Makati, October 1995.

59. *Manila Times,* May 7, 1995.

60. President Ramos responded to my question at a press conference in Malacañang Palace on September 24, 1997.

61. Thomas Hubbard, speech to the Manila Rotary Club, July 17, 1997, transcript, U.S. Information Service (Manila), p. 4.

62. Angeles correspondent Ding Servantes reported the story exclusively in the *Philippine Star,* September 25, 1997; State Department official, interviewed by the author, March 1997; CDC press release, September 25, 1997.

63. Admiral Joseph Prueher, remarks to the press, transcript, U.S. Information Service (Manila), December 12, 1996.

64. U.S. military officer, interviewed by the author, Washington, D.C., July 1996.

Chapter Ten

1. Danilo Zamudio, interviewed by the author, General Santos City, September 1995.

2. Rosalita Nuñez, interviewed by the author, General Santos City, September 1995.

3. Brother Bob McGovern, interviewed by the author, General Santos City, September 1995.

4. Ibid.

5. Donald Partridge, interviewed by the author, General Santos City, November 1996.

6. Nuñez, interviewed by the author, General Santos City, September 1995.

7. Haruo Kawai, interviewed by the author, General Santos City, September 1995.

8. Roy Ventura, interviewed by the author, General Santos City, September 1995.

9. LaVerne Humphreys, interviewed by the author, General Santos City, September 1995.

10. Brother Bob McGovern, interviewed by the author, General Santos City, November 1996.

11. *Philippine Daily Inquirer* and other Manila newspapers, November 30, 1996. Blas Ople, Senate president and a Ramos foe, was the source of this report, one of many in the Philippine press.

12. *Manila Standard,* May 21, 1996.

13. Arturo Carlos, interviewed by the author, Puerto Princesa, August 1995.

14. Captain Rex Robles, interviewed by the author, Puerto Princesa, August 1995.

15. Sanders A. Laubenthal, *A History of John Hay Air Base: Baguio City, Philippines,* Office of PACAF History, U.S. Air Force, Hickam Air Force Base, Hawaii (August 1981), tells the story of John Hay through 1980.

16. Frank Hilliard, interviewed by the author, Baguio, May 1996.

17. Igorot is derived from the Tagalog *ygolotes* or *igorrotes,* for mountaineers (see William Henry Scott, *The Discovery of the Igorots: Spanish Contacts with the Pagans of Northern Luzon* [Quezon City: New Day, 1974], p. 2.)

18. Paul Fianza, interviewed by the author, Baguio, May 1996.

19. Minnie Degawan, interviewed by the author, Baguio, May 1996.

20. Raymondo Bolos, interviewed by the author, Itogon, May 1996.

21. Engineer Catalino Corpuz Jr., "All the Mines to Give: the 1995 Mining Act and the Cordillera," *Bantayan: Environment Alert,* Year 8 (December 1995), pp. 1–2.

22. "Against the San Roque Multi-Purpose Dam Project: The People's Position is Clear," *Hapit* (official publication of the Cordillera People's Alliance), Vol. 3, Nos. 7–8 (January-April 1996), pp. 1–3.

23. Bolos, interviewed by the author, Itogon, May 1996.

24. *Philippine Daily Inquirer, Philippine Star,* other Manila newspapers, May 5, 1996.

25. Art Borjal, editorial page column, *Philippine Star,* May 23. 1996. The column was headlined, "The perfect match: Erap-Imelda."

26. Jaime Cardinal Sin, "The Way, the Truth, and the Life," homily, Manila, September 21, 1997.

27. Corazon Aquino, "Trust the Filipino," text of speech, Manila, September 21, 1997.

28. Ramos' arrival remarks and press conference at Villamor Air Base were broadcast live by the government television station, PTV, monitored by the author.

29. Estrada made this remark in a brief conversation with the author at the Manila Hotel after the rally, September 21, 1997.

30. Amando Doronila, opinion page column, *Philippine Daily Inquirer,* September 29, 1997.

31. Ramos read this statement at a press conference, attended by the author, at Malacañang, September 24, 1997.

32. Aquino, "Trust the Filipino," September 21, 1997.

Select Bibliography

Books

Aguirre, Maj. Gen. Alexander P. *A People's Revolution of Our Time: Philippines, February 22–26, 1986.* Quezon City: Pan-Service Master Consultants, 1986.

Anderson, Gerald R. *Subic Bay: From Magellan to Mt. Pinatubo.* Dagupan City, Philippines: privately printed, 1991.

Andrade, Pio, Jr. *The Fooling of America: The Untold Story of Carlos P. Romulo.* rev. ed. Manila: Ouch Publisher, 1990.

Aquino, Belinda A. *Politics of Plunder: The Philippines Under Marcos.* Quezon City: Great Books Trading in cooperation with the University of the Philippines, College of Public Administration, 1987.

Autonomous Region of Muslim Mindanao. *ARMM 5th Anniversary Souvenir Program.* Cotabato City: ARMM, 1995.

Bada, Judge Cesar V. *The Genesis of a City: The Olongapo Story.* Olongapo: privately printed, 1994.

Bello, Walden, Shea Cunningham, and Bill Rau. *Dark Victory: the United States, Structural Adjustment and Global Poverty.* Quezon City: Freedom from Debt Coalition, 1994; Oakland, California: the Institute for Food and Development Policy, 1994.

———, and Jenina Joy Chavez-Malaluan, eds. *APEC: Four Adjectives in Search of a Noun.* Manila: Manila People's Forum on APEC, Focus on the Global South, and Institute for Popular Democracy, 1996.

Blount, James H. *American Occupation of the Philippines: 1898/1912.* 1913. rpr. Manila: Solar Publishing, 1986.

Bonner, Raymond. *Waltzing with a Dictator: The Marcoses and the Making of American Policy.* New York: Times Books, 1988.

Burton, Sandra. *Impossible Dream: The Marcoses, The Aquinos, And The Unfinished Revolution.* New York: Warner Books, 1989.

Carlson, Thor. *The Twisted Road to Freedom: America's Granting of Independence to the Philippines.* Quezon City: University of the Philippines Press, 1995.

Carter, Tom. *The Way It Was.* Volumes 1–3. Manila: privately printed, 1986, 1989, 1992.

Collins, Joseph. *The Philippines: Fire on the Rim.* San Francisco: Institute for Food and Development Policy, 1989.

Chapman, William. *Inside the Philippine Revolution.* New York: W.W. Norton, 1987.

Concerned Members of the Communist Party . . . and Other Organs and Units of the Party. *Crisis of Socialism Strategies of Action . . .* (Krisis Ng Sosyalismo Istratehiya Ng Pagkilos . . .) Manila, 1993.

Fallows, James. *Looking at the Sun: The Rise of the New East Asian Economic and Political System.* New York: Vintage Books, 1995.

Gleeck, Lewis E., Jr. *The American Governors-General and High Commissioners in the Philippines: Proconsuls, Nation-Builders and Politicians.* Quezon City: New Day, 1986.

———. *President Aquino: Book 1, Sainthood Postponed.* Manila: Loyal Printing, 1995.

Gutierrez, Eric. *Ties That Bind: A Guide to Family, Business, and Other Interests in the Ninth House of Representatives.* Pasig City: Philippine Center for Investigative Journalism, Institute for Popular Democracy, 1994.

———, Ildefonso C. Torrente, Noli G. Narca, and Noel Pangilinan, eds. *All in the Family: A study of elites and power relations in the Philippines.* Quezon City: Institute for Popular Democracy, 1992.

Joaquin, Nick. *The Aquinos of Tarlac: An Essay on History as Three Generations.* Manila: Solar Publishing, 1986.

———. *Manila, My Manila: A History for the Young.* Manila: City of Manila, 1990.

Johnson, Bryan. *Four Days of Courage: The Untold Story of the Fall of Marcos.* Toronto: McClelland & Stewart, 1987.

Jones, Gregg. *Red Revolution: Inside the Philippine Guerrilla Movement.* Boulder: Westview Press, 1989.

Karnow, Stanley. *America's Empire in the Philippines.* New York: Random House, 1989.

Kerkvliet, Benedict J. *Everyday Politics in the Philippines: Class and Status Relations in a Central Luzon Village.* Berkeley: University of California Press, 1990; Quezon City: New Day, 1991.

———. *The Huk Rebellion: A Study of Peasant Revolt in the Philippines.* Quezon City: New Day, 1979.

Lacaba, Jose F., ed. *Boss: 5 Case Studies of Local Politics in the Philippines.* Pasig City: Philippine Center for Investigative Journalism, Institute for Popular Democracy, 1995.

Lachica, Eduardo. *Huk: Philippine Agrarian Society in Revolt.* Manila: Solidaridad, 1971.

Lancion, Conrado M., Jr., ed. *Who's Who in Philippine History.* Manila: Tahanan Books, 1995.

Larkin, John A. *The Pampangans: Colonial Society in a Philippine Province.* Quezon City: New Day, 1993.

Laubenthal, Capt. Sanders A. *A History of John Hay Air Base, Baguio City, Philippines.* Hickam Air Force Base, Honolulu, Hawaii: Office of PACAF History, U.S. Air Force, 1981.

Man, W.K. Che. *Muslim Separatism: The Moros of Southern Philippines and the Malays of Southern Thailand.* Quezon City: Ateneo de Manila University Press, 1990.

Manapat, Ricardo. *Some Are Smarter Than Others: The History of Marcos' Crony Capitalism.* New York: Alethia Publications, 1991.

May, Glenn Anthony. *A Past Recovered.* Quezon City: New Day, 1987.

McCoy, Alfred W. *Priests on Trial.* Victoria, Australia: Penguin Books, 1984.

———, ed. *An Anarchy of Families: State and Family in the Philippines.* Quezon City: Ateneo de Manila University Press, in cooperation with the Center for Southeast Asian Studies, University of Wisconsin-Madison, 1994.

O'Brien, Niall. *Island of Tears, Island of Hope: Living the Gospel in a Revolutionary Situation.* Maryknoll, N.Y.: Orbis Books, 1993; Quezon City: Claretian Publications, 1994.

Poole, Fred, and Max Vanzi. *Revolution in the Philippines: The United States in a Hall of Cracked Mirrors.* New York: McGraw-Hill, 1984.

Putzel, James. *A Captive Land: The politics of agrarian reform in the Philippines.* Quezon City: Ateneo de Manila University Press, 1992.

Quirino, Carlos. *Filipinos at War.* Manila: Vera-Reyes, 1981.

Rivera, Temario C. *Landlords & Capitalists: Class, Family, and State in Philippine Manufacturing.* Quezon City: Center for Integrative and Development Studies, Philippine Center for Policy Studies, University of the Philippines Press, Quezon City, 1994.

Rocamora, Joel. *Breaking Through: The Struggle Within the Communist Party of the Philippines.* Pasig City: Anvil, 1994.

Rodolfo, Kelvin S. *Pinatubo and the Politics of Lahar: Eruption and Aftermath, 1991.* Quezon City: University of the Philippines Press and Pinatubo Studies Program, Center for Integrative and Development Studies, 1995.

Salonga, Jovito R. *The Senate That Said No: A Four-Year Record of the First Post-Edsa Senate.* Quezon City: University of the Philippines Press, 1995.

Sa-Onoy, Modesto P. *A History of Negros Occidental.* Bacolod City: Today Printers and Publishers, 1992.

Saulo, Alfredo B. *Communism in the Philippines: an Introduction.* Quezon City: Ateneo de Manila University Press, 1990.

Scott, William Henry. *The Discovery of the Igorots: Spanish Contacts With the Pagans of Northern Luzon.* Quezon City: New Day, 1974.

Shalom, Rosskamm Stephen. *The United States and the Philippines: A Study of Neocolonialism.* Quezon City: New Day, 1986.

Tan, Samuel K. *Internationalization of the Bangsamoro Struggle.* Quezon City: Center for Interactive and Development Studies, University of the Philippines Press, Quezon City, 1993.

Tanggol, Sukarno D. *Muslim Autonomy in the Philippines: Rhetoric and Reality.* Marawi: Mindanao State University Press and Information Office, 1993.

Timberman, David G. *A Changeless Land: Continuity and Change in Philippine Politics.* Armonk, N.Y.: M. E. Sharpe, 1991; Makati: Bookmark, 1991.

Wilkinson, Earl K. *People Priests & Pedophiles.* Manila: privately printed, 1994.

Wurfel, David C. *Filipino Politics: Development and Decay.* Quezon City: Ateneo de Manila University Press, 1988.

Papers, Brochures, Pamphlets, Leaflets

Autonomous Region in Muslim Mindanao Investment Guide, Cotabato City: Regional Planning and Development Office, 1995.

"Bases Conversion and the Baguio District: Proposals on Alternative Uses for Camp John Hay." Baguio: Movement for a Sovereign Philippines, Ad Hoc Committee, December 1990.

De Castro, Renato. "Philippine-United States Security Relations in the Post–Cold War Era: From Bilateralism to Cooperative Security." unpublished paper, Manila, 1996.

Doing Business in Cebu. Cebu: Cebu Investment Promotion Center, 1993.

Doing Business in the Subic Special Economic and Freeport Zone Philippines. Manila: Sycip Gorres Velayo, 1993.

Factbook: U.S. Facilities and Their Alternatives. Manila: Foreign Service Institute, Research Development Center, 1989. *Foreign Investments Act of 1991 R.A. [sic] 7042 As Amended by RA 8179.* Makati: Department of Trade and Industry, 1996.

A Gateway to Opportunity: South Cotabato, Sarangani, General Santos City. Manila: Louis Berger International, Manila, ca. 1994.

Hutchcroft, Paul D. "The Political Foundations of Booty Capitalism in the Philippines." Paper presented at the annual meeting of the American Political Science Association, Chicago, 1992.

McDonough, Lolita W. "The U.S. Military Bases in the Philippines: Issues and Scenarios." Quezon City: International Studies Institute of the Philippines, University of the Philippines, 1986.

Makinano, Merliza M. "The South China Sea Dispute." Quezon City: Strategic Research Division, Office of Strategic and Special Studies, Armed Forces of the Philippines, July 1995.

Nova. "In the Path of a Killer Volcano." WGBH-TV, Boston, February 9, 1993; transcript, Journal Graphics, Denver.

"The Philippines and the South China Sea Islands." Manila: Foreign Service Institute, Department of Foreign Affairs, 1992.

Ramos, Fidel V. *Toward Philippines 2000: A Resurgence of Optimism and Growth.* Manila: Bureau of Communications Services, Office of the Press Secretary, Malacañang, 1995.

Subic Bay Freeport, Philippines: A Guide for the Foreign and Local Investors. 4th ed. Manila: Joaquin, June 1995.

The Truth About the 1991–1993 Management of the Subic Bay Metropolitan Authority (SBMA) Under the Chairmanship of Richard J. Gordon as Reported in the Findings and Recommendations of the Commission on Audit (COA)." Philippines, privately printed, 1996.

Tujan, Antonio Jr. "Bursting the Ramos Bubble: 1995 Year End Briefing, Sociopolitical Situation and Projections," Manila, 1995.

UN Environment Program–Water Branch. *Final Report of the United Nations Expert Assessment Mission to Marinduque Island, Philippines* (Nairobi: UNEP/Department of Humanitarian Affairs Environment Unit, September 30, 1996).

U.S. Agency for International Development. *Country Program Strategy: the Philippines,* Manila, n.d., 1995.

———. *How USAID's Programs Help the Philippines.* Manila [1991].

———. *USAID in the Philippines: Years of Cooperation.* Manila [1988].

U.S. Information Service. *Background on the Bases: American Military Facilities in the Philippines.* rev. ed. Foreword by Nicholas Platt. Manila: U.S. Information Service, 1988.

White Paper: The Overseas Employment Program. Manila: Department of Labor and Employment, April 1995.

Periodicals

Abueg, Jose Marte. "Philippines: The Bandwagon is Rolling." *Asian Business,* Vol. 32, No. 1 (January 1986), pp. 42–48.

"Back on the road: A Survey of the Philippines." *Economist,* Vol. 339, No. 7965 (May 11–17, 1996).

Duay, Nonoy. "Don't Go to Saudi!" *Misyon* (The Missionary Society of St. Columban), Vol. 9, No. 1 (January-February 1996).

The Foreign Post, weekly, Makati, Metro Manila.

Ibon Philippines, semi-monthly, Databank and Research Center, Santa Mesa, Metro Manila.

Kadtuntaya (Mutual Consultation and Understanding), quarterly of the Muslim-Christian Integrated Development Program, special issue on the 1976 Tripoli Agreement, Cotabato, July 1989.

Kilosbayan Magazine, monthly, Pasig City.

Kohut, John. "Kidnap Corp.," *Asia, Inc.,* Vol. 5, No. 4 (April 1996), pp. 32–39.

Life, Asian Edition. "A Week With the Huks," Vol. 43, No. 1 (July 10, 1967); Ron de Paolo, "Report of a week among Philippine killer-terrorists: the Huks," pp. 20–25; Arthur Zich, "The many faces of Philippine Communism," pp. 25–28.

Neumann, A. Lin. "The Man Who Would Be Everything." *Asia, Inc.,* Vol. 4, No. 11 (September 1995), pp. 64–69.

O'Malley, Sean. "Our Man in Manila." *Saturday Night* (Toronto), December 1991, pp. 40–45, 84–90.

Philippine Graphic: Weekly Magazine, Metro Manila.

Philippine Flyer, unofficial newspaper published by and for Americans at Clark Air Base until their departure in 1991.

Philippines Free Press, weekly, Metro Manila.

"Philippines Incorporated: Who Owns the Philippines?" Seventh Anniversary Report, *Business World,* 1994.

Philippines Yearbook of the Fookien Times, annual.

Smart File, published irregularly, issues numbered but undated, Animal Farm Publications, Makati, Metro Manila.

Subic Today, quarterly, Subic Publishing, Subic Bay Freeport.

We Forum, weekly, Quezon City.

What's On in Manila and Expat Philippines, weekly, Makati.

A Note on the Dailies

Daily journalism has exploded since the Marcos era when only a few newspapers, all controlled by Marcos cronies, notably Imelda's younger brother, Benjamin "Kokoy" Romualdez, were published. Upward of 30 "national" newspapers appear every day in Metro Manila. Copies go by plane, train, van, jeepney, bus and boat to municipalities throughout the country. However, none of the Metro Manila papers is printed at more than one site despite talk of satelliting pages for publication in Cebu and elsewhere. Total circulation of all papers, including tabloids, is about 2 million—in a country of 70 million.

Broadsheets include *Business Daily, Business World, Malaya, Manila Bulletin, Manila Chronicle, Manila Standard, Manila Times, Philippine Daily Inquirer, Philippine Journal, Philippine Star,* and *Today.* These papers are written almost entirely in English, except on occasion when quoting in crime stories. *Isyu,* a newspaper of commentary in tabloid format, appears five times weekly with articles in English and Pilipino.

Tabloids edited for broader, down-market appeal are appearing in greater profusion at newsstands and street corners everywhere. These include *Abante, Balita, Bandera, Bulgar, Daily Aliwan, Daily Libangan, Gossip, Liberty, Metro Sun, People's Journal* and *Tonight, Pilipino Star, Pinoy, Pulse, Remate, Taliba, Tempo* and the *Philippine Tribune.* These tabloids carry material in both English and Pilipino, mostly Tagalog, spoken in Metro Manila and much of Luzon and understandable throughout the Philippines.

Among the most successful provincial newspapers is a middle-market tabloid, the *Sun-Star,* which originated in Cebu and is on sale, with local editions, in a number of other centers but not Metro Manila. Another middle-market tabloid, *Gold*Star Daily,* published in Cagayan de Oro, circulates only in Mindanao. Both are in English. Local dailies and weeklies are published in regional and provincial centers, often in English but also in Tagalog and other languages. There is a dearth, however, of vernacular papers, especially in languages other than Tagalog/Pilipino.

Index